ORDEAL AT LUCKNOW

Ordeal at Lucknow

The Defence of the Residency

MICHAEL JOYCE

MANOHAR
2020

First published 1938
Reprinted 2020

ISBN 978-93-90035-40-3

Published by
Ajay Kumar Jain *for*
Manohar Publishers & Distributors
4753/23 Ansari Road, Daryaganj
New Delhi 110 002

Printed at
Replika Press Pvt. Ltd.

TO

THE LOYAL INDIANS OF ALL RANKS

WHO DIED IN DEFENCE OF THE BAILLIE GUARD

For loyalty is still the same
Whether it win or lose the game;
True as the dial to the sun,
Although it be not shin'd upon.

SAMUEL BUTLER

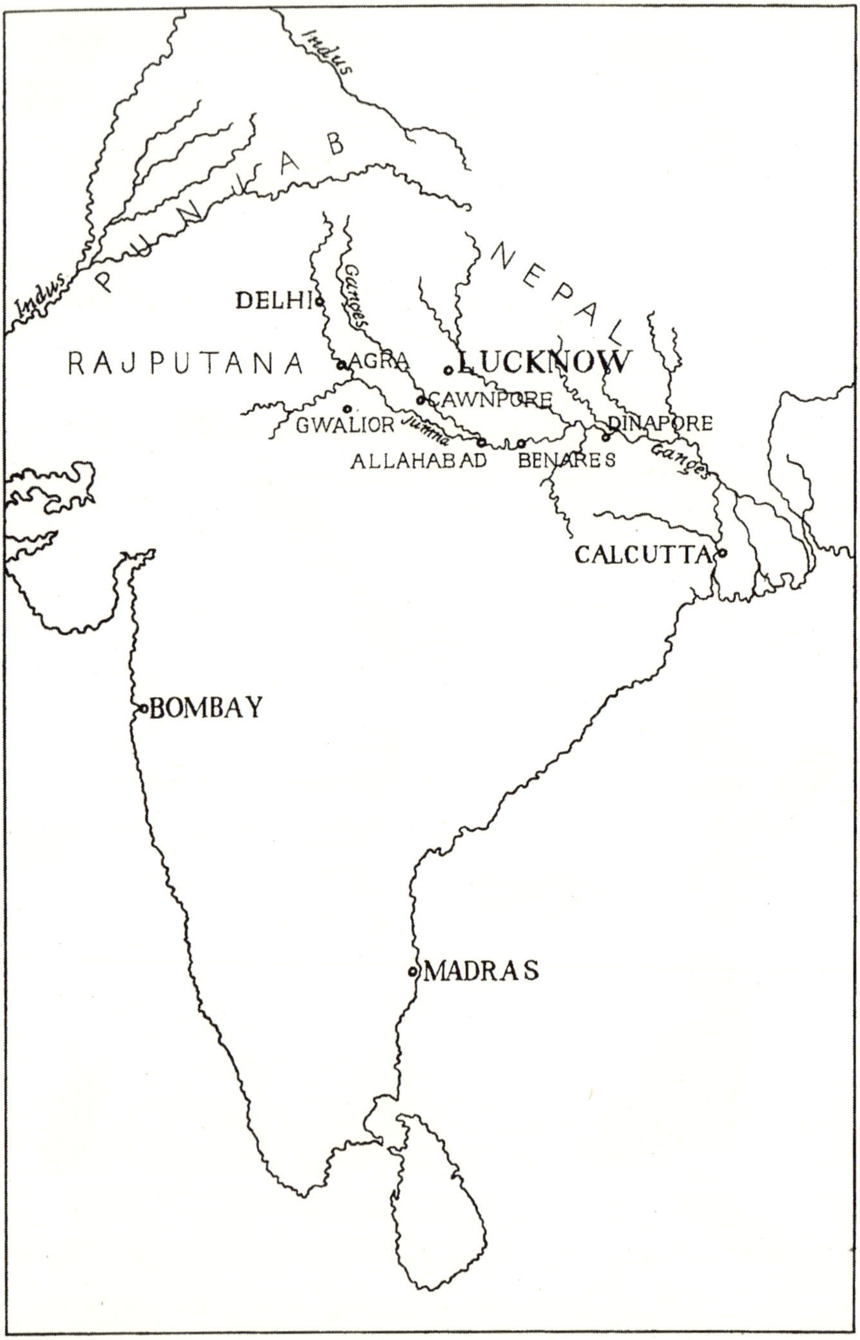

Indus
PUNJAB
NEPAL
Indus
DELHI
Ganges
RAJPUTANA
AGRA
LUCKNOW
CAWNPORE
GWALIOR
Jumna
DINAPORE
ALLAHABAD
BENARES
Ganges
CALCUTTA
BOMBAY
MADRAS

More than eighty years have passed since the outbreak of the Indian Mutiny, but the Residency of Lucknow is not forgotten: the men who held an untenable position for a hundred and forty days are still honoured by the flag that is never struck at sunset, but flies day and night above the ruins, and every morning a fresh tribute of flowers is laid on the grave of Henry Lawrence.

This is the true story of the three thousand men, women, and children who fought and suffered in Lawrence's entrenchment. It is told from their point of view, with only such intelligence of events outside as reached them through the enemy's lines—a method which does less than justice to Havelock, Outram, Colin Campbell and their men, but which may help us to share the hopes and fears that possessed the garrison from day to day.

Those hopes and fears are set down in the letters, journals, and memoirs of the time as fully as the practical details of the defence. There is as much to be learnt of the daily life of Mrs Inglis and her family as of the military dispositions of her husband, the Brigadier. We are told of Kavanagh's feelings as he made his way at night through the enemy's lines, and of Havelock's first words to the defenders when he entered the Residency at last with reinforcements. The rank and file of the 32nd Foot, the backbone of the garrison, come to life in Private Metcalfe's narrative, and even Bustle, the chaplain's terrier, has a place in history.

The Bengal Army had long been in a state of disaffection, which various causes were combining to increase, when in January 1857 *an unfortunate report, not quite unfounded, that the new Enfield cartridges were lubricated with cow's fat, gave substance to the fears of the Hindu sepoys that the East India Company were resolved to break their caste and turn them into Christians. February, March, and April were months of unrest, but it was not till the second week of May, when a savage outbreak at Meerut was followed by the seizure of Delhi and the restoration of the Mogul dynasty, that the Calcutta government awoke to find its very existence threatened.*

At the end of May the storm broke at Lucknow, where the bulk of four regiments mutinied, but were driven off by Lawrence. At Cawnpore, fifty miles to the south-west, the sepoys rose a week later and invested General Wheeler's ill-prepared position. One by one the outlying parts of Oudh were lost to British rule, until at last Lawrence was cut off at Lucknow with over five hundred women and children, one weak battalion of European infantry, and a handful of military odds-and-ends, civilian volunteers, and loyal sepoys, to hold his own, as he feared, against many thousands of mutineers, disciplined and well-equipped, and supported by a hostile and warlike population.

My story opens on the last day of June. Delhi was still held by the sepoys, and the small British force that clung to the ridge outside the city was being daily wasted by casualties and disease. Cawnpore and Lucknow could only hope for relief from Havelock's movable column, two thousand strong. Havelock himself was at Allahabad, a hundred and twenty miles from Cawnpore, but a detachment was marching up the Grand Trunk Road ahead of him in the hope of saving Wheeler: they did not know that his pitiful entrenchment had already fallen, and that he and his men had been massacred on the river bank. In Oudh large bodies of the rebels were threatening Lucknow, where Lawrence's preparations for a siege were not yet complete. Lawrence moved out to meet them.

Sir Henry Lawrence wrote to Allahabad as follows:

'*Lucknow*,
June 30*th*, 1857.

My dear Havelock,

This morning we went out eight miles to Chinhat to meet the enemy, and we were defeated, and lost five guns through the misconduct chiefly of our Native Artillery, many of whom deserted. The enemy have followed us up, and we have now been besieged for four hours, and shall probably to-night be surrounded. The enemy are very bold, and our Europeans very low. I look on our position now as ten times as bad as it was yesterday; indeed, it is very critical. We shall be obliged to concentrate *if we are able*. We shall have to abandon much supplies and to blow up much powder. Unless we are relieved quickly, say in ten or fifteen days, we shall hardly be able to maintain our position. . . .'

The city had been threatened by the mutineers who had been hovering in the eastern parts of Oudh since the rising at Lucknow on the 30th May and the mutinies that had followed in the outlying districts. By the 29th June the mutineers were reported to be moving on Lucknow by the Fyzabad road, emboldened by the news that Sir Hugh Wheeler's command had been wiped out at Cawnpore. Lawrence undertook a reconnoissance in force and found himself engaged with the main body of the rebels, six or seven thousand strong, instead of the advanced guard of six hundred, as he had expected. The odds were about ten to one, but even then he might have held his own had all his troops been staunch and fit for their work. The loyal sepoys of the 13th Native Infantry fought with spirit, but the Sikh cavalry bolted and some of the Indian gunners and drivers overturned their guns and rode away with the waggon teams.

The column had been ordered to move out at dawn, but owing to delay on the part of the artillery the sun was well up before it left the Residency. The men of the 32nd Foot, the Cornwall Regiment, who had been under arms day and night for several weeks, and some of whom had been drinking the night before, were given no refreshment before starting. They were halted by the Kokrail bridge before the final advance, but though coffee, biscuits, and rum had been brought along with the baggage by Lawrence's orders, neither food nor drink was served out to the men. When they went into action they were faint from empty stomachs and exhausted by marching over heavy ground in the morning sun. Lieutenant Colonel Case was shot down as he led his men against a native village, and they began to lose heart.

The rebel leader used his superior numbers to such good purpose that Lawrence was hopelessly outflanked. Soon the column was in full retreat, and before long the retreat was a rout. The men were tormented by thirst, for the Indian water-carriers had deserted. Some of the wounded were given a hand or a stirrup by the Volunteer Cavalry and the mounted officers, or carried on the gun limbers and waggons, but many more had to be abandoned. Others fell unwounded but fainting from fatigue, or struck down by the sun. They were all despatched by the enemy's cavalry. The Indian infantrymen covered the retreat in good order, helping the European wounded rather than their own, as if to assure their officers that not every sepoy was a mutineer.

Throughout the retreat Lawrence behaved with coolness and decision. As they neared the Kokrail bridge he checked the infantry's pursuit by ordering one of his remaining guns to be brought into action and the portfire lighted, although the gun was empty and all the ammunition had been lost or shot away. Five hundred of the enemy's horse, with two 9-pounder guns, were massing by the bridge to cut off the retreating column. Lawrence's Volunteer Cavalry had ridden out of Lucknow that morning thirty-six strong and few of them had been under fire before. Captain Radcliffe, 7th Light Cavalry, gave the orders, 'Threes Right!', 'Trot!', and the troop swept forward. When they were within a quarter of a mile of the enemy the two 9-pounders opened fire, but as the first roundshot screamed overhead Radcliffe gave the order 'Charge!', and the trumpet sounded above the din of cannonade and musketry. The thirty-six sabres rode straight for the enemy squadrons, who did not wait for them but galloped away, guns and all; the bridge was cleared and the road to Lucknow was still open.

Lawrence sat his horse bareheaded, a target for the enemy marksmen, trying to rally his men for a last stand by the Kokrail bridge; but it was too late for individual gallantry and resource to stop the rout. Some of the sepoys and Europeans retreated steadily, firing with deliberate aim when the enemy came within range, but most of them hurried on without attempting to resist. Many of the 32nd found that their muskets were foul through being loaded too long without being fired. All that could be done now was to secure the Residency enclosure, where the work of fortification was not yet complete, and Lawrence therefore handed over his command to Colonel Inglis of the 32nd and rode on ahead with his chief of staff and his aide-de-camp to make his dispositions.

That morning work had begun as usual on the defences at the Residency. The city was quiet and supplies were still coming in. Hundreds of coolies were at work throwing up batteries, erecting palisades, and digging trenches, and the place was crowded with soldiers, sepoys, carts, and guns, horses, bullocks, camels, and elephants. Then, suddenly, the workmen and the tally clerks decamped, taking with them all their tools and lists of stores. A few minutes later news was brought to Mr Martin Gubbins, the senior civilian in Lawrence's absence, that the force was in retreat. Gubbins took the messenger to the senior officer in the place, who ordered all gates and entrances to be secured and the batteries and outposts manned. Mr Gubbins met some of the Sikh cavalry and the Indian artillerymen who had just come in, their horses flecked with foam. He asked them why they had fled, since not one of them was wounded; they replied that the enemy had surrounded them. Half an hour later the rest of the survivors began to straggle in, covered with dust and blood, some riding on horseback, some on the guns, some helping each other along on foot: they dropped down in the shade, hopeless and exhausted. Many of them would never have returned but for the kindness of the Indian women who had given them cool water and milk to drink as they hurried through the outskirts of the city.

Mrs Inglis, who was suffering from smallpox, looked out of her window as she anxiously awaited Colonel Inglis' return. There was firing on the far side of the river Gumti, and through the trees she could see large bodies of the enemy. A fresh detachment of 32nd Foot had been ordered out by Lawrence to hold the iron bridge until the rearguard should have crossed the river, while an 18-pounder gun opened fire on the enemy from the Redan Battery on the north face of the defences. Thus the pursuit was checked, and by midday the remnant of the column had made good their retreat, some into the Residency and some into the Machhi Bhawan fort, nearly a mile further up the river.

Mrs Case, whose husband had gone out in command of the 32nd Foot, came to Mrs Inglis and said:

'Oh, Mrs Inglis, go to bed; I have just heard from one of the syces (grooms) that Colonel Inglis and William are both safe.'

Mrs Inglis replied: 'Why, I did not know Colonel Case was out.'

A few minutes later Colonel Inglis came in. There were tears in his eyes. He kissed his wife and then turned to Mrs Case and said:

'Poor Case!'

Mrs Case gave a pitiable cry, and Mrs Polehampton, the junior chaplain's wife, took her into her own room where she tried to quiet her.

In the Residency grounds there was chaos. Barricades were being thrown up, walls loopholed, guns dragged into position. Clothes and furniture were being thrown about. Men were hastening to their posts, women seeking the safest places for their families, children crying, and all the Europeans shouting for their Indian servants, many of whom had run away. The hospital was full of shattered men. They had been taken off the waggons and limbers at the iron bridge and brought the rest of the way on litters. They lay in rows, pale, bloody, and groaning, while the surgeons amputated, probed and dressed. Women flocked round fanning the wounded and offering iced water and stuff for bandages; the horrors of war were new to most of them.

The natives of the city were making away from the English quarter. Riderless horses galloped up and down while elephants and camels were hurried off by their drivers. The boatmen on the river worked their craft as far away from the Residency and the iron bridge as possible. Soon there was not a living creature to be seen round the outside of the entrenchment. Then from the roof tops the garrison could see the enemy fording the river lower down. Both the stone bridge, by the Machhi Bhawan, and the iron bridge were covered by the British guns, and the mutineers therefore began collecting boats for a bridge which should be out of range. Others occupied the houses round the entrenchment and rapidly cut loopholes for musketry. The walls of the native prison outside the Baillie Guard gate were seen to be thick with prisoners making their escape by ropes from the windows. The enemy began to fire from the neighbouring houses, and opened a cannonade from the far side of the river, where they had placed their own guns and the 8-inch howitzer that they had captured that morning. The garrison took cover as the musketry grew heavier, but Lawrence went round from post to post, careless of the fire.

At Captain Anderson's house on the east face of the defences the garrison were maintaining a sharp fire on the mutineers outside, when a roundshot carried away one of the pillars of the verandah, which fell with a crash, burying a civilian, Mr Capper, who was serving as a volunteer. Captain Anderson, 25th Native Infantry, and the rest came running up. Capper was buried under a mass of masonry, but they could hear a low voice saying:

'I'm alive! Get me out! Give me air, for God's sake!'

Someone said: 'It's impossible to save him,' but again they heard Capper's voice coming up as if from a vault:

'It *is* possible, if you try.'

They started work. The heavy timbers of the verandah had been checked in their fall by a single beam which had been fixed about two feet above the floor to be used as a firestep, and Capper's head was in the space between this beam and the floor. There were huge blocks of masonry to be shifted, and, as the rubble was constantly falling down and stopping up the cracks through which Capper was breathing, he kept on calling out for air. The enemy knew that something peculiar was afoot and kept up an incessant fire, but there was just enough wall to cover the bodies of the rescue party as they lay on their bellies working with both hands. After three-quarters of an hour, when they were nearly exhausted, they had uncovered Capper's body and begun work on his legs, Corporal Oxenham, 32nd Foot, exposing himself freely to get the work done quicker. When at last they hauled Capper out they were surprised to find that no bones were broken; he was only bruised and a little faint.

The troops in the Machhi Bhawan fort were now cut off from the Residency, where some of the women were in great suspense, not knowing whether their husbands had survived the retreat from Chinhat. Lawrence gave Mr Gubbins, who was in charge of Intelligence, several despatches, written in Greek character, to send across to the fort, but since many of the native runners had deserted, and those that were left did not know the city, the letters were never taken. Lieutenant Colonel Palmer, 48th Native Infantry, who was commanding at the Machhi Bhawan, contrived to send a message that he was not well supplied with either food or ammunition for his guns, though he had plenty of powder and small-arms ammunition. The fort had been held to overawe the city, and used as an entrepôt for stores and provisions. It was considered strong enough to resist a popular rising, but the walls were too old and crazy to withstand an attack supported by artillery, and Lawrence had intended to evacuate the fort and concentrate in the Residency position as soon as a siege was imminent; now, the heavy losses sustained at Chinhat had made the need for concentration doubly urgent. During the afternoon an attempt was made to signal to the fort, but the telegraph had been so badly damaged by the enemy's musketry that it was found unworkable, and nothing more could be done that day.

Mrs Inglis, who was only twenty-four, with her two small boys and baby, and Mrs Case and her sister, Caroline Dickson, had been sharing quarters in the upper storey of the Residency building; but they were soon driven down by the roundshot to the basement, where they spent the rest of the day with the gunners' wives. The windows were all barricaded and it was not safe to step outside; they could only wait and listen anxiously to the firing. Towards evening, when things were quieter, Colonel Inglis took them to a little room which opened off a courtyard in the centre of the position and which had formerly been part of a native gaol. Mrs Inglis was carried over on a sofa. They were all tired out and slept soundly.

Next morning Inglis came in and warned them to expect heavy firing soon, and a few minutes later they heard a storm of gunfire and musketry. They could get no news, for every man was at his post. The women sat there trembling, convinced that the enemy would break in and kill them all, until Mrs Case, who would not give way to her grief, knelt with her sister by Mrs Inglis' bedside and read the

Litany. When she had done they were calmer, believing that they were in God's hands whatever terrors might be in store. Soon the firing slackened and they heard that the enemy had been repulsed on every side.

Although Sir Henry Lawrence was only fifty-one, he looked ten years older and, in spite of the energy that tired out his subordinates, people already spoke of him as an old man. He was tall, thin, and wiry, with restless eyes, a straggling grey beard, and sunken cheeks. He had fretted for years after Lord Dalhousie had elbowed him out of the Punjab, but his recent appointment by Lord Canning as Chief Commissioner of Oudh had gone far to salve his pride. Since the death of Lady Lawrence in January 1854 he had seemed to his friends to be living for the next world rather than for this, although he was still active, and concerned with things about him. 'Grief', it was said, 'had made him grey and worn, but it became him like the scars of a battle.' Sometimes his face had a kind of radiance. His manner was courteous and gentle except when the old impatience broke out under unusual stress.

In March 1857, when he took the reins at Lucknow, the province of Oudh, which had only been annexed in February 1856, was already in a fever of discontent, the administration having been in the wrong hands since the departure of Sir James Outram less than three months after carrying out the annexation. Lawrence went to work with the happy blend of firmness and conciliation that had made him such a power in the Punjab, and did much—more, perhaps, than any other man in India could have done—to reassure and pacify the people: but the growing disaffection of the sepoy army was beyond his power to check.

At the beginning of May some of the 7th Oudh Irregular Infantry showed an unreasoning reluctance to use the cartridges issued for musketry practice, which were in fact quite inoffensive, and by the 3rd they were openly mutinous. Order was soon restored, and the ringleaders were placed under arrest, but Lawrence believed that this was only the beginning. On the 14th May news came by telegraph of the great outbreak at Meerut and the loss of Delhi, and on the 30th there was a second and more serious mutiny at Lucknow. Lawrence drove off the mutineers, and quelled a sympathetic riot in the city, writing afterwards to Lord Canning, the Governor General: 'We are now positively better off than we were. We now know our friends and enemies. . . . I have told you by telegraph it will never do to retire on Allahabad. We *could not* do it. Besides, I am quite confident we can hold our ground at Lucknow as long as provisions last, and we have already a month's laid in. When Delhi is taken we are all safe. If there is much delay most of our outposts will be lost.' There followed a series of risings in the out-stations of Oudh, and on the 12th June

Lawrence wrote: 'Every outpost (I fear) has fallen, and we daily expect to be besieged by the confederated mutineers and their allies from Cawnpore, Sitapur, Sikrora, etc. The country is not yet thoroughly up, but every day brings it nearer that condition.' Meanwhile he made the most of this last breathing space to forward his preparations.

He had soon acquired a remarkable hold on the affections of the English community. He was indefatigable; they could all see how much he was doing for their safety, and they knew that no person was too humble, no detail too small, for his attention. To the European troops he was a hero. One of the 32nd Foot said to Mr Polehampton, the junior chaplain: 'We'd follow Sir Henry through fire and water; he's a good un and a right good man to soldiers.' When he shifted his quarters to the Residency from across the river, the men broke into spontaneous cheers and shouted: 'Long life to Sir Henry! Long live Sir Henry!': indeed, one of them cheered so loudly that he burst a blood-vessel.

Ever since the troubles had begun Lawrence's task had been to keep the routine of government working smoothly while preparing for emergency. He had telegraphed in May to Lord Canning to ask for the chief command in the province, and had been readily granted the local rank of Brigadier General with full military powers. While occupying the Machhi Bhawan fort to hold the city in check, and the Mariaon cantonments on the north side of the river to keep the country open for supplies, he had given orders to prepare the Residency position for the final stand. Mr Gubbins, the Financial Commissioner, an intrepid, generous, energetic, and capable but wrong-headed man, had pressed for more radical measures, but Lawrence had refused, in view of the immense odds against him, to be badgered into irresponsible action. On the 2nd June Gubbins wrote to Lord Canning: 'Sir Henry Lawrence is no longer, I think, firm, nor his mental vision clear.'

The general name of the 'Residency' was given to a piece of ground, standing somewhat higher than the rest of the city, which had been allotted to the British Resident by a former King of Oudh. Besides the Residency proper—a handsome building with lofty apartments and wide verandahs, a taikhana, or basement, to shelter the residents from the summer heats, and high windows ill-adapted to defence—there was an English church, and various offices and private houses standing in their own compounds among trees and flowering shrubs. The water supply from wells was excellent.

In planning the defences Major Anderson, the Chief Engineer, and Captain Fulton, his second-in-command, had not been able to adopt what they considered a correct trace. Ignorant how soon the attack might come, they had designed a continuous enceinte which was to gain strength with each day's work at an even rate on every side. Existing walls had been included wherever possible, trenches had been dug, and palisades erected. Outside the ramparts various obstacles were placed, such as chevaux-de-frise, abattis (entanglements of branches), crows-feet (four-pointed iron spikes), and trous-de-loup (pits with sharp stakes in the bottom). Such obstructions were intended to check the enemy's storming parties and give the garrison time to bring the full fire-power of the threatened front to bear on them before they reached the defences. Some of the lower ground towards the river had to be abandoned, and the fortified position was roughly diamond-shaped, each of the four faces being about four hundred yards long, although, allowing for various irregularities and a big spur at the north-west angle, the total perimeter was quite two thousand yards.

Outside the northern defences there was open ground which sloped away towards the river; here the natural bank had been scarped down and a ditch had been dug at the foot of the escarp, the earth being used for the crest of a rough-and-ready glacis. The bank itself was crowned by a parapet seven feet high, part of which was merely a stack of firewood covered up with earth, the rest being solid and revetted with gabions (wicker baskets filled with earth) and fascines (long faggots), and topped with sandbags, with a banquette, or firestep, on the inner side. Both the ditch and the glacis were freely sown with obstacles, since this was the only front on which there was ample space for the enemy to mass his columns of assault.

The Redan battery (named after the Great Redan at Sebastopol), which was the strongest point in the whole of the works, projected sharply from the continuous curtain of the north face, which it flanked to right and left. It was supported in rear by the Residency building, where a detachment of fifty Europeans was posted as a general reserve. The Redan mounted two 18-pounder guns and one 9-pounder, and there were also some seven guns disposed along the curtain.

The banqueting hall near the north-east angle had been converted into a hospital and dispensary, the right wing being set aside as a manufactory of cartridges and fuses. Just round the corner, on the east face, was the Baillie Guard post, which included the Treasury and the main gate of the Residency grounds. The curved line of buildings that formed the Baillie Guard proper (named after Colonel Baillie, a former Resident) was outside the gate, but the name was applied by the sepoys to the whole entrenchment. Three guns were posted in rear of the gate, which was banked up with earth, to command the entrance in case the enemy broke in.

The eastern face was skirted by the Cawnpore road; there was nothing to stop the enemy from occupying the buildings and enclosures on the far side of the road, the nearest of which was only twenty-five yards away, and loopholing them for musketry, or using them as bases for mining operations. On the other hand, troops making an assault from the east would be forced to advance in column through narrow passages.

The main defence on this side was the boundary wall of the Residency grounds, supported by several houses with loopholes and parapeted roofs. Near the outer wall were the Financial Commissioner's Office, which was strongly barricaded with boxes and furniture, though the outhouses and the gateway were very insecure; Mrs Sago's house, formerly a girls' school; and the Judicial Commissioner's Office, which was defended by a bank of earth and palisades.

These posts were supported by Fayrer's house (Dr Fayrer was the Residency surgeon) and the Post Office, both of which stood on the higher ground behind. There were two guns by Fayrer's house and four in the Post Office grounds, two to rake the approach to the Baillie Guard gate and two for frontal defence.

Near the south-east angle stood Captain Anderson's post, where Mr Capper had been buried alive, a two-storeyed house, barricaded and loopholed, the compound being defended by a trench and palisade. On the angle itself was the Cawnpore battery, designed to enfilade the Cawnpore road and hamper the movement of enemy troops from the south. It was constructed of earth and palisades, and armed with two 9-pounders and one 18-pounder. Round the corner on the south face was the house of M. Deprat, a French merchant, which, with the battery, formed a single post.

The south face, too, was skirted by a narrow street, and here the buildings which were being occupied by the enemy were as little as thirteen yards away. The defence on this side depended on palisades, an almost continuous line of loopholed buildings, and flanking fire from the Cawnpore battery. Next to Deprat's was the house known as the Martinière, the temporary home of the boys from the Martinière College outside the city. Next to the right came a road blocked up by a bank and palisades, and across the road the Brigade Mess, a high building with a parapeted roof and a good command for musketry. This post was chiefly manned by the English officers of the mutinous regiments, many of whom had their own rifles and were excellent shots. The commandant, Lieutenant Colonel Master, 7th Light Cavalry, became known as the Admiral from his habit of hailing from the top.

The two enclosures to the right of the Brigade Mess were held by the Sikh troopers and known therefore as the Sikh Squares. They were surrounded by buildings with low roofs which were parapeted with boards and sandbags as the siege went on.

A lane, commanded by a 24-pounder howitzer at the inner end, separated the Sikh Squares from Gubbins' post, which formed the south-west angle of the position. Mr Gubbins had been fortifying his house since May, though at first his activity had amused his more optimistic neighbours. His compound was surrounded by outhouses adapted for musketry, and work had been begun on a battery at the extreme angle of the post. In spite of Gubbins' measures the engineers had not been satisfied that the post was tenable, and they had therefore built a bridge across the lane that separated it from the next compound, so that the garrison might retire to a more central position if they found themselves hard pressed. There was a gun on the west face of the northern corner of the post.

To the north of Gubbins' post were the Slaughterhouses, a range of low buildings along the west face which were used for sheep and cattle-pens, for butchering, and for the Indian servants' quarters. The racquet court behind the Slaughterhouses had been filled up with fodder for the cattle.

The Church with its close, which had not yet been used as a graveyard, stood on low ground at the north of the west face, commanded by three guns on the bank behind. There was only a small guard posted in the Church itself, which had been cleared to accommodate stores of grain and clarified butter. The churchyard was reckoned one of the weakest points in the defences, and indeed the whole of the western face was likely to suffer from the lack of flanking fire; fortunately, however, the ground outside the works was broken and rugged, sloping away to a ravine which ran down to join the river Gumti. Two batteries had been begun by the Slaughterhouses, but were still unfinished at the opening of the siege.

The most exposed of all the outposts was Innes' house, which stood on a spur of high ground projecting from the main body of the entrenchment. The house itself was low and weakly defended by mud walls and palisades, but its site gave it a good command of the surrounding land, and it was supported by the battery in rear of the church and by the guns at the Redan.

Besides the various guns that were permanently placed in position, there were eight 8-inch mortars and a number of field pieces which were moved about as required. There was no shortage of either guns or ammunition; indeed, there were about two hundred pieces of ordnance belonging to the ex-King of Oudh lying, unmounted, near the Redan, having been discovered in an old magazine in the city by Captain Fulton. It was there that he had found the 8-inch howitzer that had been abandoned at Chinhat—a serious loss to the garrison, since they had no other. The difficulty was to man the guns, but the artillerymen had been reinforced by some of the volunteers and regular infantrymen, who had been put through a hasty course of gun-drill before the beginning of the siege.

Lawrence had hoped that by taking the initiative on the 30th June he might delay the investment of the Residency by several days at least: his defeat precipitated it. The defences needed another week to make them as tenable as their defective trace would allow, and were not yet strong enough to stand a determined rush. Gubbins' battery, which was essential to the safety of the south-west angle, was only half finished. On the first day tables, sideboards, and even books and government records were built into the works, while on the south face the parapets were heightened by canvas screens which spoilt the enemy's aim if they did not repel their bullets.

During June a number of buildings outside the position had been demolished under Captain Fulton's orders. Lawrence had been anxious that all demolitions should be noted so that the owners might be reimbursed, and had always said: 'Spare the holy places, and private property, too, as much as possible.' By the 30th June, however, not more than a third of the work had been done, and many buildings which commanded the entrenchment were still intact. Others had only had their upper storeys destroyed, or the parapets on the roofs thrown down, since it was thought that the lower walls might protect the defences against breaching fire. The house of Mr Johannes, an Armenian merchant, on the far side of the street from the southern defences, had a turret which commanded all the neighbouring outposts, and Lieutenant Innes, Bengal Engineers, had suggested its inclusion as a flanking work to the south face. It had been decided to follow his advice if possible, and if not, to blow the place up; but it had been left till too late, and now there was nothing to stop the enemy from occupying the house and posting their sharpshooters in the turret.

The work of fortification had quite disfigured the Residency grounds. The trees and flowering shrubs were all cut down, and the garden beds were trampled hard or hidden under piles of roundshot; but the view from the top of the Residency building, where a lookout was kept, was as beautiful as ever. The city itself was dense and squalid, but the northeast quarter was rich in villas, palaces, mosques, and mausoleums. The delicate domes and minarets stood out white and gold against the green trees and gardens, and there was open country across the river.

On the 1st July, the second day of the siege, Lawrence was sitting in his room in the upper storey of the Residency with Mr Couper, his secretary, when an 8-inch shell from the howitzer that had been lost at Chinhat burst between them. Although neither was injured, Lawrence's staff begged him to shift his quarters, if only to the lower storey of the same building. Lawrence replied with a laugh that the enemy gunners were not clever enough to put two shells into one small room; but later on, when the upper storey had been struck by roundshot, he agreed to have his papers moved down on the following day.

The same afternoon some of the ladies were shifting their possessions from the outer rooms at the Residency to a more sheltered place in the centre of the building. Among them was Miss Palmer, daughter of Lieutenant Colonel Palmer, who was commanding at the Machhi Bhawan, a girl of eighteen, devoted to her father, whom she had only joined in India during the previous December. She was moving some china out of a cabinet when there was a crash, and Mrs Huxham, who was by the door, saw her fall backwards, hit in the leg by a 9-pounder shot. The girl was deadly pale and seemed stunned for a moment, but then exclaimed with a sudden effort: 'My leg is shot off; I know I shall die.' Dr Wells, who was called at once, compressed the arteries to stop the flow of blood and bound up the wound. When he had done, they carried her, screaming, to a safer room, where they laid her on a bed. Seeing two doctors now beside her, and guessing that they were about to operate, she begged them not to torture her but to let her die in peace. The doctors had their way; they gave her chloroform and amputated, though there was little work for the knife to do, since the roundshot had almost taken off the leg. The operation left her very weak, but the doctors said she might recover.

There was still great anxiety for the force at the Machhi Bhawan. Several runners had been sent out, but as it was doubtful whether they had evaded the mutineers who were swarming between the two positions, another attempt was made to work the telegraph on top of the Residency building—a primitive machine, contrived by Captain Fulton to correspond with a similar affair on the roof of the Machhi Bhawan, and consisting of a single post with a cross-bar from which was suspended a row of black, stuffed bags, fitted each with a separate halyard. It was when he had at length attracted the attention of Lieutenant Innes, the Engineer at the Machhi Bhawan, that Fulton's troubles began. The enemy opened a heavy fire of musketry and roundshot;

some of the halyards broke or were cut by musket balls; the pulleys jammed; and twice the whole machine had to be taken down and put in order. Fulton himself, George Lawrence, of the Civil Service, Sir Henry's nephew, and another officer worked for three hours under fire in the burning sun, until at last the telegraph was made to work. The message was sent: 'Spike the guns well; blow up the fort, and retire at midnight,' each letter being signalled back by Lieutenant Innes. All Lawrence could do now was to give orders that shortly before midnight the space between the Residency and the fort should be shelled by mortars, while the guns opened fire from all the batteries to distract the enemy: the rest must be left to Lieutenant Colonel Palmer.

Palmer made his dispositions with the utmost care, giving precise orders in writing to all his commanding and departmental officers. They were to withdraw what guns they could and spike the rest at the last minute. The women and children and the sick and wounded were to be carried in waggons, together with several highly-placed citizens of Lucknow who had been detained on suspicion of conspiracy: the prisoners were to be pinioned, gagged, and blindfolded, and Lieutenant Huxham, 48th Native Infantry, was to have them shot if the enemy attempted a rescue. The magazine, containing two hundred and forty barrels of powder and over half a million rounds of ball and gun ammunition, was to be blown up, Lieutenant Thomas, Madras Artillery, Deputy Commissary of Ordnance, firing the train with a twenty-minute fuse as the rearguard left the fort. Palmer's orders concluded: 'The whole to be in readiness to move out at midnight, from the eastern gate, in perfect silence, under penalty of death.'

Both officers and men had to leave their kit behind, since no baggage could be taken across; indeed, they would be lucky if they escaped with their lives. The 32nd Foot had their headquarters in the fort, and most of the regimental records from the year 1846, all the band instruments, a valuable collection of music, and almost all the paymaster's and quartermaster's books had to be abandoned.

At ten o'clock the sentries were strengthened and preparations were made to move the guns. As midnight approached the troops were paraded in the central courtyard, where the entire personnel was formed up in one unbroken column of infantry, artillery, women and children, sick and wounded, prisoners, and camp-followers. When all was ready the sentries were withdrawn and the last beam of the barricade removed from the eastern gate. At twelve o'clock to the minute the column marched out, headed by the detachment of the 32nd. The waggons got away without mishap, but the wheel of one of the guns jammed against the gateway. It was a critical moment. The horses were restive, and many of the Indian drivers had deserted the night before; but some of the European officers took their places, and in a few minutes the wheel was cleared and the rest of the column moved out without a check. Palmer was in the rear with two light field-pieces, loaded with grape, and as soon as the last gun was through the gate he called to Lieutenant Innes to pass the word to Lieutenant Thomas to fire the train.

Outside all was quiet but for the boom of the 18-pounder at the Redan, which was firing grape parallel to the right flank of the column in case of an attack from the city. The men had all expected they would have to fight their way through, but not a shot was fired, the enemy being busy, as it seemed, looting the bazaars.

Only one man was left behind, an Irish private of the 32nd who was drunk. One of the sergeants had done his best to get the man out, but he was only abused for his pains, and had to leave him lying there since there was no time to waste on stragglers when once the train was lighted.

By a quarter-past twelve, five minutes ahead of time, the leading files had reached the Water Gate of the Residency. The gate was locked and the man who had the key was missing. Impatient at the delay, someone in the column shouted: 'Open the gates.' There were guns inside covering the entrance, loaded with grapeshot, and the gunners, thinking they heard the order 'Open with grape', were about to fire when, just in time, an officer put them right. At last the gate was opened, and, as the rearguard passed through, the Machhi Bhawan went up. Windows were broken inside the defences and doors shaken off their hinges, children screamed with terror, and some of the women believed that the enemy had sprung a mine and might break in at any minute. The earth rocked, and after the flash and the explosion a column of black smoke rose high into the air. The 32nd gave a cheer, while those of the enemy who were within earshot, thinking perhaps that their own people had blown up the fort with a lucky shell, retorted with shrieks of triumph.

The column was soon surrounded by the relatives of the men who had been missing since the retreat from Chinhat, and who might—it was the last hope—have returned to the Machhi Bhawan instead of the Residency. There was a sad answer to most of the enquiries. Palmer came in to find his daughter dying, perfectly resigned and only begging the chaplain to take care of her father when she was gone.

In the morning there came an unexpected shout from outside the Water Gate: 'Arrah, by Jasus, open your gates!' The men on duty inside looked out to see the drunken Irishman standing there stark naked, leading a pair of bullocks with a waggon of ammunition. He had fallen asleep after the sergeant had left him, had been blown into the air, had come down unhurt, and had gone to sleep again, waking at last to find himself lying in a heap of ruins. He had walked over to the Residency, picking up the stray bullocks on the way. The men roared with laughter and let him in. They asked him if he had not met the mutineers. 'Sure', he said, 'I didn't see e'er a man in the place.' Either the enemy had not yet returned from the native quarter; or they had been driven away for the time by the explosion; or else they had seen the man in the half light, naked and grimed with dust and powder, and mistaken him for an Indian beggar.

Lawrence's losses at Chinhat had been as follows:

	Killed and Missing	Wounded
Europeans - - - -	118	54
Indians - - - -	175	24

He had withdrawn the detachment that had been stationed on the north side of the river on the 29th June, and now that the Machhi Bhawan had been evacuated he had an effective strength of sixteen hundred and forty, a further eighty being sick and wounded, to man the perimeter of at least two thousand yards. The numbers were made up as follows:

British Officers (including medical)	133
British N.C.O.'s and Men - -	671
Christian Drummers (mostly Eurasians) - - - - -	51
Volunteers (all civilians capable of bearing arms) - - - -	153
Total of Christians - -	1008
Indian Troops - -	712
Total -	1720

The non-combatants numbered twelve hundred and eighty, as follows:

Christians:		
	Women - - -	240
	Children - - -	270
	Boys - - - -	50
	Others - - -	40
		600
Indians:	- - - - -	680
	Total -	1280

The 32nd Foot and a detachment of fifty of the 84th were the only Queen's troops, the rest being drawn from the East India Company's regular army and the Oudh Irregular Force. The 32nd were the backbone of the garrison, though, man for man, many of the officers of the mutinous regiments were more formidable, being armed with rifles while the rank and file had only smooth-bore percussion muskets: 'Brown Bess' was not a weapon of precision and was of little use for firing into loopholes. The detachment of the 84th had been sent up from Cawnpore by Major General Sir Hugh Wheeler only three days before he was himself attacked by the Nana Sahib and the mutineers; these were the first of the reinforcements that had been working their way up from Calcutta before being detained by the troubles at Allahabad.

All the able-bodied civilians had been enrolled

as volunteers, together with certain merchants and others who chanced to be in Lucknow at the time. Some of them had joined the troop of Volunteer Cavalry that had helped to stave off disaster during the retreat from Chinhat, and the rest had been drilled as infantry by sergeants of the 32nd. Their instructors considered it hopeless to turn them into self-respecting troops. There were tall, athletic Englishmen and fat Eurasians, all belly and no chest, some little more than boys and others bent with age. They looked quaint enough to raise a smile when marching, and when they advanced at the double their antics constrained the military men to laugh outright. Some of them took time to become accustomed to discipline, thinking it beneath them to be drilled with muskets like the common soldiers, but by the end of June they were pretty handy with their weapons and could be relied upon to put up a good fight from behind the parapet. Many of them had sporting rifles of their own, as well as shot-guns which would be destructive at close quarters.

Among the Indian troops were the sepoys of the 13th and 71st Native Infantry that had marched from their lines on the night of the mutiny and fallen in on the flank of the 32nd, the 13th bringing their colours and treasure chest; the remnant of the 48th Native Infantry that had marched with the colours into Lucknow on the same night, after some hesitation; and a number of pensioned sepoys and artillerymen who had been brought in by Lawrence from the outlying districts, some of them old and infirm, but all staunch and willing. There were also the Sikh cavalry that had broken at Chinhat, besides some native levies raised by Mr Gubbins.

The fifty boys were pupils at the Martinière College, founded by General Martin, a famous French adventurer. Mr Schilling, the Principal, had brought them into the entrenchment from the General's palace outside the city and housed them on the south face of the defences. Although not included in the official numbers of the combatants, some of the elder boys were armed with muskets, and helped the masters to defend their own building. Of the younger, some were lent to the various houses to help in domestic work, some were employed in taking messages or carrying ammunition, and some fanned the flies from the wounded in the hospital.

Each outpost was manned by an independent garrison, the commandants, some of whom were very junior officers, being specially chosen for the duty. The troops from the Machhi Bhawan were at once distributed among the various posts—a welcome reinforcement, which put a little heart into the original garrison, still shaken as they were by the defeat at Chinhat. Lawrence superintended these dispositions himself, and went round at dawn inspecting every post, explaining what was wanted of the men, and steadying them all to their duty.

Towards eight o'clock that morning, the 2nd July, he returned to the Residency building with his nephew George after a final round of inspection. As it was already very hot they lay down in their clothes on their beds, which were side by side in the same room a few feet apart. There was a cooly sitting on the floor pulling the punkah. Lawrence asked Captain Wilson, his Deputy Assistant Adjutant General, to draw up a memorandum on the issue of rations. Wilson reminded him of his promise to move to a lower room, but Lawrence replied that he was too tired at present and would rest for a couple of hours before having his things carried down. Wilson then retired into the next room, returning in half an hour with his memorandum. He stood between the two beds, on the right hand side of Sir Henry's, with one knee resting on the bed. He had read out what he had written, and Lawrence had just begun to suggest certain alterations, when a second shell burst in the room. There was a red glare and a shattering report; then darkness. Wilson was knocked onto the floor, where he lay for a few seconds, stunned. On scrambling up he found that he was slightly wounded in the back, half of his shirt being blown away. There was nothing to be seen for the smoke and dust, nor was there any sound from either bed. He asked in great alarm:

'Sir Henry, are you hurt?'

There was no answer. He said again:

'Sir Henry, are you hurt?'

There was still no answer, and he asked a third time:

'Sir Henry, are you hurt?'

Then Lawrence replied in a low voice: 'I am killed.'

As the dust and smoke began to clear away Wilson could see the white coverlet on Sir Henry's bed, crimson with blood. George Lawrence was covered with bricks but unhurt, though one of the punkah cooly's feet had been carried off by a splinter. Several privates of the 32nd rushed in, placed Lawrence on a chair, and carried him down to the drawing-room, where they laid him on the table. George Lawrence ran across the way for Dr Fayrer.

The doctor found Sir Henry faint and depressed from shock. His face was pale, his voice low, and his speech hurried. He asked: 'How long have I got to live?' Fayrer replied: 'For some time, I hope,' as he began to remove the torn clothing and examine the wound. He found that the upper part of the left thigh had been lacerated by a fragment of shell, which had passed through it, comminuting the head of the bone and causing extensive injury to the soft parts. The femoral artery, however, was not injured. Lawrence said: 'I want a distinct answer. How long shall I live? I have a deal to do.' On Fayrer's replying that he gave him about forty-eight hours, Lawrence seemed satisfied and sent for Colonel Inglis and Major Banks.

Presently he rallied under the influence of cordials and was able to talk freely. As the Residency building was still under a severe fire of shot, shell, and musketry, it was thought best to remove him to Dr Fayrer's house which, it was hoped, would be less exposed. They carried Lawrence across under a storm of bullets and placed him in the north verandah; but it seemed that the enemy had intelligence of his movements, for almost at once they opened fire on the very place where he was lying, and it was only by keeping strictly under cover of the pillars and the end walls that the principal officers and civilians in the garrison who surrounded his deathbed could themselves be safe. Mr Harris, the senior chaplain, administered Holy Communion to Lawrence and to Inglis, Banks and the rest, many of whom were moved to tears, while the women looked on through the windows commanding the verandah. The words of the Communion Service were accompanied by the din of the enemy's musketry and cannonade, and the booming of the guns that were firing in the compound outside. When the service was over Lawrence was moved to an inner room.

The office of Chief Commissioner would in the ordinary course have devolved upon Mr Martin Gubbins, the Financial Commissioner, but, while admiring his courage and energy, Lawrence had decided early in June that he was too headstrong for high office, and had telegraphed to Lord Canning as follows: 'If anything happens to me during present disturbances, I earnestly recommend that Major Banks succeed me as Chief Commissioner, and Colonel Inglis in command of the troops until better times arrive. This is no time for punctilio as regards seniority. They are the right men, in fact the only men for the places. My secretary entirely concurs with me on the above points.' Now, in the presence of many witnesses, Lawrence confirmed Major Banks and Colonel Inglis in these appointments, instructing them to form a Military Council of three, with Major Anderson, the Chief Engineer. Major Banks took notes of Lawrence's orders for the defence, as follows:

Reserve fire, check all wall firing.

Carefully register ammunition for guns and small arms in store. Carefully register daily expenditure as far as possible.

Spare the precious health of Europeans in every possible way, from shot and sun.

Organize working parties for night labour.

Entrench—entrench—entrench—erect traverses, cut off enemy's fire.

Turn every horse out of the entrenchment, except enough for four guns. Keep Sir Henry's horse 'Ludakee', it is a gift to his nephew Geo. Lawrence.

Use the state prisoners as a means of getting in supplies by gentle means if possible, or by threats.

Enrol every servant as bildar, or carrier of earth. Pay liberally, double, quadruple.

Turn out every native who will not work. Save menials, who have more than abundant labour.

Write daily to Allahabad or Agra.

Sir Henry Lawrence's servants to receive one year's pay, they are to work for any other gentlemen who want them, or they may leave if they prefer to do so.

Put on my tomb only this—'Here lies Henry Lawrence who tried to do his duty. May God have mercy on him.'

Take an immediate inventory of all natives so as to know who can be used as bildars, etc.

Take an immediate inventory of all supplies and food, etc. Take daily average of expenditure.

There was nothing to be done for the dying man beyond checking what little haemorrhage was present, supporting the injured limb with bandages and pillows, and giving stimulants to counteract shock. When the pain became excessive Dr Fayrer gave him chloroform. He consulted Dr Partridge and Dr Ogilvie on the question of operating, but they both agreed that it would be hopeless. They were satisfied, after a further examination under anaesthetic, that the pelvis was fractured, and that it would therefore be useless to amputate at the hip joint. Even if the thigh bone alone had been broken, it was doubtful whether the patient could have stood the shock of amputation.

During his periods of consciousness Lawrence's

judgment was still clear. He adjured his officers never to treat with the enemy, to do all that was in their power to save the women and children, and to husband their food and ammunition. He spoke of his family and of the provisions that would be found in his will. He spoke, too, of his dead wife Honoria, breaking into passionate tears as he pronounced her name. Summoning those among the garrison for whom he had a special affection, he talked with them about the future, telling them how much he was expecting of them: he had always had a keen eye for promise in the young. He sent, too, for those to whom, in the stress of the last few weeks, he felt he had spoken harshly, and asked them to forgive him. He reminded the company at large of the worthlessness of human distinction, such as his own high office, in the face of death, recommending them to fix their thoughts on the world to come. Again and again he spoke of the danger that threatened the women and children.

He told George Lawrence that he had been like a son to him; there had been a time, he said, when he had thought him selfish, but he had found that he was wrong, and now he gave him his blessing. He spoke humbly of his own merits and dwelt on his shortcomings. He hoped that he would not be maligned, and said that he had undertaken the advance on Chinhat against his own judgment, from the fear of man—a statement which was thought by some to refer to Mr Gubbins, who, though he might not have advised that particular operation, had been the untiring advocate of an aggressive policy.

Lawrence feared what his death might mean to the schools for children of European soldiers that he had founded and sustained with princely contributions. 'Remember the Asylum,' he said, 'do not let them forget the Asylum.' He told Mr Harris that he was to be buried without any fuss, in the same grave with any men of the garrison who might die about the same time. Later he said: 'I forgive everyone—I forgive my brother John.' There had been painful friction between the two brothers in the Punjab before Dalhousie had decided that Henry should go to Rajputana while John stayed at Lahore, but since then they had met on friendly terms in Calcutta.

After the evening of the 2nd July Lawrence spoke little, though sometimes he joined in the psalms and prayers that Mr Harris read to him. Dr Fayrer attended him frequently, giving him chloroform and opiates from time to time. George Lawrence was constantly beside him, Dr Ogilvie keeping him company, while Mrs Harris, Mrs Dashwood, and Mrs Clarke helped to nurse him. He seemed to Mrs Harris to be suffering the utmost agony, but Dr Fayrer did not believe that the pain was intolerable.

During the 3rd July Lawrence was gradually sinking, and took nothing but a little arrowroot and champagne. At eight o'clock on the morning of the fourth he died, so quietly that his nephew, who had just been shot through the shoulder and was sitting at his feet, did not know that he was dead until Dr Ogilvie told him.

Soon Mrs Harris was forced to ask that the body should be removed from the room where she was attending to George Lawrence's wound, for the climate did not admit of any lying-in-state. Mr Harris called in four men of the 32nd, who were serving the guns outside, to carry the bed out onto the verandah. One of them lifted the sheet from Sir Henry's face and the four of them in turn bent down and kissed the dead man's forehead. He was buried after dark without fuss, as he had wished, in a trench with several gunners who had been killed during the day. Mr Harris read the burial service under a heavy fire. So many of the garrison wished to attend the funeral that Inglis, knowing how few could be spared from their posts, and thinking it invidious to pick and choose, gave orders that only some of the staff should be present.

The authorities were in no hurry to inform the garrison of Sir Henry's death, but the news soon got about and was received with grief and alarm by both Europeans and Indians. They did not blame him for the reverse at Chinhat, but remembered that if any of them came through the siege alive it would be thanks to his foresight, since no one else would or could have made such effective preparations. Some of them wondered how the defence would be conducted now that they were without the leader whom everyone had trusted, and many of them felt that they had lost a friend, almost a father. It was said among the troops that his last words had been: 'Dear Inglis, ask the poor fellows whom I exposed at Chinhat to forgive me. Bid them remember Cawnpore and never surrender. God bless you all!'

Meanwhile, the garrison had been working day and night to complete the defences. At the south-west angle a bastion was already under construction, designed by Lieutenant Hutchinson, Bengal Engineers, but when the siege began the parapet was still too low to be tenable, while a large gap had been left for the entrance of the coolies with their baskets of earth. Believing the flanking fire of this bastion to be essential to the safety of his post, Mr Gubbins determined to finish the work at all costs. On the evening of the 30th June he assembled his native servants and levies, informing them of his intention and offering two rupees (four shillings) a night to all who would bear a hand. Lieutenant Hutchinson promised to superintend, and several other Europeans offered to help. Since the bastion was outside the compound walls nothing could be done before nightfall, but as soon as it was dark Mr Gubbins' volunteers opened a window in one of the out-houses and let themselves quietly down into the earthwork.

Their first task was to secure the gap in the parapet by means of a retrenchment, or inner line of defence, and a rough-and-ready palisade. Fortunately the enemy had no notion of what they were about, and they were therefore able to steal out and collect various planks and timbers that were lying in the open. Mrs Gubbins and Mrs Brydon, one of her guests, sat up through the night to keep the men supplied with tea and brandy-and-water. After a good night's work they all climbed back through the window, just as day began to break, and barricaded it after them.

Mr Gubbins paid the Indian workers their two rupees each in cash as soon as they had finished. The pay was high, the ordinary day's wage of a labourer being one-eighth of a rupee, and soon there were as many as seventy-five men working in the bastion every night. Indeed, there were complaints that indispensable servants were being attracted from the other outposts, and some of them had to be turned away. One woman and several children joined in the work, being paid at half the men's rate.

The second and third nights passed as quietly as the first, and it was still safe to search for planks and battens in the open; but on the fourth night, discovering what was afoot, the enemy occupied and loopholed the surrounding houses, the nearest of which was within twenty-five yards of the bastion. There was a liberal exchange of abuse in the vernacular, followed by shots from the enemy which killed one of the workmen and wounded others, but the work went on steadily.

It was not long before the whole garrison were

regretting that the demolition of the neighbouring houses was incomplete, for the entrenchment was commanded by hundreds of loopholes manned by excellent marksmen, some of whom were armed with single- and double-barrelled rifles. There had been no time yet to tackle the problem of defilade, and, until some sort of traverses could be improvised, the only hope of crossing safely from one post to another lay in moving faster than the sharpshooters could aim: more than one of the garrison owed a sudden death to the pride that would not let them run in the face of the enemy. It was fortunate for the defence that Johannes' house, with its turret commanding the south and south-east sides of the position, was not occupied by the enemy for the first few days, in consequence, it was said, of a rumour that it had been undermined.

It was believed that from eight to ten thousand men were firing into the entrenchment at once. There had been over six thousand mutineers at Chinhat, both soldiers and military police, besides the armed retainers of three of the Talukdars, or Barons of Oudh; and on hearing of Lawrence's defeat the last regiments of native infantry in Lucknow had mutinied, letting their officers escape to the Machhi Bhawan, while the sepoys' example had soon been followed by the last of the police. Most of the Talukdars were still neutral, both they and the villagers having treated the fugitives from the outlying districts of Oudh with considerable kindness, but they had all been arming their retainers for some time past; the countryside was overrun with disbanded soldiers of the ex-King who had found no place in the new Oudh Irregular Force or the Military Police; among the city's six or seven hundred thousand inhabitants were many tradesmen who had depended on the vices and luxuries of the court and had now lost their livelihood; and, besides those who had good reason to hate the British rule, there were the badmashes, or scum of the bazaars, who welcomed violence for its own sake.

Many of the Talukdars' retainers were Pasis, low caste Dravidian tribesmen, who were reckoned faithful to their masters although they were the chief robbers in the province. They were small, sleek, and supple, quick-eyed, and expert bowmen. Many of them ranged the jungle, keeping pigs and hunting game, while others lived in small groups in the villages where they were employed as guides and messengers. They were highly valued as mercenary troops and noted for their skill in mining. Some of them were armed with matchlocks, but many of them preferred the bow, with which they could drive a shaft, at short range, clean through a man's body. Sometimes they used arrows fitted with flaming wicks for incendiary purposes.

Each of the mutinous corps was still a regiment in being, with its own Indian officers, and only lacking the accustomed European leadership; they had plenty of guns, though they were short of mortars for high-angle fire; and it was clear that, whatever the total numbers of the enemy, which probably varied throughout the siege between ten and fifty thousand, the odds on their side were so immense, and the garrison's allowance of less than one man per yard of the perimeter so scanty, that only competent leadership was needed to carry the defences by a coup-de-main or by breaching with mines or artillery.

Lawrence had left the conduct of the defence in good hands, and Mr Ommanney, the Judicial Commissioner, had cheerfully accepted his own supersession by Major Banks. Mr Gubbins, on the other hand, was indignant at being passed over, and announced at a meeting on the 2nd July that so long as Sir Henry lived he would not record any objection to the appointment of Major Banks, but that, if it pleased God to take Sir Henry, he would then urge his claims to the office of Chief Commissioner. It was agreed that the question should be left over, and Banks added to the account of the meeting in his diary: 'Sufficient for the day is the evil thereof.' After Lawrence's death Gubbins wrote several contentious letters to Banks, and even addressed protests to the authorities at Calcutta, but received no satisfaction.

Major Banks, the Commissioner of the Lucknow division, was an excellent linguist and a capable administrator. In ability and energy he was scarcely superior to Gubbins, but he and Major Anderson, the Chief Engineer, were both shrewd and level-headed men. Anderson's health was bad, but fortunately Captain Fulton, his Executive Engineer, was able to take much of the work off his shoulders.

Colonel Inglis of the 32nd was known throughout North-West India as a keen regimental officer, a crack shot, and an ardent sportsman. He was active and conscientious, and his own men liked and trusted him, though some of the engineers held him in contempt. He was not outstanding in either intellect or ability, but was well served by his subordinates and could take advice. He now held the local rank of Brigadier, subject to confirmation.

Inglis himself, his staff, and the engineer officers were even more exposed to the enemy's fire than the rest of the garrison, since each post was manned by an independent unit, the members of which were kept under cover as far as possible, rarely leaving their own positions except at night when on fatigue. Each separate garrison had to repel attacks, attend to their own defences under the engineers' supervision, and make any local sorties that were needed. The only reserve was the detachment of the 84th, posted in the Residency building, and there were no reliefs. Officers and men stood sentry without distinction. The Brigadier made his rounds once a day and once a night. Captain Wilson also inspected the outposts, and at daylight every morning Lieutenant Birch, 71st Native Infantry, Inglis' Aide-de-Camp, collected the returns of casualties for the previous day.

After the Residency was invested none of the combatants ever spent a restful night in bed. When they slept it was in their clothes with their arms beside them; but there was not much sleep, for, besides standing guard on the defences, the men had a score of other duties, most of which could only be executed after dark. So many of the Indian servants had deserted that the neglected commissariat and battery bullocks were wandering about the entrenchment, searching for food and tumbling down wells or being shot by the enemy. The artillery and cavalry horses broke loose, driven half mad by lack of food and water, and many of these, too, were shot. The stench of carcases was so overpowering that fatigue parties were sent after dark to drag them into shelter and bury them; Mr Couper, Lawrence's secretary, spent an arduous night disposing of a camel. There were dead men to bury, too, and the sick and wounded to carry to the hospital; there were guns and mortars to be dragged into place, screens and traverses to be erected against the enemy's fire, batteries and embrasures to be repaired, and stores to be shifted into less exposed positions.

All ranks worked side by side, officers, non-commissioned officers, and men, clerks and responsible civilians. The troops had not yet recovered from the mauling they had had at Chinhat. There was drunkenness among both the volunteers and the rank and file of the 32nd, while many of the officers let it be seen that they had quite lost heart. The man that everyone was shouting for was Captain Fulton, the Executive Engineer, who soon impressed the whole garrison by his courage and capacity. All the Indian troops worked loyally except the Sikh cavalry, who sat about sulking and sneering at the rest.

Gradually the entrenchment began to assume some kind of order. The cattle were driven to their sheds, and the best of the horses were picketed while the rest were turned out at night and driven away. Most of them wandered back, however, to be shot down by the enemy just outside the defences, where they rotted to the great discomfort of the garrison. In Captain Anderson's compound alone five horses were wounded. It was impossible to approach them by daylight and not easy at night, but when some of them died the air became so rank that Anderson took out a party after dark to drag them away and throw them down a well. Those that were still alive were driven out. One of them had a broken leg, and, rather than let him die there, Anderson crept out on hands and knees, cut the rope he was tethered by, and ordered one man to drag him by the halter and another to urge him from behind, until he had hobbled into the open on three legs.

Some of the cattle that had strayed outside the defences were driven in by two of the volunteers, one of whom was Mr J. A. Casey, a civil engineer. Mr Casey knew very well that he was courting death, but tried to comfort his wife by suggesting that some of the coolies that had worked for him before the troubles might persuade the mutineers to hold their fire. He returned with a severe wound in the left shoulder which soon began to mortify.

The issue of rations was being made under difficulties, Lieutenant James, Sub-Assistant Commissary General, having been wounded at Chinhat, his native clerks having run away with all their papers, and his subordinates being new to the work. The first depots that were opened could only be approached under fire, and, while some of the servants did not know where to apply for food, others who found the way were killed or wounded. As soon as possible the stores were shifted into less exposed positions and a scale of rations was fixed for every man, woman, and child in the place, Christian, Mohammedan, and Hindu. It was the duty of the commandants of the various posts to return their strength every morning to the Commissariat, which sent back the necessary supplies in bulk, leaving each garrison to make its own arrangements for cooking and distribution.

Supplies had been collected hurriedly, some by the civil, some by the military authorities, under the direct orders of Lawrence himself. There was abundance of grain, livestock, and fodder, much of the first having been sent in, at Lawrence's suggestion, by influential Indians who had professed sympathy with the British cause, and whose contributions had been stored in the large plunge bath under the Residency banqueting hall. Rum and porter had been liberally provided; large stacks of firewood had been built; and stores of lime and charcoal had been distributed about the position for sanitary purposes.

The women and children were accommodated in the less exposed outposts and in buildings nearer the centre of the position. The Residency itself housed a number of officers' families, and the women of the 32nd Foot were quartered in the taikhana or underground suite. Many of the ladies had arrived during June as fugitives from the out-stations of Oudh, bringing neither servants nor baggage, and, however generously they were treated by the English residents of Lucknow, they inevitably suffered great discomfort. In a country where a junior chaplain, for instance, living very quietly with his wife and no children, had been used to employ twenty-three servants, it was hardship indeed for the wives of officers and civilians to clean their own rooms, draw their water, wash their clothes, attend to their children, and cook their food—all in a trying climate and in such cramped quarters that there was little privacy or comfort.

Mrs Bartrum, a doctor's wife, who had been living in one of the outlying districts, had been sent into Lucknow in the early days of June by Lawrence's orders. She herself would have preferred death by her husband's side to the uncertainty of separation, but Dr Bartrum insisted that she must leave him, if only for the safety of their child. He accompanied her as far as Sikrora, where the convoy was to start from, and said as he helped her onto her elephant: 'Good-bye, dear Kate, keep up your spirits—we shall soon meet again; and take care of my little darling.'

She begged him to come with her and the baby, but, though he longed to be with them and distrusted the sepoy escort, he could not leave his regiment. On reaching Lucknow after a hazardous and exhausting journey, Mrs Bartrum was quartered with a party in a squalid, ill-furnished room in the Begam Kothi, a large building in the centre of the position which had once been the residence of a European wife of the King of Oudh. The heat was intense, there was no punkah, and there were swarms of flies and mosquitoes. For the first time in her life Mrs Bartrum had no one to look after her: she was among strangers, and ignorant of her husband's fate. On the 12th June, however, she was cheered by a note from Dr Bartrum which told her that the troops at his station had mutinied but that he had escaped with the other officers. Towards the end of the month, when all the available servants had deserted, and most of the other women were either too ill or too wretched to keep things in order, Mrs Bartrum made herself responsible for cleaning and tidying the room. She found that, in spite of the discomfort, it was a blessing to be forced to work, since it kept her from brooding on her troubles and fears.

The Lucknow residents were generally more fortunate than the refugees. Mrs Inglis, for instance, had several servants, among them an Indian butler who had been with Inglis through the siege of Multan, where he used to take him his dinner in the trenches under fire: he and many more were faithful to their masters. Those who had fled had much to excuse them: there was little enough shelter for the Europeans, and nothing but odd sheds and corners for the Indians themselves; they did not know what arrangements were being made to feed them; they were aware that the mutineers had already beaten the Europeans in the field; and some of them had wives and families in the city. Many who might have been faithful were left outside the entrenchment when the siege began, and could not have got back again if they had wished.

Now that the Residency was strictly invested there was no news from the outside world beyond the rumours among the Indian garrison. The Sikh troopers, who were suspect from the beginning, were often in touch with the enemy, and some of their news leaked through to the authorities; but this was, of course, the merest hearsay which told them nothing about the general state of India. Major Banks sent out several messengers with letters for Agra and Allahabad, but none of them came back, and what became of them and their despatches was never known. Besides keeping a sharp lookout from the surrounding buildings, the enemy posted pickets further out and searched every passer-by that aroused the least suspicion: it was said to be death to be taken with despatches.

As early as the 16th May, Lawrence had advised Lord Canning to ask for help from Nepal, and when the siege began Brigadier Inglis was still hoping for assistance from the Gurkhas. It was known that the stream of reinforcements from Calcutta had been held up for a time by the troubles at Benares and Allahabad, that order had at last been restored, and that a small force had marched for Cawnpore. Delhi, they knew, was still in the hands of the mutineers, who had proclaimed the restoration of the Mogul dynasty, although a British force was holding the Ridge outside the city. On the 26th June news was received that Delhi had been captured, and royal salutes were fired from the Residency, the Machhi Bhawan, and cantonments before it was discovered that the news was false.

At Cawnpore, nearly fifty miles away, the mutineers had cut the wire to Lucknow and broken up the bridge of boats across the Ganges. On the 6th June they invested Major General Wheeler's earthwork, which was not so much as bullet-proof at the crest of the parapet. Lawrence was asked for help, but was forced to refuse even Wheeler's last appeal: 'Surely we are not to die like rats in a cage.' When word came to Lucknow of the column that was marching up the Grand Trunk Road from Allahabad, Lawrence at once passed on the intelligence to Cawnpore, hoping that all might yet be well. But the news had come too late. On the 28th June Lieutenant Colonel Master received a scrap of paper with the following note from his son, Lieutenant Master, 53rd Native Infantry, at Cawnpore:

'*June 25th*, 8½ *p.m.*

'We have held out now for twenty-one days, under a tremendous fire. The Raja of Bithur [the Nana Sahib] has offered to forward us in safety to Allahabad, and the general has accepted his terms. I am all right, though twice wounded. Charlotte Newnham and Bella Blair are dead. I'll write from Allahabad. God bless you!

Your affectionate son,

G. A. Master.'

When Lawrence heard of this he at once predicted treachery on the part of the Nana Sahib, against whom he and Mr Gubbins had already warned General Wheeler. The same evening two runners returned from Cawnpore, where they had not been able to deliver their despatches. It was plain that they brought bad news. Taking the men aside, Mr Gubbins learnt that Wheeler's force had been annihilated on the river bank, but that many of the women and children were still alive and in the Nana's hands. The runners had witnessed the massacre themselves.

Lieutenant Colonel Master was not the only one in Lucknow to whom the news brought anxiety and grief, for Wheeler's force had included the invalid depot of the 32nd, and many of the women and children of the Regiment had been with them. Now that the Lucknow Residency, too, was besieged by mutineers, the defenders swore that they would sooner die at their posts than make terms with a treacherous enemy. But what of the non-combatants? Some of the men began to ask each other whether they must kill their wives and children in the last extremity. An officer in his own garrison took Mr Gubbins aside one evening and said that he and his wife had determined that he should shoot her if the enemy broke in. He asked Gubbins to agree that, if one of them were killed before the other, the survivor should perform this last act of mercy for both their wives. Gubbins refused, saying that the need had not yet arisen, and that, besides, he could never bring himself to do it.

Mr Harris, the senior chaplain, and his wife had been anxious for the safety of their white terrier, Bustle, who had shared not only their travels but their joys and sorrows for the past three years. During June the authorities had ordered that all dogs found about the Residency, outside their owners' compounds, were to be hanged, and, rather than tie up Bustle at Dr Fayrer's house, where they were staying, they sent him out of the city to the Martinière College; but when Mr Schilling, the Principal, seeing the dog pining for his master, brought him back again, Harris decided to keep him at Fayrer's house for the present, since it appeared from the number of curs that were straying round the entrenchment that the order had not yet been enforced. Now that the siege had begun, however, some of the ladies in the taikhana were looking askance at the dog, and it was doubtful whether there would be food to spare for pets; so, taking Bustle out one morning on the chain, Harris asked a soldier to destroy him. The man replied that he would shoot the dog, as he wanted to discharge his piece and clean it.

Private Henry Metcalfe, 32nd Foot, who was

sitting on the verandah at the time, overheard the conversation and asked if he might have the dog. Harris objected that he would not be able to spare him food from his rations, but on Metcalfe's replying that he would take the risk Bustle's life was spared. A few days later Harris told the dog's new master that when he had been serving on the North-West Frontier he and Mrs Harris had been given Bustle as a puppy by a dying soldier whom they had befriended. Mrs Harris had undertaken never to part with him except from sheer necessity. 'And now,' said Mr Harris, 'if you and Mrs Harris and I survive the siege, will you promise to give the dog to Mrs Harris again?'

Metcalfe passed his word, and from that time the dog and he were inseparable. Sometimes when the soldier dozed away on sentry, worn out with overwork, the dog would catch his trousers between his teeth and shake him till he awoke. Metcalfe was now twenty-two, having enlisted at the age of thirteen; during his first year in India he had been nearly carried off by fever, but was spared, as he said himself, for rougher work. Harris was so touched by his care for the dog that he asked one day if there was anything he could do for him. After some thought Metcalfe replied that his pipe had been stolen and that he would be glad to have another. Harris was taken aback by this request, for he had been hoping to forward the lad's prospects in the Regiment, but he answered that though he was no smoker himself he would see what could be done. He went back into the house, where the story of Metcalfe's modest want raised a general laugh, and soon returned with no pipe but a box of fine cigars.

Meanwhile the enemy had maintained a constant fire on the entrenchment day and night, until even the ladies had become expert in judging the weight of the roundshot and distinguishing between that and shell. During the first week, there were from fifteen to twenty deaths a day. Either Polehampton or Harris, or both, held a funeral service every night, usually under fire, the bodies being wrapped in sheets and laid in a common grave. It was not always easy to find labour, and when, on the first day of the siege, Mrs Soppitt's little boy died of cholera, Polehampton could only induce the coolies to dig the grave by threatening them with his revolver; nor were their fears unfounded, for a servant of Mrs Soppitt's who was helping them was wounded in the arm. The child had been two years old, though his mother was only nineteen on the 3rd July. With her boy dead and her husband constantly on duty, her only comfort was the hope of the second child that she believed was on the way.

There were both cholera and smallpox among the garrison, but fortunately neither disease seemed to be spreading. The hospital had a full complement of surgeons, Dr Scott being the senior medical officer. He was sometimes crusty, especially towards patients who winced under the knife, but he was well liked and trusted, and to any man who bore the pain cheerfully he gave a nod of approval or even a cheroot. It was less than three years since the first female nurses had been admitted to British military hospitals, and Miss Nightingale's reforms had not yet borne fruit in India; but her example was followed by Mrs Polehampton, whose only child had died in January, and Mrs Gall and Mrs Barbor, both of whom had lost their husbands during June. The authorities gladly accepted their offer to assist the orderlies, and they were moved into a small room on the south side of the hospital, where Mr Polehampton joined them, and where all four ate, slept, and dressed. They could only avoid the musket balls that were continually entering the room by making the most careful arrangements. They removed the glass from the window frames, for fear of splinters, and slept between the two windows, under cover of the wall, waking almost every morning to find a number of bullets on the floor.

Miss Birch, whose father had been shot in the back by one of his own men at Sitapur, came to help in the hospital later on, but though she was kind and willing her health was so poor that Dr Boyd, who was in immediate charge of the hospital, sent her back to Mr Gubbins' house. Among others who came to help were Mrs Parry, Mrs Erith, Mrs Bates, and Miss Alone. Mrs Parry used to take a can of tea from her private store to the hospital every morning and evening, and sometimes gruel, too, having robbed herself to make it. The sick and wounded welcomed every such addition to their monotonous fare.

The state prisoners who had been brought across from the Machhi Bhawan were quartered in the same building as the hospital, in the hope that their presence would lessen the danger to the patients; for, judging by the rapid way the enemy had shifted their fire from the Residency building to Fayrer's house when Lawrence was moved across on the 2nd July, the garrison supposed them to be informed of all that went on in the entrenchment.

Mrs Inglis, who was now recovering from the smallpox, was beginning to settle down in the small white-washed room to which the Brigadier had brought her on the night after Chinhat. Mrs Case and her sister, Caroline Dickson, had braved the infection to throw in their lot with hers. The room was only twelve feet by six, with open arches in place of doors and windows, but they soon made it tolerably private by means of screens and curtains, and they had the luxury of an outhouse which could be used as a bathroom. They were fortunate, too, in possessing their own goats and fodder, besides a store of such comforts as tea, sugar, and arrowroot.

Mrs Inglis slept on one sofa and Mrs Case on another, while Miss Dickson and the three Inglis children—Johnny, Charlie, and the baby—lay on the floor on mattresses which could be rolled up and put away neatly in the day-time. Mrs Case saw that the room was kept clean and tidy, and Mrs Inglis took charge of the rations, weighing them all out scrupulously herself. Sometimes she gave away a little arrowroot or sugar to a sick child outside her own quarters, or made simple puddings for invalids who were less fortunate than she.

At Dr Fayrer's house the domestic work was shared between the women and two of the Martinière boys whom Mr Schilling sent across to help, Mrs Harris taking charge since Mrs Fayrer's health was feeble. There were eleven women and seven children living in the taikhana. They slept on the floor, fitting their mattresses together like the pieces of a puzzle so that they might all be as near as possible to the punkah. During the day the beds were rolled up and piled against the wall. There was only room for a few chairs, all of which were reserved for the invalids, and the rest of them took their meals sitting on the floor. Even in the day-time the room was so dark that they had to eat by candle-light. Sometimes about sunset, when the enemy were preparing their supper and the firing slackened, the women were allowed to come up and sit in the portico for half an hour to enjoy the fresh air. Mrs Harris, who was still nursing George Lawrence, was allowed upstairs during the day, and also Mrs Dashwood, whose husband, Lieutenant A. J. Dashwood, 48th Native Infantry, had been badly knocked about by falling bricks at the Cawnpore Battery. The men slept upstairs in a long verandah on the side of the house that was least exposed.

Rations were now being issued of meat, flour, rice, attah (stone-ground wheat), dal (a kind of lentil), and salt. The regular fare was stew and chapatties (flat cakes made by kneading flour or attah with water, beating the mixture out between the palms of the hands, and baking it on iron girdles). There was no bread at all, for all the bakers had deserted, and no one else had leisure to learn the trade, even if yeast could have been procured. The stews were unpalatable and often nauseous, and most of the Europeans disliked the chapatties; neither were tempting to delicate children who were suffering from the heat. Milk was very scarce, and the garrison were cut off from the pits in which their supply of ice, collected from earthenware saucers in the cold weather, was stored. There were few punkahs and fewer coolies available to pull them, and the mothers themselves often sat up for hours to fan their children, who found it hard to sleep in such cramped and comfortless conditions. Sometimes when there was a night alarm the order would go round: 'All lights to be put out.' and the children would wake up and cry in the darkness, while their mothers sat beside them trembling, wondering how long it would be before the enemy broke in. The women at Fayrer's house always slept in their clothes.

Those who were staying with Mr Gubbins fared better than the rest, for their host had not only begun to fortify his house long before the siege, but had also laid in a generous store of provisions. The bottled beer, which was considered the greatest luxury, was reserved for the sick and wounded and the ladies who were nursing them, but one glass of sauterne was served all round at luncheon every day, and at dinner one glass of sherry and two of champagne or claret. They drank tea three times a day, with milk and sugar. Sometimes at dinner they were able to treat themselves to a rice pudding, and there were even memorable occasions when a plum or a jam pudding was announced, to which Mrs Gubbins helped the others so liberally that often there was none left for herself. A few poultry were still kept, some goats, and two cows, all of which were half starved during the siege. There were times when members of less fortunate garrisons envied this profusion, or would have envied it had they not been disarmed by the generosity with which Mr Gubbins gave to the hospital and to the poorer people outside his own house.

As the days went on the volunteers began to shake down to their work, though some of them were still drinking heavily. One day a small civilian approached Captain Anderson and gravely asked him: 'What are we to do, sir, if we are charged by elephants?' Anderson could not help laughing, but replied as seriously as he was able that this was a difficult question; he was confident, at all events, that, whether it would be possible or not to keep them out, Government would expect every man to make the attempt.

One of the keenest fighting men in Anderson's garrison was Signor Barsottelli, who had lately imported and disposed of a consignment of alabasters from Florence. He used to go on duty with a musket in one hand and a double-barrelled rifle in the other, a huge sabre at his side, and his cartridge pouch slung across his chest like an Italian hand-organ. The pouch was much in his way, and when someone pointed out that it would be better on his back he was delighted, since he had trouble enough in keeping his sabre from getting between his legs. He did not approve of the nocturnal visits of the staff, and used to say: 'I think these "grand round" officers do this for their own amusement.' One night when one of the other volunteers was anxiously wondering whether he could present arms correctly, Barsottelli consoled him: 'Never mind, sir, make a *leetle* noise; who's to see in the dark?'

One day an officer who was passing the much exposed Cawnpore battery with a friend heard the following conversation—presumably about the Brigadier—between two of the garrison, one of whom had just returned from a neighbouring post:

'Well, Bill; anything up?'

'No.'

'Jack been here?'

'Yes.'

'What did he do?'

'Oh, he looked through this here keek-hole, and then through that there keek-hole.'

'And then?'

'He said we must trust to the British bayonet only.'

'And then?'

'Why, then he hooked it.'

'*Judicious* Hooker!' said the officer to his friend as they passed on.

Before the siege, while Lawrence was still hoping to hold the ground between the northern defences and the river bank, a mass of powder and ammunition had been stowed away in pits outside the hospital post; and when the place was invested a number of tents had been left standing close to these stores, besides a large stack of fodder for the cattle. On the night of the 3rd July the enemy set fire to the stack, and it was feared that if once the flames reached the tents the magazine would go up. Lieutenant Fletcher, 48th Native Infantry, took out a party of officers and cut the tents to the ground in time to prevent the fire from spreading. On this day Mr Ommanney, the Judicial Commissioner, was mortally wounded by a roundshot in the Redan battery.

On the 4th July three Irish privates of the 32nd and a handful of volunteers made a swift sortie from Innes' post to silence a 9-pounder gun which the enemy had planted behind a small mosque on the way to the iron bridge. Stealing out in the early afternoon they found most of the enemy asleep or at their dinner, only the sentries being armed. Private William Cooney rushed the gun and drove home a spike in the vent, while Private William Dowling killed an Indian officer, and Private Michael Smith fired his musket and bayoneted a couple more of the enemy. The volunteers acted as a covering party, and they were all away again before the enemy could collect themselves. They reached Innes' post without a scratch though followed by a heavy fusillade. That night thirteen of the Sikhs deserted.

It was clear from the screams and shots that could be heard after dark that the mutineers were still plundering the bazaars, and it was rumoured that some of them were already leaving for their homes to secure their loot. The garrison had reason to be thankful that they had been thus distracted during the first and most critical days of the siege, for had they been more aggressive in following up their success at Chinhat there would never have been time to organise the defence.

In the early morning of the 5th July there was heavy rain, which washed away some of the accumulated filth from the entrenchment, though it left enough unburied and decaying carcases to raise an incessant stench. During the day the enemy's cannonade slackened so sensibly that the garrison hoped they were running short of ammunition; but the musketry was still as intense as ever, and when the mutineers ran out of bullets they fired nails and ramrods from their smooth-bore muskets. Some of them were seen in the open near the Cawnpore battery, picking up bullets from the ground. Mr Rees, a Calcutta merchant, shot one of them dead, but regretted it afterwards when the body began to rot.

Next day the cannonade was as heavy as ever and the enemy could be seen digging trenches all round the position. They seemed to have overcome their fears that Johannes' house was undermined, for now their sharpshooters were posted in the upper storeys, which commanded the Cawnpore battery, the barracks behind it, Anderson's post, the Post Office, the entrance to the Begam Kothi, and, in reverse, the Hospital on the far side of the position. For the first few days the sharpshooters had it all their own way: the range was short and the casualties in the garrison were heavy. One of the African eunuchs of the ex-King of Oudh made such good practice with his double-barrelled rifle that he became known as 'Jim the Rifle', or 'Bob the Nailer', because he nailed a man with every shot.

On the 7th July it was resolved to make a sortie against Johannes' house. A party of fifty of the 32nd and twenty Sikhs was to be led by Captain Mansfield, Lieutenant S. H. Lawrence, and Ensign Studdy, all of the 32nd, and Ensign Green of the 13th Native Infantry, accompanied by Captain Fulton and Lieutenant J. C. Anderson of the Engineers. The sortie was timed for noon, when the men had had their dinner. After the Brigadier had addressed a few words to them they filed out through an improvised sally-port in the wall by the Martinière post, while a brisk cannonade was opened from the neighbouring batteries, and the officers on the roof of the Brigade Mess kept Bob the Nailer busy with their rifles. The house was soon occupied, Sam Lawrence being first up the ladder and in at one of the windows. Bob the Nailer was so absorbed in his contest with the Brigade Mess that he was taken by surprise and quickly despatched. The engineers were already preparing charges of powder to blow up the house when the sortie was recalled by Brigadier Inglis, who could see the enemy gathering in force outside. The party regained the defences with none killed and only three wounded. Among the latter was Private Cooney, who had distinguished himself again to-day, and who received a tot of brandy and a word of praise from the Brigadier. Sam Lawrence had one of his trouser legs blown away, but was himself untouched. The enemy had lost from fifteen to twenty killed, and the affair had improved the spirits of the garrison; but Johannes' house was still standing and there was nothing to prevent its reoccupation.

On the 8th July a little girl was playing with a roundshot in the courtyard outside the Begam Kothi when she was hit in the head and instantly killed. On the same morning, early, Mr Polehampton received a note from Miss Ommanney, telling him that her father was dead and begging him to come and comfort her mother. He went across at once, and, after persuading Mrs Ommanney to leave the bedside, washed the body and laid it out. He then returned to his room, had his morning shave, and was stooping down to roll up his bed when he felt a sudden stunning pain. After a second or two he realised that he had been hit in the side, by a spent shot as he believed until, on examining the place, he found a hole in the flesh. He then began to fear that the ball was still in the wound, but soon, to his relief, Mrs Barbor found it on the floor. After making him lie down, Mrs Polehampton fetched Dr Boyd, who wished to have him carried to the hospital receiving room. Polehampton insisted on walking, but had to be supported and fainted away before long. After a rapid examination his hurt was pronounced not dangerous, the bullet having entered his side and come out of his back without touching any vital part. As soon as the wound had been dressed he was put to bed in the front ward.

The air in the hospital was now becoming ranker every day. The building was so exposed that the upper rooms could not be used and almost all the doors and windows had to be barricaded. The heat was intense, the wards were crowded, and many of the patients' wounds were sloughing and offensive. Flies were swarming everywhere. Attempts were made to clear the air by such means as burning camphor, but with little success.

In spite of these unfavourable conditions Polehampton soon began to mend, and hoped to be about again before long. He was a simple, manly fellow—an old rowing blue—and his reassuring presence was greatly missed outside the hospital. Mr Harris—who had rowed for Brasenose—had double work to do now that his colleague was on the sick list. Mrs Harris used to await his return from the graveyard every evening in deep anxiety, for the burial of the dead was a hazardous duty.

To add to the fatigues of the garrison one of the walls of the racquet court, which had been filled up with fodder, now collapsed, and every available officer and man had to work for many hours on two successive nights, shifting the chaff back into place and covering it with tarpaulins. Each able-bodied man was on duty from thirteen to twenty hours a day. The bullocks and the horses were now under control, but there were still carcases to be buried, stores to be shifted, parapets to be repaired, and drainage to be dealt with. There were guns to be moved, too, and the wounded to be carried away, and, though the enemy had not yet made any concerted assault on the position, there were constant alarms at night which forced the garrison to stand to arms.

There were times when the Europeans turned sullen and even refused duty, too tired to care what became of them. When Mr Gubbins told the men at his post not to expose themselves more than they could help, they replied that they had as lief die now as later. One night at the Post Office a private who was due to go on sentry threw down his musket and folded his arms. Captain M'Cabe, 32nd Foot, called the sergeant of the guard and said: 'Put him to bed.' The order was obeyed. Knowing his man, M'Cabe was certain that he would not refuse duty again after such an indignity.

As time went on the issue of rations began to work more smoothly and efforts were made to husband the supplies, the officers being put on short allowance every third day. Flour was already scarce but there was plenty of wheat, which was ground in hand-mills by the Indian servants; on the other hand, no provision of tobacco had been made, and the lack of it increased the general depression.

On the night of the 8th July twelve more Sikhs deserted. At four o'clock next morning the enemy bugles sounded the Advance. A force about three hundred strong attacked the Baillie Guard gate, from which they were driven off by a few rounds of grape and canister, and a steady fusillade from the loyal sepoys, while a half-hearted assault near the Cawnpore battery was as easily repelled. On the same day Lieutenant Dashwood, who had been injured some days before by falling bricks, died of cholera after a few hours' illness, leaving his widow with two children and a third on the way. Next morning his brother, Ensign Charles Dashwood, 18th Native Infantry, wounded himself in the leg while cleaning his pistol, and as the surgeon could not extract the ball he was likely to be laid up for some time.

There were now repeated rumours that the enemy were undermining the entrenchment. Since they were only just across the road on the east and south fronts, it would be simple for them to sink shafts in the houses they were occupying, drive galleries underground as far as the defences, charge the mines and blow them up, thus making practicable breaches with little danger to themselves and no great labour: on the southern face, for instance, a forty-foot gallery would do the work. Major Anderson and Captain Fulton were agreed that it would be foolish to take the initiative and thus suggest mining to the enemy, with their immense command of labour, but all the sentries were instructed to listen for the sound of the pick.

On the 10th July, Major Banks wrote to Allahabad as follows: 'We have now been besieged for eleven days. The enemy has not done much harm to our defences, though many men have been killed and wounded. We find that we have food for fully six weeks, nevertheless we look for relief when possible. To-day we hear that Cawnpore is in the hands of our troops. I am writing thither. The enemy's fire is slackening, and his attacks are diminishing in number; why, we cannot tell. We have no reports from outside reliable. I cannot get a messenger for Agra.'

It was rumoured that a general assault was to be delivered in the small hours of the following morning, and the garrison therefore stood to arms from one o'clock onwards, but there was no attack. The besiegers' fire, which had never wholly died away by day or night, grew heavier with the dawn as usual.

During the 12th July the enemy were preparing gun emplacements outside the south-east angle. It was Sunday; in the evening the ladies at Fayrer's house sat under the portico, singing. Captain Weston, 65th Native Infantry, the commandant, came round to join them, but just as they had finished the first verse of the evening hymn there was a burst of firing and the garrison were called to arms. The enemy advanced, three hundred strong, against the Baillie Guard gate, from which they were soon repulsed by shellfire and musketry. At midnight they threatened Gubbins' post. The bugles sounded the Advance again and again, while the mutineers could be heard abusing one another for not advancing. After half an hour they retired and spent the rest of the night firing into the Cawnpore battery.

On the 13th July Johannes' house was reoccupied by the enemy, whose sharpshooters were soon raking the lane between the Brigade Mess and the Martinière post, and could not be dislodged by musketry or shellfire. In the evening the mutineers fired several carcasses, or incendiary shells, into the entrenchment. The Residency building caught fire, but the flames were soon extinguished.

Next day the enemy were reported to be digging in the Captan Bazaar, about a hundred yards from the Redan. One of the engineers crept out after dark to listen for sounds of mining, but could hear nothing.

The heat is greatest at Lucknow at the end of May and the beginning of June, when the thermometer has been known to read over 117° in the shade, but the mean temperature in July is only 6° less than in June; the monsoon rains begin in June, are heaviest in July and August, and only cease in October. Fighting or working, the garrison were exposed alternately to burning sun and drenching rain, conditions for which they were ill-equipped since many of them had no clothes but what they stood up in. There was this to be said for the rain, however, that it discouraged the sharpshooters outside and drained away from the Residency position, which stood on higher ground, into the enemy's trenches.

During the second week of the siege casualties had been decreasing, for the men had begun to know their way about the position and were learning how to take cover. Slowly, since labour was scarce, parapets had been raised, trenches deepened, and roads defiladed by traverses and screens. The knowledge that there were large stores of food and ammunition was beginning to remove the sinister impression created by the failure at Chinhat, the commanding positions of the enemy, and the absence of news from outside.

When the Europeans were first concentrated at the Residency, Dr Ogilvie, as Sanitary Commissioner, had been able to keep the place decent, but now there was so little labour available for his department, the troops being otherwise employed and the Indian sweepers deserting daily, that little could be done to allay the constant reek of carrion and ordure. The health of the garrison was beginning to suffer: there were several cases of cholera and a number of deaths among the children; many of the Europeans had painful boils on the face and head; and in not a single case had the amputation of a limb saved the patient's life.

A few of the officers had allowed the constant discomfort and fatigue to impair their temper, but the rest were usually able to maintain their spirits. Fulton, the indefatigable engineer, could always find time to be pleasant; M'Cabe, a rough customer who had risen from the ranks, was uniformly cheerful; Sam Lawrence, commanding at the Redan, was as good-humoured as he was good-looking. The Indian infantrymen, especially those of the 13th, fought as well as the Europeans, whom they even surpassed in the patience and energy with which they worked.

Meanwhile the investing forces were occupying houses nearer and nearer to the defences. With the enemy just across the road the only hope of safety lay in constant vigilance, and staff-officers were continually visiting the outposts with the solemn warning: 'The Brigadier requests you will be *particularly* on the alert.' At night, while the others rested, a handful of mutineers, firing blank cartridge, could raise an alarm which would force every man in the entrenchment to stand to arms. The enemy had not yet pressed an attack home, but the garrison knew that, when the time came, each outpost must hold its own whatever force might be brought against it, since if one post were overwhelmed there would be little hope for the rest: the general reserve had numbered, when the siege began, fifty men only, and their strength was decreasing every day. It was resolved that, whatever might befall, there should be no surrender, and that the enemy should not boast of a second Cawnpore. If once the defences were carried, every man must die at his post while the women and children were blown up with the magazine. Dr Fayrer, who divided his time between the bedside and the parapet, had a heavy sabre ground to a fine edge and point, fitted with a leather thong for the wrist, and hung up ready to hand, being determined to give a good account of himself if the enemy broke in. He refused, however, to give men poison for their wives.

The enemy sharpshooters were still a constant menace. They used to darken the rooms from which they were firing, so as to be less visible through the loopholes, but before long the officers learnt from Captain Fulton that they could be seen with a glass by one man, while another kept his rifle trained on a loophole and fired when his observer gave the word. The private soldiers' muskets were not accurate enough for this kind of work. The quickest way to dislodge the sharpshooters was to put a roundshot through their post, but this could only be done by special permission of the authorities, who knew that the enemy were short of ammunition and would pick up the shot at once and fire it back: indeed, many of the roundshot went backwards and forwards time after time, while unexploded shells were fitted with new fuses and returned. Sometimes the enemy would make good practice from a point which could not be covered from any existing loophole in the defences. The garrison would leave them alone for a while, to give them confidence, and then one night they would make new loopholes, wait until the enemy had occupied their usual position in the morning, and take them by surprise.

The mutineers did not seem to have received further reinforcements from the Talukdars, or Barons of Oudh, since the concentration at Chinhat, but they had been joined by all sorts of malcontents, including certain disaffected Afridis from Malihabad. They were a noisy crew, especially the Talukdars' men and the badmashes, or city rabble, who used to shriek and beat their drums and blow outlandish horns to the great annoyance of the garrison. One night when the men were all turned out for the usual alarm, one of them said:

'I say, Bill, I'm blowed if these here badmashes don't yell like so many cats.'

'Yes, they do,' said Bill, 'and I only wishes I was behind them with a tin pot of biling water as they opens their damned mouths.'

At that moment there was a shrill blast from the horns outside, and another said:

'I only wish I had a holt of the black rascal as plays that; I'd not kill the vagabond, I'd only break that infernal hinstrument over the bridge of his nose.'

Every morning the mutineers' bugles could be heard sounding the Assembly and their regimental calls, while both morning and evening their bands paraded in sight of the Residency and mortified the garrison by playing popular English airs such as 'The Standard Bearer's March', 'The Girl I Left Behind Me', and 'See the Conquering Hero Comes', always winding up with 'God Save the Queen'. The Union Jack, which was flown from the top of the Residency building, was the favourite target of the enemy marksmen. Their bullets riddled the bunting, cut the halyards, and splintered the staff; but after dark the flag was patched and refitted, and in the morning it was always flying.

Fifteen of the elder boys of the Martinière College, who were armed with muskets, took their turn on sentry and stood to arms to repel the enemy's assaults. Sometimes they would climb onto the roof with a supply of ammunition and blaze away through the loopholes at anything in sight. It was so tantalising, cut off from green food as they were, to see the pumpkins growing in the garden of Johannes' house, that they used to fire at them and spoil them for the enemy. Later on, when two of the boys had been wounded, this light-hearted musketry was forbidden. The rest of the garrison had already learned to save themselves and their ammunition by only firing when they could cover their man.

After the trials of the day the ladies at Dr Fayrer's house would sometimes refresh their spirits in the evening by singing part-songs as they sat in the portico, though Mrs Germon, whose husband was commanding at the Judicial post, found the accompaniment of roundshot and musket balls flying overhead too dismal for her taste. By now, Mrs Inglis and her party had settled down to a pretty regular life. The servants were still loyal, though the ayah was uneasy because her husband and children were outside in the city. The Brigadier slept in the Residency building, but came across every day to breakfast and dine with the family. Every morning, too, he read the proper psalms and prayers with them, which heartened them to meet whatever the day might bring. One morning he told them that his servant, Vokins, of the 32nd, had been hit by a roundshot while standing in the portico of the Residency, which had hitherto been considered safe. His leg was amputated. He was too weak to take chloroform, and, at his own request, the Brigadier himself held him during the operation.

On the 16th July Inglis decided to change his quarters, since a roundshot had traversed his room just after he had left it in the morning, and he was convinced that the enemy knew where he was sleeping. It was Johnny Inglis' birthday; he was four. Fortunately they had been able to buy some toys for him from a merchant in the entrenchment. On previous birthdays Mrs Inglis had entertained the children of the 32nd, and to-day she naturally wondered how those of them were faring that were in the power of the Nana Sahib. In the evening Mrs Case complained of a sore throat and headache; Mrs Inglis and Caroline Dickson made her lie down and fetched Dr Scott to see her.

On the same day one of Major Banks' spies came in. He reported that the force that had marched from Allahabad too late to save Cawnpore had engaged and routed a body of mutineers, but that the column was too weak to advance further up-country and had halted to await reinforcements. He reported, too, that the investing forces were short of food, and that the Sikh deserters would be glad to return to the entrenchment if they could. Banks believed that the news of Havelock's column might well be true, but some of the garrison thought that the first relief was more likely to come from Delhi. Nothing more had been heard of the Gurkha regiments.

By the 17th July Mrs Case was very ill. Dr Scott said she was suffering from suppressed grief; she had refused to break down when her husband was killed, and now nature would be denied no longer. They gave her port wine to keep her strength up, and dined in the outhouse, where the boxes and the goats were kept, to avoid disturbing her. A little before midnight they gave her a sedative, but just as she was falling asleep the enemy attacked Gubbins' post and the heavy firing woke her up. Mrs Inglis sat on the bed, holding her hand to reassure her, although she was trembling with fright herself. The firing soon died away, but the shock left Mrs Case in an alarming state of weakness.

The enemy were still busily engaged in cannonading the outposts, throwing up new batteries, and digging trenches. They occupied a commanding position on part of the Farhat Bakhsh, opposite the Baillie Guard gate, from which Second Lieutenant Bonham, Bengal Artillery, dislodged them with a few rounds from an 18-pounder at the Post Office. Bonham had already distinguished himself by his devotion to his guns at Sikrora during the early days of June, and by his efforts to save the 8-inch howitzer at Chinhat before he was wounded and carried off on a limber.

On the morning of the 18th July a dead body was seen lying outside the Baillie Guard gate. Thinking that perhaps a messenger had been shot as he tried to enter, Inglis led out a party after dusk to drag in the corpse, but no letters or papers of any kind could be found on the body, which was a woman's. During the night the enemy fired a carcass, or incendiary shell, into the room that Inglis had vacated two days before, setting it alight.

At half-past nine next morning, when several officers were at breakfast in the Residency building, a roundshot struck the table and passed right through the room; no one was hurt except Lieutenant Harmer, 32nd Foot, who had his leg broken by a piece knocked off the table. In the afternoon an 18-pound shot entered Dr Fayrer's drawing-room and smashed a valuable copper-plate engraving of Raphael's 'Transfiguration'.

On the same day Mr Polehampton, who was rapidly recovering from his wound, was attacked by cholera. His sufferings were great and it was soon apparent that the disease was mortal, but he said with his frank smile to his visitors in the hospital: 'I am not in the least frightened, and I know exactly how I am.' As Mrs Polehampton tended her husband during the last day and night of his life, she was upheld by a sense of unearthly peace which swelled into triumph as the end approached, for she felt that she was watching him enter into the joy of his Lord, and she was able to share his joy. He died on the morning of the 20th July. It was usual to bury the dead in sheets or blankets from their own beds, but Mrs Polehampton was anxious to procure a coffin; Mr Harris found her one at last, stowed away under a staircase with some old boxes. He read the funeral service to the widow alone, before the body was taken away with the others to the churchyard, where it was buried in a separate grave.

Mrs Polehampton was sustained by the sense of triumph until, as the days went on, she awoke to the emptiness of life with neither child nor husband: then the radiance began to fade. Still, as the siege continued and times grew harder, she was glad that her husband had been taken early, finding comfort in the promise to Josiah: 'Behold therefore, I will gather thee unto thy fathers, and thou shalt be gathered into thy grave in peace; and thine eyes shall not see all the evil which I will bring upon this place.'

After midnight on the 19/20th July the enemy were unusually quiet, and at daybreak nothing out of the way was to be seen. Since the beginning of the siege an officers' lookout had been posted every day in a turret on the Residency building and on the roof of the Post Office. This morning at half-past eight it was reported by the Residency lookout that the enemy were massing within a few hundred yards of the defences. The outposts were warned at once and the whole garrison called to arms, but the enemy made no move though their bugles were sounding continually. Inglis sat down to breakfast with his family, after arranging to be kept informed of the enemy's movements. At 10.15 there was a sound which was new to many of the garrison, like a great gun being fired under their feet; some of them believed that one of the magazines had exploded. Inglis rushed away from the breakfast table, knowing that at last the enemy had sprung a mine, and the women were left to dwell upon the horrors they might expect if the mutineers broke in.

The mine had been intended to blow up the Redan, but since it was a hundred and ten feet short and twenty degrees out of bearing the battery was untouched. This was the signal for the first general assault. The smoke from the crater and from the guns in the Redan, which immediately opened fire, was so thick that the enemy could not see before them. Their storming party came up the glacis at the double expecting to find a practicable breach, but were checked by the obstacles outside the defences, and suffered heavily from grapeshot and musketry from the battery and the north curtain. At the first check one of their leaders stuck his cap on the point of his sword, waving them on with a shout. They advanced again, but their leader was hit by a musket ball, they were shelled by mortars, and the grapeshot tore wide gaps in their ranks. The attack was supported by a fusillade from a neighbouring house, and the firing on both sides was so heavy that a number of expectant birds of carrion fell dead from the surrounding trees.

Meanwhile the whole position was under an intense fire of musketry and artillery. Mr Harris was in his bath when the mine went up, and almost at once an 18-pound shot broke through the wall, covering him with dust and plaster. Mrs Harris was much alarmed until he shouted 'All right' and crept, all but naked, out of the wreckage. For the first few minutes Mr Rees, the Calcutta merchant, was frightened by the firing, the clouds of smoke on every side, and the advancing masses of the enemy; he thought with many others that there was little hope of seeing out the day. But as the firing grew severer yet and the enemy were still advancing, his fear gave place to excitement and to the desire to kill. Many of the sick and wounded staggered or crawled out of the Hospital to help in the defence. They were pale and trembling from debility, some of them bleeding from reopened wounds, but they seized the nearest muskets and fired them as long as they could. Those who were wounded in the legs threw away their crutches and knelt to fire, while the weakest loaded for the others. One of them who had lost an arm was seen hooking himself up to the parapet with a musket in his remaining hand, but he soon collapsed and died.

Lieutenant Loughnan was holding Innes' post on the north-west angle, with twelve men of the 13th Native Infantry (his own regiment), twelve of the 32nd, and a number of volunteers. The post jutted out so sharply from the main position that Loughnan had been given orders to retire if it became untenable. As the enemy came on in great force some of his men began to speak of retreat, but Loughnan refused to hear of it and cried: 'Give a shout, my boys! A loud one and a strong one!' At that the men cheered lustily and the enemy's advance was checked. But not for long, for they soon made another rush which took some of them right underneath the walls, where they were safe from the musketry of the defenders. Once there they could get no further but shouted for scaling ladders. The garrison were ready: as the ladders came up they fired at the men that brought them, and if they hit only one of the three the other two carried him away rather than stay to face the musketry. The men under the walls, tired of waiting for the ladders, attempted to scale the works without them, but those that reached the top were thrust down again at the point of the bayonet.

Loughnan was anxious, however, for he had no hand-grenades—which would soon have cleared them out—and it was death to lean over the parapet and fire down at them; but two of the volunteers, Mr Erith and Mr Alone, pelted the enemy with bricks and mortar and all sorts of filth until they had forced them out into the open, when they were soon dispersed by musketry.

Mr Hardingham, another volunteer, was firing as fast as he could when he heard a bullet whistle by his ear from behind. As he turned round he saw one of the Indians regarding him with terror. He at once suspected treachery, and was making for the sepoy with his bayonet when Loughnan stopped him. 'Never mind, Hardingham,' he said, 'don't bayonet him yet, there's lots of time afterwards.' So the man was spared and was able to convince Hardingham, when things were quieter, that the shot was accidental. The Indian troops understood the mutineers better than the Europeans did: as the enemy's advance began to threaten the neck of the position, the men of the 32nd were afraid they would be cut off, but the sepoys said: 'No fear of that, they will never get so far.' The post was still being raked by a severe fire, and a corporal of the 32nd had his stripes torn off by a musket-ball.

One corner of Innes' post was held by two men of the 13th Native Infantry and a little fellow named Bailey, the son of a native Christian who had been a captain in the service of the King of Oudh. Seeing the mutineers taking cover in some huts not five yards away from the palisade, Bailey began to abuse them in fluent Hindustani, and they, supposing him to be one of the loyal sepoys, offered to spare his life if he deserted.

'Come over to us,' cried one of them, 'and leave those cursed Europeans, whose mothers and sisters we have defiled, and whom we shall kill this day. Come over to us; what have you to do with them? Will you be made a Christian too? Or have you already lost your caste?'

'Take that,' Bailey shouted back, firing his musket; 'do you think that I have eaten pig's flesh like yourselves? Do you think that I too shall disgrace myself by proving unfaithful to my salt? Take that, thou son of a dog! Thou whose grandfather's grave I have dishonoured.'

The two loyal sepoys joined in the abuse as they loaded the muskets for Bailey to fire, until at last they ran short of ammunition. Bailey did not know what to do. He could not leave the post himself, nor could he spare one of the men, while if he shouted loudly enough to be heard by the main body, the enemy might learn what straits he was in. Fortunately his position was flanked by the guns in the Redan, and the enemy were held back by shellfire until he had attracted attention. A fresh supply of ammunition was brought up by Hardingham under heavy fire, and presently the post was reinforced. One of the two Indians was wounded, and a musket ball smashed Bailey's lower jaw, passing out again through his neck; it was thought at the time that the injury was mortal, but he recovered.

The south side of Gubbins' post was also attacked in great force. Some of the enemy reached the unfinished bastion on the south-east angle, only to be killed on top of the parapet. Others attacked Grant's bastion on the east corner of the outpost from which they were driven off by hand-grenades. Lieutenant Grant, 5th Oudh Irregular Infantry, had his hand shattered by one of the grenades, which burst too soon. The same explosion wounded Captain Forbes, 1st Oudh Irregular Cavalry, who was in command of the outpost and who now handed over to Captain Hawes, 5th Oudh Irregular Infantry. Lieutenant Grant died some days later, having already lost his wife and one daughter from cholera, and leaving a small girl and a baby in charge of Mr and Mrs Gubbins.

At the south-east corner the enemy advanced against the Cawnpore Battery and Anderson's post, with bugles sounding, bands playing, and flags flying. With the first rush nine of them penetrated the palisade, and, bending double as they ran, had almost reached the inner ditch before they were shot down. The leaders tried desperately to urge the rest of them on. Again and again they surged forward, to be driven back by shellfire and the steady musketry of Captain Anderson's and Captain Germon's garrisons. Their leaders shouted: 'Come on, come on; the place is ours, it is taken!' and a fanatic bearing the green banner of the Prophet led another charge with the cry: 'The Faith, the Faith! Kill the Europeans!' but fell at the palisade, hit by several balls at once. The green flag remained, caught up in the defences, until one of the enemy rushed up to retrieve it. His right arm was broken by a musket-ball, but he extricated the flag with his left hand and carried it away. From minute to minute the cry went up: 'More men this way!' as the enemy pressed home their attack on this side or on that.

Mr Capper, who had been rescued from the ruins on the first day of the siege and who was now Captain Anderson's second-in-command, was in charge of the volunteers in what was left of the house, while Anderson himself guarded the junction between his post and the Cawnpore battery. Monsieur Geoffroi, hearing one of the enemy leaders shouting: 'Come on brothers, there's nobody here,' shouted back: 'There are plenty of us here, you rascal,' and shot the leader dead. Signor Barsottelli distinguished himself by his zeal and energy, rushing from one loophole to another with his musket and asking his commanding officer: 'Here we dominate—shall I strike?' The garrison were inspired by the example of Major Banks, who carried up shot and shell with his own hands through the hottest fire. He always refused to stoop, however low the breastwork, and, short though he was, his head was often exposed to the enemy marksmen.

Captain Sanders, 41st Native Infantry, was commanding at the Financial post, from which there was a clear view for two hundred yards down the street outside. It was empty when the mine exploded, but soon he saw a bale of cotton, followed by another and another, rolling slowly towards the defences, apparently of their own accord since there was still not a man to be seen in the street. Meanwhile the attack was developing elsewhere, and Sanders went on firing until his shoulder was black from the kick of his rifle. Suddenly a head appeared from behind the leading bale. Sanders killed his man with a snap shot and the bales did not move any further. The fighting at this post and at Sago's post, under Lieutenant Clery, 32nd Foot, was so heavy that Captain M'Cabe sent a small detachment of the 32nd from the Post Office to reinforce Sanders, while Dr Fayrer and Captain Weston maintained a destructive fire from the roof of Fayrer's house. The enemy took cover under the outside wall of the compound, throwing over showers of logs and brickbats to distract the garrison and spoil their aim. At longer range they fired their guns and muskets, howling, beating their drums, and blowing their bugles; while inside the defences the silence was only broken by gunfire and musketry and a few necessary orders.

By three in the afternoon the firing had begun to slacken, and by four o'clock the enemy were retreating sullenly, carrying with them many dead and wounded. Before long they begged permission, under a flag of truce, to remove the rest of their casualties, a request which was granted readily, if only for sanitary reasons. Their dead and wounded were taken away in cartloads. The garrison were all exhausted, having been under arms throughout the heat of the day, but they were in the best of spirits. It was clear that the enemy had lost many hundreds, whereas among the defenders only four Europeans had been killed and twelve wounded, with about ten casualties among the Indian troops. Even these small losses had been mostly due to the men's exposing themselves needlessly as soon as they saw that the enemy were beaten. When Mrs Inglis taxed one of the 32nd afterwards with recklessness, he replied: 'Yes, but it's not in the way of Englishmen to fight behind walls.'

After thanking Heaven for a whole skin, Mr Rees sat down with a wonderful relish to his meal of chapatties washed down with brandy-and-water. Tired out as he was, and thickly grimed with dust and powder, he observed after a wash, a rest, and a cigar, that he had not been so happy for a long time, even before the siege began.

The following order was issued after the fighting was over: 'The Brigadier commanding congratulates the force on the determined manner in which the attack made on the position was repulsed. When all behaved well, it is invidious to draw comparisons; but the manner in which the garrison outposts drove back the enemy is worthy of the highest commendation.' Inglis also wrote a strong letter to Major Banks, begging him not to expose himself more than was right and necessary in his position.

All was quiet during the night that followed the general assault, but in the morning the enemy opened their usual fire of artillery and musketry. At ten o'clock Major Banks was at Fayrer's house talking to the doctor when they heard the groans of a man who had just been hit in the spine. Banks said to Fayrer: 'I hope, when my time comes, I shall not suffer like that.'

The same morning the enemy made a further attack on Gubbins' post. They occupied the houses on the south side in great force and made their way into a long, low range of buildings, known as the Goindah lines, in an enclosure which was separated from Gubbins' compound by a narrow lane. Breaking out of the enclosure, they entered the lane itself, where they were only opposed by a low wall precariously heightened by a canvas screen. When Mr Gubbins heard of this he took a couple of double-barrelled rifles to a loophole on an outhouse roof, from which he could enfilade the lane, except where his line of fire was interrupted by the pillars of a portico underneath Grant's bastion. The enemy took cover at once, some running back into the Goindah lines, some sheltering behind the pillars.

Meanwhile, a private of the 32nd helped Gubbins to barricade a second loophole which was more exposed.

The enemy in the enclosure now began to throw picks and shovels over the wall to those who had made a lodgment under the portico, hoping that they could dig their way into Grant's bastion. At this moment Gubbins heard a European voice behind him and, still keeping his eye on the lane, he asked that the wall of the Sikh Square, which projected in rear of the enemy, might be loopholed for musketry. The man behind seemed to be coming nearer, as if to observe the enemy, when suddenly Gubbins heard a heavy fall. Looking round he saw Major Banks lying there with a bullet through the temple: he had his wish, for he died without a groan. Gubbins remained at the loophole, attended only by an Indian orderly to load his rifle, firing at the enemy whenever they exposed themselves, until at last a mortar was brought up. As soon as the shells began to burst among the crowds in the enclosure they ran to a safer distance, while the men under the portico dashed out and leapt across the lane, followed by a destructive fusillade from the roof of the Brigade Mess.

It was not till late in the afternoon that Major Banks' body was taken away; it was buried the same night, sewn up in a sheet. His loss was deeply felt, for, though he had not held the office of Chief Commissioner long enough to make his mark on the defence, he was both zealous and active, besides being perhaps more clear-headed than the Brigadier.

On the same day the enemy tried to make lodgments for mining outside the Redan and in the shops adjoining the Martinière building. The first attempt was made by a small party which crawled up before daylight and was driven off at dawn by musketry and grape from the Hospital post and hand-grenades from the Redan. The threat to the Martinière post was more serious, for the enemy had actually begun to undermine the outside wall when the garrison cut loopholes above the miners' heads and dropped hand-grenades on them, killing some and dispersing the rest. They then enlarged one of the holes into a sally-port and occupied the shops, which they barricaded so strongly that they now formed part of the fortified position instead of being neutral ground as before.

On the same day a stray bullet entered Gubbins' house by one of the south windows while the inmates were at dinner, severely wounding Dr Brydon, who was in charge of the Native Hospital, and who was already known to history as the solitary horseman that appeared before the Kabul gate of Jalalabad on the 13th January 1842 with the news that Elphinstone's army had been annihilated in the Afghan passes. It was now determined to remove the women from the south side of the upper storeys, but the rooms on the opposite side were still considered safe. Next day, however, Mrs Dorin, whose husband had been killed before her eyes in the mutiny at Sitapur, was standing in her room on the north side of the upper storey when a matchlock ball penetrated a south window and traversed two suites of rooms before wounding her fatally in the head. After this all the south windows were carefully barricaded with bookcases and wardrobes.

The garrison were still anxiously awaiting reliable news of the relieving column from Allahabad. For the present, however, they were becoming more confident in their ability to repel the enemy's assaults. As a rule the Hindustani sepoy had a passive contempt for death which might have put the bravest European to shame, but without his accustomed leadership he lacked the aggressive gallantry needed to storm the weakest fortifications when defended with resolution. Adequately led, the investing forces could at any time have broken their way in by sheer weight of numbers, but apparently they feared to attack the most vulnerable parts of the defences, since, it was said, they believed them to be undermined. Although they had more than enough guns to breach the works by converging fire, they preferred to shoot at random from odd nooks and corners, aiming at individual marksmen in the upper storeys rather than cannonading the lower walls to destroy the buildings. Often their guns were laid at such high angles of elevation that the shot cleared the entrenchment altogether and plunged into their own posts on the other side.

Although the nearest of the enemy's guns were within fifty or sixty yards of the defences, it was not easy to silence them. Sometimes the gunners dug narrow trenches eight feet deep in rear of each gun, so that the teams could take cover when they were shelled by the 8-inch mortars, and even when they were serving the guns there was nothing but their hands to be seen. Sometimes they posted a gun round the corner of a building, ran it out into the open to fire, dashed back to cover before the garrison could reply, and hauled back their cannon into shelter with a drag rope. Sometimes they kept the gun at the bottom of a ramp, ran it up to the top to fire, and let the recoil send it flying down again to the bottom. They dug shelter trenches for musketry, too, and kept up a continual fire from these as well as from the buildings, so that the garrison were constantly losing men shot in the head at loopholes and embrasures.

Since the 20th July there had been a new source of anxiety for the garrison. The mine that had been driven so unskilfully against the Redan was a hundred and sixty feet long: on the south face, where there was good cover within forty feet of the defences, the chances of missing would be more remote. The men in the outposts were now haunted by the fear of being blown up at any moment, and Inglis and his staff were anxious lest the enemy should succeed in breaching the defences and pour through in overwhelming force. The garrison had from the first been short of labour, their numbers were decreasing day by day, and they had an enceinte of well over a mile to defend; on the other hand, the enemy's supply of labour was almost unlimited and included the low caste Pasis, many of whom were expert miners. Moreover the garrison were short of tools, for the coolies who had been employed on the works before the siege had decamped with their picks and shovels when they heard of the defeat at Chinhat.

Major Anderson, the Chief Engineer, was in such poor health that the active responsibility of the defence against mines devolved upon his second-in-command, Captain Fulton, who entered into the underground warfare with a boyish zest. The commandants of the outposts were ordered to train their most intelligent men to listen for sounds of mining, and countermines were to be driven out wherever the enemy were at work; while at those points which were most exposed to attack shafts were to be sunk and galleries begun at once. Fortunately there were some Cornish and Derbyshire miners in the ranks of the 32nd Foot, and a squad of specialists was quickly organised to instruct the various garrisons and to assist in the most urgent work. Many of the Sikhs showed great aptitude for mining and dug much better than they fought.

One day Lieutenant Innes, Bengal Engineers, was discussing the shortage of tools with another officer, when a civilian who chanced to overhear told him that there was a mass of hardware on the roof of Deprat's shop on the south face. Innes sent away for a ladder, but being too impatient to wait for it, he climbed up by an outside staircase onto the roof, where he was in full view of the windows of Johannes' house. There were all kinds of useful gear on the roof, such as picks, spades, and tarpaulins, and after having a bed of straw laid on the ground below to deaden the noise, Innes pitched them all down and descended by the ladder without being observed by the enemy.

Each of the garrison's countermines consisted of a vertical shaft and a horizontal gallery. The shaft, which was some four feet in diameter, was sunk inside the defences to the depth of from twelve to twenty feet, and the gallery was then driven out towards the enemy's working. The miners were generally grouped in gangs of ten, five of them relieving the other five at intervals of half an hour, or sometimes even less, since the heat underground was terribly oppressive. Number One worked in the gallery with a short pick or crowbar, loosening the earth in front of him so as to make a tunnel high enough to clear his head when squatting down, and wide enough to give him elbow room. Number Two sat close behind him with an empty packing case, which he filled with the earth that Number One brought down. When the box was full, Number Two jerked a cord as a signal to Number Three, who stood at the bottom of the shaft, to drag the box towards him. He in turn gave the word to Numbers Four and Five at the top of the shaft, who hauled up the box, emptied it, and lowered it down again. Officers and men, high officials and Eurasian clerks, worked side by side, the engineer officers attending as often as possible to advise and to assist. Fortunately for the garrison, the ground was so stiff that the galleries did not need to be lined with casing or any kind of supports. It was fortunate, too, that none of the mines were long enough to require ventilation, since there were no bellows or airtubes to be had.

It was a formidable task for a novice to visit the far end of a mine. He must let himself down the shaft by a rope, barking his knuckles on the side, and crawl along the dark gallery on hands and knees, unable to defend himself from the hordes of mosquitoes, whose high-pitched drone was all that could be heard. He would bump his head as the gallery took a sharp turn to left or right, and sometimes the roof would be so low that he must go on his belly. Reaching the end at last, he would sit still and listen until his ear became attuned to the prevailing quiet and caught the sound of some simple domestic task—one of his own garrison, perhaps, chopping firewood above him. At that he would wriggle out as swiftly as he could with the news that the enemy miners were at work, and an older hand would be sent down to find out whether it was a false alarm.

Sometimes an officer would sit for hours by himself at the end of a mine, listening to the faint sound of the pick and trying to determine the direction of the enemy's working. Fulton developed to a high degree both an intuitive and a reasoned understanding of the enemy's methods. When the sound of the pick was drawing close he would sit alone in the gallery, pistol in hand, waiting for the first man to break through. One day when he was wanted above ground a sergeant was asked whether he was down a mine. 'Yes, sir,' said the sergeant, 'there he's been for the last two hours, like a terrier at a rat hole, and not likely to leave it either, all day.'

Listening became a second nature to the garrison. A couple of officers might be seen in casual conversation at the Brigade Mess or the Sikh Square when suddenly one of them would fling himself down with his ear to the ground. Sometimes a dried pea was placed on a drum on the floor, in the belief that, if it moved, it would show that there was mining underneath. Often the engineers stole out at night to listen in the no-man's-land outside the defences. Lieutenant Innes, whose only uniforms were white, used to borrow less conspicuous clothes to wear on these excursions, with a grimly humorous apology to the owner in case he did not live to bring them back.

On the 21st July it was found that mines were being directed against the Cawnpore battery, the Brigade Mess, and the Sikh Square, from behind walls or ruins less than sixty feet from the defences. Shafts were sunk at once at the threatened posts and countermines driven out. This prompt action seemed to cow the enemy, whose miners were not heard again for some time. By Major Anderson's orders, however, all the countermines on the south face were driven to at least twenty-four feet outside the defences. The gallery at the Cawnpore battery was taken thirty feet, and branches were dug to right and left to intercept the enemy's mine should they resume work, the ends of the branches being charged with powder, which was kept ready to be exploded in case of emergency. At the Brigade Mess the countermine had reached a length of thirty-eight feet when it became clear that the enemy had ceased work altogether.

On the 22nd July it was decided to break into the Goindah lines, from which the enemy had made their lodgment at Gubbins' post the day before, to see if they were being used as a base for mining. At sunset the enclosure was shelled until the enemy were driven out, when a party made up of men of the 32nd, Sikhs, and other Indians, led by Brigadier Inglis himself, made a sortie through a hole which had been dug in the wall of Gubbins' compound. They met with no opposition, but a private of the 32nd, advancing too far in the falling light, was mistaken for one of the enemy by the garrison of the Brigade Mess and killed by a shot from the roof. Lieutenant Hutchinson, Bengal Engineers, explored the enclosure but could find no trace of mining. The roofs of the buildings were set alight, and as soon as the flames had taken a good hold the party retired through the same hole in the wall, which was then stopped up with a barrel, secured with earth and mud.

On the same evening a working party of officers and civilians opened up the underground magazine outside the Hospital post, which still contained two hundred and forty barrels of powder. It was pitch dark and raining heavily, and the ground outside the defences was knee-deep in mud. The barrels had to be lifted out of the pit, passed over the parapet, and taken to the new magazine that had been constructed inside the entrenchment. With immense exertion the work was completed in two nights; the enemy did not interfere.

On the evening of the 22nd July Mr Gubbins, who was still in charge of the Intelligence Department, turned in early, being indisposed. Soon after midnight he was woken up with the news that a messenger had just come in. The man's name was Ungud: he was one of the Indian pensioners who had been recalled by Lawrence, and he had been sent out on the 29th June to observe the movements of the Nana Sahib, who was then expected to cross the river and join the investing forces. Ungud had been detained by the enemy for thirteen days but had at last reached Cawnpore, which he had only left two days ago. He brought no letters but declared that Havelock, with a mere handful of men and twelve guns, had defeated the Nana Sahib in three engagements, had retaken Cawnpore, and was now preparing to cross the river and raise the siege of Lucknow.

At first Gubbins hardly dared believe the news, but a careful examination of the messenger soon convinced him that it was true. Ungud was taken across to headquarters, with an abstract of his intelligence and a note from Gubbins asking whether Inglis wished to write a letter to Cawnpore. The

Brigadier sent back Ungud with word that he did not propose to write himself, whereupon Gubbins prepared a despatch addressed to the Governor General, under cover to Havelock, stating the numbers of the garrison and the computed strength of the enemy, and setting forth the state of the siege. When the despatch was nearly ready, Lieutenant Birch, Inglis' aide-de-camp, appeared with a message that, since the Brigadier was unable to sleep, he would write after all if the runner had not yet started, and Gubbins therefore undertook to keep him till the letter was brought across. Inglis wrote as follows:

'*To the Officer Commanding the Relieving Force.*

Lucknow, July 22nd.

My dear Sir,

It is with deep regret I have to announce to you the death of Major Banks, chief commissioner, who was killed yesterday. I now write to inform you the enemy have pushed up to some of the walls of our defences, and keep up a heavy musketry fire day and night from loopholes. As yet their artillery have done us not much mischief. On the 20th the enemy appeared in force on all sides, and at 10 A.M. blew up a mine in the vicinity of one of our batteries facing the river, and made an attempt to storm our position, but were repulsed with great loss. Our casualties were few, considering the heavy fire we were exposed to, for three hours. Since the commencement of operations on the 30th ult. there have been 151 casualties in the 32nd Foot, including several officers, and there are from 70 to 80 in hospital. The present strength of the regiment's fighting men is 380 of the 32nd, and H.M.'s 84th detachment muster 36 men. We are most anxiously looking for succour, and I trust you will lose no time in pushing on to assist us. I am most desirous to hear from you. We have not heard any news from any quarter since the 27th ult. Aid is what we want, and that quickly. Our defences are straggling, and our numerical strength quite inadequate to man them. Our artillery is weak, and the casualties heavy.

J. Inglis, Brigadier.'

Meanwhile the rain had set in so heavily that Ungud proposed to go at once, while the enemy's sentries were busy finding shelter. Gubbins tried to keep him, but since he insisted that he must either start now or wait till another night, he was allowed to make his way out with the despatch that had already been prepared. When Gubbins sent across to tell the Brigadier what had happened, his messenger met Birch on the way with Inglis' letter, which was just too late. Gubbins had acted to the best of his judgment, intending no discourtesy, but it seemed afterwards that Inglis felt he had been slighted.

When daylight came there were fewer of the enemy in sight than usual, possibly because some of their troops had been drawn off to oppose Havelock's advance into Oudh. There were heavy showers of rain throughout the day. A single shower was welcome since it cooled the air, but continual rain was followed by a suffocating humidity, while the nights were often cold enough to make the sentries shiver in their wet clothes. That afternoon the enemy's bridge of boats across the Gumti was cannonaded from the entrenchment and broken up. At midnight it was reported that four hundred of the enemy had forced their way into the churchyard, which was one of the weakest points in the defences. The Brigadier was turned out at once, but it proved to be a false alarm. Mrs Inglis used to fear that the constant strain and the lack of rest would break her husband down, but he always seemed cheerful when they met.

Mrs Inglis had a new anxiety now, for Caroline Dickson had been sent to bed with smallpox, and it seemed likely that Mrs Case, who was better but still very weak, would catch it from her. It was a relief to find, as time went on, that, although they lived at such close quarters, not one of the party was infected. Mrs Inglis found it a blessing to have so much of her time taken up by the children, who were still keeping pretty well. Sometimes in leisure moments she read aloud to the others, but they all found it so hard to think of anything outside the entrenchment that in the end the readings were given up.

At Dr Fayrer's house Mrs Harris was busy looking after Mrs Dashwood, whose husband had died of cholera on the 9th July, and who was expecting her confinement before long. Mrs Dashwood was far too unwell to look after her own children, Ally, a boy of two, and Herbert, a baby of ten months old, both of whom, as well as little Bobbie Fayrer, were suffering from diarrhoea. Down in the taikhana the scurrying of rats and mice made it difficult to sleep. The ladies took turns throughout the night to sit up and watch —what for they hardly knew, but they were always expecting something terrible to happen, and the rest could sleep more easily if they knew that one of their number was awake.

After the death of Major Banks Mr Gubbins restated his claims to the office of Chief Commissioner, but Inglis opposed his succession in the following terms:

'*Lucknow, July* 23*rd*, 1857.

Sir,

I am directed to acknowledge the receipt of your letter No. 1 of this date, in which you report that you have assumed charge of the office of Chief Commissioner for the affairs of Oudh and in reply to state that Sir Henry Lawrence superseded you in the post by the late lamented Major Banks, and he also expressed his opinion to Lord Canning and to more than one living member of this garrison that you should on no account be permitted to hold the office of Chief Commissioner. Under the above circumstances, the Brigadier, with the entire concurrence of Major Anderson, thinks it his duty to inform you and to publish in this day's orders, for general information, that the office of Chief Commissioner is for the present vacant, and that Martial Law, and the highest Military Authority will be paramount in Oudh, until a successor to Sir Henry Lawrence shall be duly appointed by the Governor General in Council.

The Brigadier therefore requests that you will for the future abstain from sending any message to the relieving force, or performing any act whatever connected with the public service without previously communicating what you propose to do for his information.

As your messenger was despatched without waiting for the Brigadier's letter to the officer commanding the Relieving Force he requests you will furnish him with a copy of your communication.

T. F. Wilson, Capt.
Offg. A.A. Genl.

To: M. Gubbins Esq., C.S.
Lucknow.'

Gubbins was candid enough to admit afterwards that there was in fact no occasion for the exercise of civil authority, since there was no intercourse with the outside world, while the garrison itself was under martial law.

On the 24th July advantage was taken of a slight

lull in the firing to repair some of the defences which had suffered from the heavy rains, though the garrison, reduced in strength and harassed by day and night, were incapable of great exertion. During the day the enemy were seen at work in a deep trench about forty yards from the Redan battery. Sam Lawrence, who was convinced that it was a mine, gaily told the Brigadier that he and his men expected very shortly to be up amongst the little birds; but one of the engineers, Lieutenant Hutchinson, maintained that it was only a communication trench to enable the enemy to pass to and fro at a corner much exposed to musketry. Accepting Hutchinson's view, the Brigadier refused to authorise a sortie to destroy the working. That evening after dark Hutchinson and Birch, A.D.C., crept out to reconnoitre and established that the engineer was right.

Next morning the enemy fired several shells into the position, one of which fell clean through the roof of the Post Office, landing on the officers' breakfast table without exploding. Seeing the enemy at work again by the Redan, Sam Lawrence and his men were still convinced that they were mining.

At eleven o'clock that night Mr Gubbins' messenger returned with a letter from Lieutenant Colonel Fraser Tytler, Deputy Assistant Quarter-Master General with Havelock's Force, and those who had not given credit to the news he had brought before were now confounded. The letter read as follows:

'My dear Sir,

Your letter of the 22nd has reached us. We have two thirds of our force across the river, and eight guns in position already. The rest will follow immediately. I will send over more news to-night or to-morrow. We have ample force to destroy all who oppose us. Send us a sketch of your position in the city, and any directions for entering it or turning it that may strike you. In five or six days we shall meet. You must threaten the rear of the enemy if they come out, and we will smash them.

Yours truly,
B. Fraser Tytler.

P.S. We have smashed the Nana, who has disappeared, and destroyed his palace, Bithur. No one knows where his army has dispersed to, but it has disappeared.'

Ungud's arrival with this authentic news raised the spirits of the whole garrison, and especially those of the Indian troops. Remembering the false report of the capture of Delhi that had been circulated before the siege, they were incredulous at first, but after crowding round Ungud and asking question after question, to every one of which he had an answer, few of them doubted any longer. The Europeans, too, plied Ungud with questions as he sat in the centre of an animated circle at Gubbins' house, the single light in the room being carefully screened lest it should be a mark for the enemy's bullets. The men pressed round him listening eagerly, laughing at his good news and his jeers at the enemy's reverses, while in the shadows further off stood the women of the household, who had slipt out of bed to see and hear the messenger.

Not all the news was good. Ungud reported that the Nana had butchered the last of the women and children, the day before Havelock had fought the battle of Cawnpore to save them; the garrison could only hope that he was wrong. He told them, too, that the first general appointed by the mutineers had been killed by a rifle bullet while reconnoitring from a loophole; that a young boy, a son of the ex-King of Oudh, had been set on the throne, his mother, the Begam, acting as Regent; and that the Maulvi (doctor of the law) of Fyzabad, who was already known as an agitator, was with the investing forces.

Early next morning another runner was sent out with the following acknowledgment:

'*Lucknow*, 26*th July*, 1857.
1 *a.m.*

My dear Tytler,

Your note to Mr Gubbins has been received. We are inclined to believe that but a small force has gone out to meet you but that the enemy are disposed to meet you here and will make a final assault on our position. Our Europeans being now little more than 300 we shall be able to afford you little assistance except by shells.

The bearer of to-day's letter will start from this to-morrow with a completed plan of the entrances to the city with a memo by the engineers.

J. Inglis, Brigadier.

To Lt. Col. Tytler.'

After a day's rest, Ungud went out again with a packet containing a letter from the Brigadier, plans of the position and its approaches, and memoranda drawn up by the engineers. The bulk of these despatches added greatly to the bearer's danger, and Ungud, who had refused all reward on his first return to the Residency, was promised five hundred pounds for their safe delivery. Inglis' letter read as follows:

'My dear Sir,

At Bashiratganj there are about 1000 matchlock-men, and about as many more at Nawabganj. It is said that the 3rd Oudh Irregulars left this to oppose you on the night of the 24th, and was followed yesterday by the 22nd Native Infantry. The bridge at Bani is believed to be entire, but being a good defensible position, it is likely that the enemy will oppose you there. There is another bridge, however, at Mohan, about eight miles higher up the stream, though the road is indifferent. The bearer, however, will give you later information of the state of the road, and force on it. I send you a plan of the town and our position, and a memo by the engineers. The distance from the entrance to the city to our position is about a mile and a half. We can assist you by shelling your flanks for the last 1,500 yards or more. In the event, however, of the enemy disputing your entrance, you might endeavour to work round his left flank by diverging to the right towards the Dilkusha Park, and making your entrance by the European barracks. The road, however, will be very heavy and difficult for guns, and is likewise lined with houses. I would suggest the direct route. If you have rockets with you, send up two or three at 8 P.M. on the night before you intend to enter the city, by way of warning to us, at which signal we will begin shelling the houses on both sides the road. Ignorant of the strength of your force and its formation, I can only offer these suggestions with the assurance that the utmost of which our weak and harassed garrison is capable shall be done to cause a diversion in your favour as soon as you are sufficiently near. Should the bridge at the entrance of the town be broken down, there is another on the side of the Dilkusha Park. It is a good mile and a half from the first-mentioned bridge to our position. Please write to the Governor General from me and say no recognised successor has been appointed to succeed Major Banks, appointed by Sir Henry Lawrence, and who superseded Mr Gubbins by Sir Henry Lawrence's orders.

J. Inglis, Brigadier.

To Officer Commanding the Relieving Force.'

The evening of Sunday the 26th July found the garrison in high spirits, for they had been promised relief in five or six days, and hoped to see Havelock's rockets before many nights had passed. Captain Boileau, 7th Light Cavalry, commanding at the Slaughterhouse post, was singing, 'Cheer, boys, cheer!' with Mr Rees and some other officers and volunteers, when word came in from the sentry that the enemy were about to attack. There was no time to finish the song for the singers were called to arms at once. The firing was so intense that Mrs Inglis believed the enemy had broken in at last, until the Brigadier came and set her fears at rest. The besiegers constantly harassed the defenders by making these sham attacks, marching from one house to another without ever coming to grips with the garrison, and maintaining a brisk fire, often with blank cartridge. This time the only casualty was Lieutenant Shepherd, 7th Light Cavalry, who was killed in a square near the Brigade Mess by a careless shot from one of the garrison on the roof of the building.

At 7 o'clock next morning the road by Johannes' house was seen to have two planks laid across it which had not been there the night before. Presently a man's hand appeared from below, and soon after that there was a fall of earth which proved that the enemy had undermined the road to within six feet of the palisade; the gallery had evidently been dug too near the surface and the heavy rains had broken down the roof. The countermine that had already been begun was pushed on as fast as possible, while the riflemen on the roof of the Brigade Mess directed a steady fire into the opening. In the afternoon, however, the enemy contrived to cover up the sap with boards, and Captain Fulton decided to make a sortie and blow the whole thing up. He took an empty pillowcase to Second Lieutenant Bonham, who was in charge of the 8-inch mortars by the Cawnpore battery, and asked him to fill it up with powder; but Bonham suggested that they should try what could be done with a shell before risking valuable lives outside the defences. Fulton agreed. A mortar was brought up and lined on the enemy's working, which was so close to the defences that the piece had to be laid at an almost vertical elevation; indeed there was a risk that if the charge of powder were too small the shell might burst inside the position. Bonham began by firing over the mark, and after three or four rounds, the charge being slightly reduced each time, he lobbed a shell right into the gallery, which was so much damaged that the enemy gave it up.

On the same day a small Indian boy was captured

just outside the works. He said that he earned his living by picking up bullets and selling them to the enemy at twelve for an anna, or three halfpence.

That night some of the garrison broke into a locked room in the Residency building and stole a large number of jewels belonging to the ex-King of Oudh, which had been brought in from his palace, the Kaisarbagh, two days before the siege began. There was also about £230,000 of treasure in the position, but this was perfectly safe, being buried in the open in front of the Residency building where no one could dig it up without being seen. Banks had wished to have the jewels buried in the same way, but Inglis had not been able to spare the men for the job.

On the 28th July there was great activity underground. When the countermine at the Sikh Square had been driven out to the prescribed length of twenty-four feet, the enemy's miners had been heard again. The gallery was therefore turned so as to intersect the line along which the enemy were supposed to be working, and by 5 o'clock in the afternoon the sound of the pick was drawing close. When the enemy were only a few more strokes away Captain Fulton broke down the partition with a crowbar. The enemy's miners bolted. Fulton entered their gallery, followed by a sergeant, took away a candle they had left burning, and crept along the gallery to the shaft, which had been sunk in one of the houses on the other side of the road. After making sure that the coast was clear, Fulton returned to his own gallery and sent Lieutenant Hutchinson to guard the shaft with his revolver. He then had a barrel of powder taken right through to the enemy's shaft, tamped the gallery—that is, packed earth or rubble round the charge to prevent the force of the explosion from spending itself along the gallery—fired the charge and, as he wrote in his diary afterwards, 'destroyed the whole with great éclat and enjoyment of the fun and excitement, to say nothing of the success.' When Major Anderson heard of this he threatened, only half in earnest, to place Fulton under arrest for entering the enemy's mine.

Next day it was rumoured that large numbers of the enemy were marching down the Cawnpore road to meet Havelock's column, and that only two or three regiments of infantry and some of the military police had been left to invest the Residency. It was impossible to verify the news by observation, for the enemy were seldom to be seen in force, but kept under cover in the surrounding buildings. During the afternoon the garrison could hear gunfire on the Cawnpore side. At about 6 o'clock, after another burst of firing in the same direction, one of the officers on lookout came running down to say that he could see European troops near the Martinière College on the east of the city. Another cannonade was heard on the north side of the Gumti and several hundred mutineers dashed across the iron bridge, followed by a couple of shots from an 18-pounder in the entrenchment.

Word went round the garrison that Havelock was at hand. The European troops began to cheer, the Indian soldiers cried that the British army had come at last, the sick and wounded turned out of hospital to help, as they said, the poor fellows coming in, and many of the ladies crowded onto the roof of the Brigade Mess, where they stood watching in a most exposed position till they were sharply ordered down. Inglis was sitting at dinner with his family when they heard the cheering. As they rushed out they were met by Lieutenant Colonel Palmer, who shook hands with Mrs Inglis, congratulating her on her deliverance. She picked up her baby, meaning to run across to see a sick friend, when she heard her husband saying angrily: ‘It’s the most absurd thing I ever heard.’ He ordered them all back to dinner, looking so put out that they did not like to ask him what had happened. At length he told them that the officer on lookout had made a fool of himself, and that it was all a mistake. The excitement was naturally followed by depression, and the authorities feared that the disappointment might have a serious effect on the morale of the Indian troops. It was heard afterwards that the enemy had been firing salutes in honour of the little King of Oudh.

That evening there was a fall of earth outside Sago’s post on the east face. The enemy had driven another mine too near the surface, and this time the collapse was so complete that there was no need for a mortar to put the finishing touch.

Next day large numbers of the enemy were seen entering the city by the Cawnpore Road, and as there were several native bedsteads carried beside them, on which it was supposed were wounded men, the garrison hoped that they had been engaged with Havelock's column and defeated. During the day a beautiful peacock alighted on the parapet at Anderson's post and sat there for a little preening its feathers. The men would have killed it for the pot had not Captain Anderson told them to spare it as a bird of good omen.

The same day Caroline Dickson was able to get up for the first time since being taken ill. She was still weak, but all traces of the smallpox were disappearing rapidly. Second Lieutenant Bonham was now suffering from the same disease, at a time when his services with the guns and mortars could ill be spared.

On the day of the general assault, Mrs Clarke, a delicate, gentle creature who had escaped from Gonda with Mrs Bartrum, had borne a child in the little room in the Begam Kothi where she lived with eight others. She never rallied. By the 29th July it was thought that both she and the baby were dying, but on the 30th she seemed easier. She told Mrs Bartrum that she wanted to sit up, and asked for her boxes to be packed as she was going on a long journey and must have everything ready.

Mrs Bartrum humoured her by sorting her things and packing them away. Mrs Clarke said: 'Thank you, now I am quite ready: the dooly (litter) is here, but the bearers have not come.' Mrs Bartrum brought her a little arrowroot, after taking which she dozed away. In the evening Mr Harris, finding her sinking rapidly, read some of the prayers for the Visitation of the Sick and went on to baptise the baby. Since the father was not in the entrenchment and there was no one to ask what the child's name should be, they could only call her after her mother. Mrs Clarke died during the night, the baby surviving her by three days; her little boy, who had long been sickly, died a fortnight later. On the last day of July Mrs Bartrum's child was seized with cholera.

Fraser Tytler's letter had presumably been written about the 24th July, and the five or six days he had spoken of were now past. A watch had been kept every evening for signal rockets, but none had yet been seen. The military authorities believed that Mr Gubbins' despatch of the 22nd had been too sanguine—no doubt they remembered his generous but impracticable impulse to send aid to Cawnpore—and that Havelock was therefore taking his time; but Gubbins maintained that he had given a faithful account of the siege, and suggested that the relieving column had been opposed by the enemy in great force, or possibly delayed by a broken bridge at Bani, between Cawnpore and Lucknow.

Sometimes at night the enemy would call out to the garrison that their friends had all been beaten and that their own turn was coming next. The garrison shouted back that the rebels had better tie up their bundles and be off, for the British army would soon be coming, to which the enemy replied with showers of abuse and musketry. Meanwhile July had gone out and August had come in without any further sign of relief, yet eight o'clock each evening found both officers and men still watching for the trail of a rocket in the southern sky.

At the end of June Lawrence had written: 'Unless we are relieved quickly, say in ten or fifteen days, we shall hardly be able to maintain our position.' It was now the end of July and, thanks to his preparations, not one of the enemy had crossed the parapet nor had a yard of ground been yielded; on the contrary, the defences now included ground that had been neutral when the siege began. Retrenchments had been constructed in rear of the front line defences to localise any successful assault, and communications from one post to another had been improved by erecting traverses and screens, and knocking holes in the walls of adjacent buildings so that the way ran through instead of round them. The heavy rains had damaged the defences and hampered their repair, but on the other hand, the drainage being good, some of the accumulated filth had been washed away, while the water had filled the enemy's trenches and soaked into their mines.

The troops were steadier now than they had been at the opening of the siege. All the liquor in the shops had been either disposed of or impounded by the authorities, and there was no getting drunk on the daily rations of rum and porter. The men were, however, in a constant state of exhaustion, and sometimes the sentries were so done up after working with fatigue parties, down the mines, or in the batteries, that they were scarcely fit for duty; yet their officers were forced to be strict, however sympathetic, since the safety of every man, woman, and child in the entrenchment depended on the vigilance of the outposts.

One night when he was on his rounds Captain Anderson came upon a sentry whose head was bent and who seemed to be asleep, since he gave no challenge as the officer approached. Anderson watched him for a little and then said in an undertone: 'Sentry.' The man started, but soon recovered himself and answered calmly: 'I was just thinking, sir, how sad it is that one half of the world does not know how much the other half suffers.' Anderson had not been expecting such a sententious reply, and as the man's character was good, and it was possible that he might have been awake but meditating, he said no more about it.

The sentry went on to tell him about himself: he had once been known among his mates as 'a man of pleasant temper', but after the loss of his wife and his little girl he had learnt to hate his fellow men. 'Ah!' he said, 'you never saw such a queer, old-fashioned wee thing as my little daughter was, sir; it was just like me, and that's why I liked it so much. The poor little creature used to know me so well, and run after me, calling out "Papa"; and the soldiers used to say she was the very image of me. I used to *love* that child, sir, and when it died I became a wretched man, and cared for nothing.'

As the days passed many of the garrison grew so despondent that they hoped for nothing but to kill a few of the enemy before being killed themselves, and glanced almost enviously at the dead that were carried to the churchyard every evening. Despondency led to recklessness: many were shot in the head, in spite of constant warning, through peering out of the loopholes, after firing, to see if they had scored a hit. There were frequent casualties, too, among the officers as they reconnoitred, until they learnt to pass an old hat across the loophole to draw the enemy's fire, and then look out quickly before they had time to reload.

There were many curious escapes among the garrison. One day a friend of Private Metcalfe's, known as Jem, came on a visit from another outpost and asked if he could let him have some rum. As it happened, Metcalfe had a tot to spare, and, thinking that he could always get some more from Mr Harris, he handed it over to his friend. Jem poured it into a small bottle, remarking: 'This will do nicely for when I'm going on sentry,' and returned to his post. At ten o'clock that evening Metcalfe was on sentry himself. It was a fine night, with less firing than usual, and when the enemy threw in a solitary shell, Metcalfe watched its fiery trail and reckoned that it was travelling in Jem's direction. He was right. Jem was resting at the time, with a pillow under his head, and the rum underneath the pillow. The shell burst so close that the bottle was shattered and the pillow torn to bits, but while several men round him were wounded, Jem was only blown into a trench and stunned. When he came to himself his first words were: 'Is my dram of grog all right?' An officer who was standing near replied: 'I'm afraid not, my man. But never mind; I'll give you one, since that's all you care about.' Next morning Jem told Metcalfe that, after that, he was sure he would never be killed; but the same night his leg was shattered by a roundshot. The surgeons amputated, but after great suffering he died.

One day when Metcalfe was on outpost duty, accompanied as usual by the dog Bustle, he and a sergeant were keeping lookout from the loopholes and firing an occasional shot at a party of the enemy who were working on a trench outside. Metcalfe had just fired his piece when a shell entered through the loophole and burst on the wall behind him, throwing up a shower of bricks and mortar. Down went Metcalfe, with Bustle running about, barking furiously, until he found him underneath a heap of rubbish. The officer in charge shouted: 'Is there anyone hurt?' The sergeant shouted back: 'Yes, I think young Metcalfe is killed.' At this moment Metcalfe called out that he was safe and emerged with nothing worse than scratches, but looking, as he said, more like a miller than a soldier; indeed, he was in such a mess that the others could do nothing but laugh, but Bustle put their callousness to shame by licking and pawing him all over.

Every casualty made more work for those that were left, and the heavier the work the less was the resistance to disease. The men were so well aware of this that they often insisted on coming out of hospital and reporting for duty long before they were fit. When Captain Anderson protested, they said: 'Well, sir, in these times every man must do his best.' There were many cases of fever, cholera, smallpox, and dysentry, although none of these diseases had spread as widely as might have been feared. There was also a scorbutic complaint which was so prevalent that it became known as 'Garrison Disease', its chief symptoms being painful eruptions, low fever, diarrhoea, spongy gums, and loosened teeth.

The hospital was always full. There was no shortage of surgeons, but there were far too few attendants; linen and soap were scarce, and the sick and wounded were often verminous; sometimes there were not even enough beds. The air in the wards was still fetid and oppressive, since all the doors and windows were barricaded; yet even then one of the convalescents was shot in his bed as he smoked his pipe, and there were several narrow escapes from bursting shells. Antiseptic surgery was unknown, and the surgeons poked their bare fingers into open wounds as they probed for the bullets. Few if any of the amputation cases survived; the attendants came to know a certain leaden look about the face that always foretold the end.

In spite of the rains the whole entrenchment was still reeking of ordure, carrion, and offal. So far as possible all offensive matter was thrown into deep pits and covered up with earth, but cattle still broke loose from time to time and were killed in the most exposed positions, from which their carcases could not safely be removed, while the offal from the slaughterhouse on the west face was simply thrown over the defences, since labour was so scarce, and left to rot outside. The flies were still increasing, making it impossible to sleep during the day, blackening the tables, for ever falling into the food, and causing, besides discomfort, disgust at the thought of what they were breeding on. One of the officers at the Brigade Mess used to amuse the ladies by rolling himself up in a mosquito net before sitting down to dinner.

Personal cleanliness was not easy to maintain. Owing to the hasty concentration in the Residency position most of the garrison were short of clothes. There was plenty of well-water but little soap, and almost all the native washermen had deserted, while the few that were left did the work badly at excessive prices. Some of the officers possessed one flannel shirt each, which they washed themselves when off duty, and hung up to dry, though in the damp monsoon weather the moisture seemed to cling to the stuff. Most of those who had white uniforms had dyed them a dust-colour, known as khaki, which had been used before on the North-West Frontier—'They look such queer figures!' wrote Mrs Harris—and some of the privates arrived at a most useful tint by mixing blue and red ink, which they looted from the public offices.

There was not yet any serious shortage of supplies, but the food was coarse and lacking in variety, and the Indian garrison were deprived of the condiments that were so necessary to their comfort. The staple food of the Europeans was corn, ground by hand with the husks unsifted, a kind of lentil mash, and indifferent beef with a large proportion of bone: the cooking was generally bad. The smaller children lived chiefly on barley, ground up and made into a sort of porridge, and eaten without milk. In the most favourable conditions European children are difficult enough to rear in the plains of India, and conditions in the entrenchment were now becoming such that many died. Bobbie Fayrer, who was just over a year old, had been compared before the siege with Murillo's St. John the Baptist: now he looked like a little wizened old man. His mother's feeble health prevented her from looking after the child, but fortunately Miss Schilling, daughter of the Principal of the Martinière College, was devoted to him. One day when she had him on her lap on the verandah, a ricochet bullet struck the child on the leg, cutting the skin and drawing blood, the ball being found afterwards in Miss Schilling's dress.

Now that the garrison were settling down to the siege they found it as monotonous as life on shipboard. Sundays were observed as far as possible, divine service being held at the Residency taikhana, the Brigade Mess, and the hospital, and also at Fayrer's house, where Mr Harris read prayers every day. There were prayers, too, at Gubbins' house each morning after breakfast, and on Sundays at the same time a short sermon was read after Morning Prayer. It was hard work for Harris now that Polehampton was dead, for there was no other Protestant clergyman in the place, though there were two Catholic priests, both Capuchins, Father Adeodatus of Perugia and Father Bernard of Pistoia. Father Adeodatus was a saintly old man of sixty-eight, who had been in India continuously since 1822, and who hoped that when his time was come his bones would be laid to rest in the Church of St Mary, which he himself had built at Lucknow. He suffered much from the discomforts of the siege, becoming bedridden at length through gout.

Since the investment of the Residency the Brigadier and his staff had always taken their scanty rest booted, with their arms beside them. Mrs Inglis used to look forward to seeing her husband first thing every morning, when he shared whatever news the night had brought while drinking a cup of tea outside the door. This was the happiest hour of her day, for she knew that Inglis often became painfully exhausted later on, and that he was always anxious at night, especially if there were no moon.

It was so firmly believed that the mutineers had outraged the Englishwomen who had fallen into their hands at Meerut, Sitapur, and elsewhere, that the women in the entrenchment were now openly discussing the question already canvassed by their husbands: What was to become of them if the enemy broke in? Some of them were armed against the worst with laudanum and prussic acid, but both Mrs Inglis and Mrs Case set their faces against suicide, believing that, if the hour of trial should come, their God who had sent it would put it into their hearts how they should act. In spite of their troubles and anxieties the women got on comfortably together for the most part, though sometimes at Dr Fayrer's house there were quarrels about domestic management, and once there was a pitched battle between Mr Harris and one of the ladies, who ended in hysterics.

On the 20th July the doctors had insisted that the hospital was no longer fit for Mrs Polehampton, Mrs Gall, and Mrs Barbor to work in. That evening Lieutenant Colonel Palmer escorted them to the Begam Kothi, where they were allowed three-quarters of a room, the other quarter of which was screened off for Lieutenant Thomas and his little girl, Mrs Thomas having died of smallpox a few days before. The three women, all widows, were thrown very much upon their own resources, although both

Palmer and Harris did what they could to make them forget their forlorn condition. They never went out except under cover of night, when they used to walk up and down the narrow pavement outside their door in spite of the stench from a drain on the opposite side. Mrs Polehampton took a strange pleasure in walking there alone on starlight nights, listening to the bullets flying overhead, and longing sometimes for the summons to join her husband. The monotony was only broken by the enemy's assaults. For Mrs Polehampton there was something grand and exciting in the night attacks when the firing was at its height. The women used to jump out of bed, run onto the verandah, and stay there listening until, sometimes, they were driven back to shelter by bullets which struck the ground beside their feet or the wall above their heads.

One Sunday when Harris was holding a service at Fayrer's house, a member of the local garrison burst into the room during the prayers, shouting: 'Holy jabers, boys, the devils are firing cook-houses at us!' There was a great commotion, and the intruder was most upset, having forgotten what day it was and rushed in on the impulse. The missile that had so appalled him was a huge block of wood, which had come swinging through the air with a loud whirring noise and landed inside the entrenchment. The enemy frequently used these wooden shot, which were sometimes bound with iron hoops; they were thrown to a great height and were heavy enough to crash through the roof and all the floors of an ordinary house. In view of their size it was supposed that the enemy had dug funnels in the ground, inclined towards the entrenchment at an angle of, say, forty-five degrees, and charged them with powder as if they were mortars. At length the things became a joke, and the men used to sing out when they appeared: 'Here comes a barrel of beer at last.'

Sometimes the enemy threw in shells made of brass and stone, but when their fuses dropped out, as they often did, these crude projectiles made a curious shriek which gave the garrison ample warning to stand clear and earned them the name of 'Whistling Dicks'. The enemy also fired shrapnel from a howitzer, it was believed, with a very high elevation, carcasses, and an occasional rocket. They invented strange fireworks, too, which were given the generic name of 'Stinkpots'. Some were constructed merely of shell splinters, with a core of powder and a husk of flax and resin, and, though they made a loud hissing and a great stench, the final explosion was only effective at the shortest range. Another and more deadly missile was made by taking a shrapnel shell which had been fired from the entrenchment and had fallen blind, placing it in a canvas bag filled with powder, and fitting both parts with fuses. First the bag exploded, scattering charred canvas, while the shell itself only burst after an interval. Before the danger was understood, two non-commissioned officers, who had taken cover from one of these double-action shells, emerged to look at the fragments after the first explosion, and were both wounded, one of them mortally, by the second. It was observed that most of the enemy's roundshot were hammered, instead of cast, but however rough the workmanship they were effective at the short ranges for which they were required.

Every shell fired from the entrenchment meant danger to the garrison: if it failed to explode, the enemy would draw the fuse, fit a new one, and fire it back: while, if the shell burst, the gunner's target was often so close to the defences that many of the splinters would be blown back over the parapet. One evening as Mrs Inglis was standing in her sheltered courtyard with the baby in her arms, talking to the ayah, a stray fragment whizzed past her ear and buried itself ten inches in the earth.

By the beginning of August there seemed to be a lull in the enemy's underground offensive, but the garrison continued to sink shafts and drive out listening galleries at the most exposed positions. The enemy had now placed a heavy gun near Hill's shop, about two hundred yards north-west of Innes' post, on the road to the iron bridge, a point which commanded a complete diagonal of the position. One of their roundshot broke the leg of a chair in the Post Office while a lady was sitting on it, became entangled in her dress as she fell to the ground, unrolled itself without hurting her, and ran away along the floor. Another grazed the temple of a sleeping engineer officer and only broke the skin.. Much of their practice, however, was more destructive.

On the 1st August Mrs Giddings, wife of the paymaster of the 32nd Foot, told Mrs Case that the last man to see Lieutenant Colonel Case alive was Lieutenant Cooke, who had tried to take a locket from round his commanding officer's neck but had been driven off by the enemy's fire. Mrs Inglis considered that Mrs Giddings would have done better to keep this to herself, since though it seemed clear that he was mortally wounded, no one could say for certain whether Case was taken by the enemy dead or alive, and a fresh story such as this could only remind his widow of her fears. So far from giving way to her sorrow, however, Mrs Case tried, as she always did, to be bright and helpful. She and Caroline Dickson were constantly agreeable in spite of the discomfort of living at such close quarters with three small children, whom they were always ready to care for or to amuse.

Mrs Bartrum had been told by Dr Wells that her little boy could not recover from the cholera, and the child was now so ill that he took no notice of his mother; but she and Mrs Polehampton applied the strongest remedies that could be safely given to a child, and, after kneeling at his bedside throughout the night, Mrs Bartrum was rewarded by seeing him sit up, though still very weak. Next day she was taken ill herself and was racked with anxiety lest she should die, leaving the child alone.

On Sunday the 2nd August the stack of fodder in the racquet court, which had given trouble before when the walls collapsed, tumbled down altogether, burying twelve gun-bullocks. A fatigue party was told off to dig them out, but only seven could be saved. This meant a serious loss of food to the garrison, since the five carcases could not all be eaten at once; nor could the necessary labour for extricating and burying them be well spared from the mines and the defences. Lieutenant Birch and

Mr Couper, Lawrence's secretary, who was now acting in the same capacity for Inglis, both volunteered for the work, although, as members of the staff, they could claim exemption from fatigue duties.

The same day saw the death of Mr Casey, who had been wounded in the arm on the 2nd July while driving stray cattle into the entrenchment. It was not long before his youngest son died of a decline. The eldest was killed by a shell; his head was smashed and he fell across his mother, who was spattered with his blood and brains. The little girl, Lavinia, who was not quite four and a half, was wounded in both feet.

On the 2nd August Inglis wrote as follows:

'My dear Mr Gubbins,

Not having received any intelligence of our reinforcements, and no distant firing being heard, I naturally feel anxious of its whereabouts. In your letter to the Officer Commanding to which you have received an answer did you give him a probable estimate of the Force likely to oppose him en route to this place and did you mention the strong position of the Bani Bridge? I am aware you kept no copy of your letter but perhaps you can remember the two questions above mentioned.

Yours sincerely,

J. Inglis.'

No satisfactory reply having been received from Mr Gubbins, the following letter was despatched:

'*Lucknow, August 2nd,* 1857.

My dear Sir,

I wrote to you on the 22nd, 25th, 27th and 30th ultimo, and sent 2 plans of our position and a memo by the Engineers, but have received no reply, and indeed only one letter, that of Colonel Tytler's from Cawnpore received on the 25th and addressed to Mr Gubbins. Unfortunately Mr Gubbins wrote without consulting the military authorities, and having kept no copy of his letter, we know not what he wrote you and we can only conjecture the strength of the Force gone against you. We suppose they have broken down the bridge at "Bani" and thus succeeded in arresting your progress here. Few of the enemy are in sight here, but they keep so much under cover it is difficult to form an estimate. We are still well off for provisions (say 20 days) both for Europeans and Natives, but our force is fast diminishing and we can no longer man all our guns. Our hopes have been very great, and we look for your arrival with great anxiety, fearing if it is much further delayed, the natives, hitherto faithful to us, will desert.

Yours truly,

J. Inglis, Brigadier.

The Officer Commanding the Relieving Force.'

Mr Harris' nightly duties at the churchyard were now becoming as repulsive as they were dangerous and distressing, for, owing to the shortage of labour, the graves were dug so shallow that they soon became offensive. On the doctors' pronouncing the stench to be dangerous to health, Harris read the burial service over the bodies in the church porch without going to the graveside at all, recognising that he had duties to the living as well as to the dead, and that if he were to sicken there would be no one left to take his place. This departure from routine displeased Inglis, who had already, at Harris' request, given orders that the graves should be dug to the proper depth and thickly spread with charcoal. On the 3rd August Harris received the following letter:

'Sir,

I have the honour by direction of the Brigadier Commanding to forward the enclosed letter this day received and with reference to its contents to state that to prevent all doubts on the subject he has himself just returned from a minute inspection of the burial ground in which he observed a four feet deep grave ready for the reception of a corpse; he also failed to observe any smell sufficient to deter you from the performance of your legitimate duties as Chaplain to this Force.

I have the honour, etc.

T. F. Wilson, Capt.

Offg. A.A. Genl.

To the Revd. P. Harris,
Chaplain to the Force,
Lucknow.'

Harris' reply called forth the following rebuke:

'Sir,

In reply to your letter of yesterday's date, in answer to mine of the 3rd instant No. 79, I am desired by the Brigadier Commanding to ascertain whether you purpose continuing to read the Funeral Service over the bodies in the Hospital, instead of the Grave Yard, in which case, he will feel it his duty to appoint an officer to officiate at the Burial Ground.

2. With regard to the latter part of your letter (3rd paragraph) in which you state that in your ministerial capacity, you are not subject to correction from any Military Authority, I am directed to inform you, that the Brigadier Commanding entirely disapproves of a Burial Service being read anywhere, but at the place appointed, and to remind you, that under present circumstances, Military Rule is supreme, and that the subject will be brought before the proper authorities, at the earliest opportunity.

I have the honour, etc.
T. F. Wilson, Captain,
D.A.A. Genl.

To the Revd. J. P. Harris,
Chaplain of Lucknow.'

On the 3rd August a new loophole was made at the Brigade Mess to command a lane outside which was much frequented by the enemy. Lieutenant

Sewell, 71st Native Infantry, succeeded in clearing the lane at a distance of over seven hundred yards with his double-barrelled rifle, until at last the enemy were forced to build a high barricade to screen the passers-by. The same day two men of the 32nd and two volunteers belonging to Innes' garrison sought to relieve the tedium of the defence by making an unauthorised sortie. They surprised one of the enemy's pickets by creeping up behind a wall and dashing out suddenly, firing their muskets. The enemy fled, pursued by the two privates, who captured a young cooly. The prisoner was brought in and carefully examined, but could give no information of any value.

Next day, as he was making his midday rounds, the Brigadier was seized with giddiness. He was suffering severely from the heat as well as the responsibility of his position, yet he was always at pains to seem confident in public, and only his staff were aware of his misgivings that the food would not hold out, and that the Indian troops would not be staunch for ever. During the day the servants declared that there were guns to be heard in the distance, but among the Europeans only Mrs Inglis and Mrs Case believed them. That evening as they were sitting at dinner the cooly who was pulling the punkah outside suddenly leapt into the room, and a moment later a shell burst in the courtyard. Mrs Inglis rushed out in terror, for the children were playing outside, but none of them were hurt.

On the 6th August Ensign Studdy of the 32nd, one of the leaders of the sortie of July 7th, was hit by a roundshot from the gun by Hill's shop. He was crossing a room in the Residency building when the shot entered and caught the end of the fringe on the punkah, acquired a circular motion in tearing it away, and so swathed the fringe round Studdy's body that it took some time to unwind. His chest was severely contused, and one arm was so badly injured that the surgeons were forced to amputate. As he was too weak to take chloroform they gave him a bottle of champagne to drink, and he bore the operation without a word or even a groan.

On the 4th August another letter had been written to the officer commanding the relieving force, but it was said that anyone found leaving the entrenchment would be killed by the enemy out of hand, and no runner could be found although the despatch was so small that it could be stuffed into a piece of quill. Next day, however, a messenger was available and the letter was sent out.

At about nine o'clock on the evening of the 6th August Aodhan Singh, a sepoy of the 1st Oudh Irregular Infantry who had been sent out with despatches some time before, returned with important news. He reported that he had reached Havelock's camp and been given a despatch in a quill, but had lost it while creeping over the broken and flooded ground outside the entrenchment. Havelock, he said, had crossed the Ganges and routed the enemy at Unao, nine miles along the Lucknow road, and at Bashiratganj, six miles further on, taking many guns, but had then fallen back on Mangalwar, a village within five miles of the river, where he was digging himself in to await reinforcements.

Aodhan Singh's intelligence seemed to be reliable, for he was able to name several officers whom he had talked with, and who had given him various personal messages to deliver. Ungud had already puzzled the garrison by his description of soldiers with blue capcovers and others with square buttons; now Aodhan Singh stated that Havelock had one Sikh and four European regiments, and that one of the latter had curious music played in front of it. The authorities were anxious to know what had led to Havelock's retirement after such brilliant successes on the north side of the river, and it was tantalising to think that the letter containing the explanation had been lost in the last few hundred yards of the journey from Mangalwar.

The same evening a sepoy of the 48th Native Infantry, who had been sent into the city for news two days earlier, returned with intelligence which confirmed Aodhan Singh's; he reported, too, that the enemy were confident of either blowing up or starving out the garrison. The Brigadier told Mrs Inglis that, though Havelock might be able to reach the Residency from Mangalwar within three days, relief was not to be expected for another eight. Some of the garrison were delighted with the latest news, while others, worn out by lack of sleep and the constant dread of mines exploding under their feet, took a less hopeful view.

At Innes' post that night a battery for an 18-pounder was hastily thrown up, the parapet being made of earth protected on the outside by a brick wall and revetted inside by wooden piles. By morning the gun was mounted, and before long the enemy's 24-pounder near Hill's shop was silenced. Inglis soon decided, however, that Innes' post was too exposed for the 18-pounder, which was therefore withdrawn the following night. Throughout the day there was heavy rain, which flooded the trenches, to the great discomfort of the troops. The water also soaked into one of the mines near the Cawnpore battery, which was already charged and provided with the usual canvas hose, filled with powder and laid along the gallery to explode the charge when necessary; all the tamping had to be removed and the powder hose replaced. The enemy's cannonade brought down part of the verandah of the Residency building, and also the verandah of Deprat's house by the Cawnpore battery.

On the 8th August heavy smoke was seen in the far distance towards Cawnpore, and two officers at Gubbins' post reported that they could hear firing in that direction. During the afternoon a battalion of infantry about six hundred strong was seen marching through the city towards the Cawnpore road with drums beating and colours flying. On this day, for the first time since the siege began, there was no casualty in the garrison.

The Residency building had been so badly knocked about by the enemy's roundshot that by now most of its inmates had been evacuated. Mr Gubbins' house was consequently fuller than ever, and the enemy seemed to be well aware of this, for their gunners began to pay it more and more attention. Throwing up a 9-pounder battery in a lane on the south side, to which no effective reply could be made owing to the lie of the land, they pounded the house until all the parapets on that side of the roof were in ruins and the walls themselves were holed in many places. The bastion on the south-west corner had by this time been completed and armed with a 9-pounder, but the gun was not to be fired without special permission, for fear of supplying the mutineers with shot. The enemy took advantage of this to cannonade the south-west angle from a battery in a neighbouring garden, until at last the authorities agreed that the defences were suffering too heavily and sent down Lieutenant Thomas, who silenced the opposing battery with eight well-directed rounds from the 9-pounder.

The Commissariat now began to issue a preparation of burnt wheat in place of tea and coffee. The men were glad of something to drink when they came off duty at night, and the stuff was not unpalatable, though it was believed to cause dysentery. Another child died in Mrs Bartrum's room at the Begam Kothi. She and the mother washed and dressed the body and laid it in a small box sent over for the purpose by one of the officers. Mrs Bartrum was beginning to feel that she would go mad if she stayed any longer in the same room, but fortunately a place was found for her party at Mr Ommanney's house, where they were much more comfortable. Her little boy was recovering rapidly from the cholera.

On Sunday the 9th August one baby was born—a fine boy—and two died. Young Studdy died also, to the great regret of the garrison. At midday Lieutenant Loughnan took out a detachment from Innes' post and spiked one of the enemy's guns, returning without loss. A successful sortie was always cheering to the garrison, but it was found as time went on that, however effective spiking guns might be in the field, where time was all-important, it was almost useless here, since the mutineers commanded expert craftsmen who could drill out the spike in a few hours or turn the gun over and bore a new vent on the other side.

At ten o'clock in the morning of the 10th August the officers on lookout reported unusual activity among the enemy. Guns, waggons, and litters were being moved from place to place; troops of cavalry were escorting notables on elephants; and both the regular infantry and the Talukdars' matchlockmen were on the march with colours flying. Soon after ten a large force was seen approaching the bridge of boats from the cantonments on the north of the river. The outposts were warned and the whole garrison stood to arms.

At half-past ten the enemy fired a shell, apparently as a signal, into the Begam Kothi in the centre of the position, and immediately a mine was sprung on the south face. Mrs Inglis and her party were startled by the roar of the explosion, which seemed to last for several seconds, and looking out they saw a cloud of dust and smoke by the Brigade Mess. Mr Thornhill, of the Civil Service, ran past, calling out that all the ladies were safe, and soon Mrs Couper and Mrs Radcliffe brought their children to take refuge in Mrs Inglis' little room. There was heavy firing and before long they heard another explosion. A roundshot struck the wall outside, coming to rest beside the door. The Brigadier, running past, called to Mrs Inglis to take shelter at the far end of the courtyard in a large storeroom which had no windows and was therefore comparatively safe. Seizing the children, the women ran across the open as fast as they could.

The first mine had been sprung opposite Johannes' house, carrying away the outer palisade over a length of sixty feet, pitching a heavy baulk of timber onto the roof of the Brigade Mess, blowing up the verandah of the Martinière house, and making a large breach in the wall. One of the outer rooms, which by the merest chance was empty at the time, was laid bare to the enemy, and the explosion blew open the door into the next room, which was occupied by Mr Schilling and the schoolboys with some of the sick and wounded. Mr Schilling slammed the door, which was quickly secured, but two private soldiers, who had come down with the Brigadier to the scene of the explosion, were dangerously wounded by bullets which smashed their way through the panels.

As soon as the dust and smoke had cleared away, the enemy occupied the surrounding buildings in force and opened fire on the entrenchment, while a small storming party made for the breach, to be repulsed by a biting fire from the roof of the Brigade Mess and from one of the retrenchments. About thirty of them, led by a man in pink, made a lodgment in the ditch of the Cawnpore battery, within a few feet of the guns, but Captain Fulton shot the man in pink, and they were driven out and across the road by hand grenades.

The second mine was sprung outside Sago's post on the east face, destroying several outhouses and blowing up two privates of the 32nd who were on picket duty. One of the men came to earth inside the defences, a little bruised, while the other, who was pitched into the road outside with his musket in his hand, jumped up unhurt and escaped into the compound at Germon's post, climbing the wall under a hail of bullets. The enemy did not find it so easy to pass the defences, but as they came on in great force Harry Metcalfe was sent to Captain

M'Cabe at the Post Office to ask for help. 'Well, Metcalfe,' said M'Cabe, 'I can't afford you any help from my post. We're as badly off as yourselves. Go back and tell your officer he must keep the post at every risk.' In the end, however, he decided to go along with Metcalfe. On the way they passed a young Eurasian who was on his knees in prayer. M'Cabe gave him a cuff on the ear which knocked him off his knees, and said: 'What do you mean, you damned swab—now is no time for praying, when the position is nearly in the hands of the rebels.' At Sago's post they found Lieutenant Clery and his garrison hard pressed. Metcalfe gave a yell and M'Cabe shouted as loud as he could: 'Number One will advance to support Number Three reserve—Charge!'—a ruse which seemed to discourage the enemy. Later on the outpost was reinforced.

The enemy advanced with scaling ladders against Innes', Anderson's, and Gubbins' posts, but were repulsed on every side with heavy loss. So many spare muskets were available that all round the defences there were two or three for each man, ready loaded and to hand, which increased the fire-power of the garrison immensely. Mr Gubbins, a sportsman and an excellent shot, was surprised to find how hard it was to hit a fleeting target with a single rifle bullet from a loophole; a smooth-bore musket, loaded with eight or ten pistol balls, was far more destructive at close quarters.

The enemy maintained an intense fire of roundshot and musketry for two hours after the last assault had failed. Then suddenly, at five in the afternoon, they made a rush on the Financial post, pressing the attack home more stubbornly than any that had yet been made. A number of them passed the compound wall and climbed up outside the verandah, while the most daring seized a bayonet which was sticking out of a loophole and tried to wrench it off the owner's musket: he was instantly shot. There were several hundred more of them lying on their faces on the far side of the road, waiting to rush in if once the stormers obtained a footing; but after twenty-five minutes they were all driven off, and the firing gradually died away. At nine o'clock in the evening, they made a further assault with no better success, and by ten o'clock all was quiet.

Inside the defences only three Europeans and two Indians had been killed, and twelve men wounded, whereas the enemy's losses seemed to be even more severe than they had been on the 20th July. After an exhausting day the whole garrison stood to arms throughout the night. The failure of this assault left the rank and file more than ever contemptuous of an enemy who, with overwhelming numbers and ample *matériel*, had lacked the stomach to carry such trumpery defences in six weeks' fighting: there was surely little to fear from such opponents, above ground.

On the day after the general assault Major Anderson, the Chief Engineer, died of dysentery, from which he had been suffering since before the siege. For some time past Captain Fulton had been doing most of his work, but Anderson's death deprived Inglis of one of his shrewdest advisers. He died peacefully, saying to his successor as he pressed his hand again and again: 'Well, Fulton, it must have come at last. If I had lived to go home, we might never have met again. God bless you!' Fulton helped to stitch up the quilt in which he was buried and to lay him in his grave, marking the place with a stick.

Every day the difficulty of housing the troops and the non-combatants was increasing as the enemy's ordnance pounded the more exposed positions. Anderson's and Deprat's houses, on either side of the Cawnpore battery, were in ruins, and the state of Innes' post was little better. The Residency building, which had always been one of the enemy's favourite targets, was riddled with roundshot, and all the upper storeys had already been vacated though there were still some privates of the 32nd and a few women and children living on the ground floor. On the 11th August there was a high wind. During the morning the enemy fired a number of roundshot into the building, and about noon the greater part of the left wing collapsed, burying six privates who were sleeping in one room. Every effort was made to extricate them under heavy fire. Four of the men were lying under such masses of bricks that their case was hopeless, but the rescue party succeeded in clearing the rubble from the heads of the other two, who were able to speak a little after having brandy poured down their throats. It took two hours' hard work and dangerous work to bring them out alive.

That evening the enemy's miners were at work again opposite Sago's post. Next morning Lieutenant Clery made a sortie with twelve men of the 32nd, accompanied by Lieutenant Hutchinson of the engineers, but was met by such a brisk fusillade from a strong covering party that he was forced to retire and was lucky to regain the defences without loss. This was the first sortie that had been made without success. It was afterwards determined to work day and night in the countermine in the hope of blowing up the enemy's gallery before it could reach the defences.

From daybreak that morning the enemy had raked the Cawnpore battery with a fire of roundshot and musketry which gradually became so deadly that the garrison could not fight the guns any longer. The shutters on the embrasures were destroyed by gunfire, and at last the battery was abandoned by all except one sentry; the guns were not withdrawn, however, for fear of encouraging the enemy. Later in the day the sentry was killed by a roundshot. As soon as it was dark, working parties were sent into the battery to withdraw a 9-pounder which had been disabled by the enemy's fire, and to repair and strengthen the works as far as possible.

The same evening, an old Indian woman was sent out with a note addressed to Havelock and rolled up in a quill. Since the beginning of the siege some twenty letters had been despatched by various hands, but so far only one reply had been received.

All that night the countermine at Sago's post was being driven out as fast as possible, while the enemy, who were now only a few yards away, did their utmost to hinder the work by throwing squibs, rockets, and brickbats over the wall. They even tried to set fire to the outhouses by means of flaming wicks tied onto long bamboos, but the garrison cut off the ends as soon as they appeared. Next morning the enemy miners could be heard at work so close that Lieutenant Hutchinson decided to load the countermine. While the charge was being tamped some of the garrison threw clods at the enemy to distract their attention, and both sides pelted each other across the wall.

At ten o'clock the engineers sent word to the neighbouring outposts that the countermine was ready to be sprung. Lieutenant F. W. Birch, 59th

Native Infantry, doing duty with the engineers, threw several brickbats into the yard of the house where the enemy's shaft was sunk, to see whether it was occupied, and as he stepped aside a shower of bricks came flying back. The charge in the counter-mine was then fired. A mass of earth was thrown into the air and the enemy's house collapsed. The garrison gave a loud cheer which was answered by a furious but harmless fusillade. A few of the enemy emerged from the ruins, only to be despatched by musketry, and a number of their miners, who were still at work with the pick, were buried in their own gallery—the garrison could hear their groans.

In the afternoon the Brigadier led another sortie into the Goindah lines, on the south side of Gubbins' post, to discover what the enemy were about. His party did what damage they could to a long, deep trench which led towards the defences and was probably intended only for shelter, demolished some of the walls, and regained the entrenchment without meeting any resistance.

On the 12th August Mrs Inglis and her party had potatoes for dinner, the first for over a month, but they were only a few odd ones which had been found in an obscure corner. Mrs Bartrum's child was steadily gaining strength, and fortunately she was able to get him a little milk every day. She was still a very bad cook, but was improving. Often the Commissariat beef was so tough that, after beating it with a heavy stick for half an hour, she had to cut it into shreds with her nail-scissors before putting it into the pot. The cooking was done in little brick fireplaces on the verandah of the Begam Kothi. There was a shortage of firewood, and what little she could find was often too wet to burn. Once one of the soldiers broke down some railings for her, but she had nothing larger than a dinner-knife to chop them up with. Besides the cooking there were clothes to wash and the child to attend to. While he slept she would sit beside him, fanning away the flies and mosquitoes, and reading the psalms and lessons for the day; and when he awoke she would talk to him about his father, who might now be dead for all she knew. As the siege went on her fingers became covered with boils. Dr Darby, who came to lance them, brought the child a little sugar which he declared he had stolen. The Doctor's wife had last been heard of in Wheeler's entrenchment at Cawnpore, her confinement being due, and his anxiety had been more acute than ever since Ungud's last report.

One day a respectable-looking woman with a baby in her arms knocked at the door of Mrs Inglis' room and asked for the Brigadier's lady. She said that her baby had been born on the first day of the siege, and that her husband, who had been an overseer of roads, had been shot through the lungs and had died almost at once. She had lost her milk through grief and anxiety. She was longing to rear the child—it was the last of four—and take it safely back to

England. Her father was a clergyman in Kent. She had all she wanted except nourishment for the baby, and hearing that Mrs Inglis was still keeping her goats she had come to beg for a little milk. She told her story in such an unaffected manner that it went to Mrs Inglis' heart to refuse her, but she had only just enough milk for her own children, and she believed that her baby would die without it. The woman seemed to understand that she would have given it if she could.

On the 14th August an Indian sweeper came in with the report that Havelock was at Unao awaiting reinforcements, but that a column nine hundred strong had advanced and engaged the enemy again. The garrison did not know what to believe, but it seemed clear that there was to be no relief for some time to come. That night six Indian water-carriers attached to the 32nd deserted, as well as several servants.

Next morning the enemy fired salvos from their 18-pounders into the Cawnpore battery, bringing down the outer wall of the adjoining house which was used as a guardroom, and driving all the garrison, except the sentry, out of the battery. Once again the sentry was killed by a roundshot later in the day. Second Lieutenant Bonham received a severe contusion in the side from falling bricks, and Second Lieutenant J. Alexander, also of the Bengal Artillery, was wounded in the arm while laying a gun at the Hospital post, leaving only two effective artillery officers, Second Lieutenant Cunliffe and Lieutenant Thomas. Of the gunners, about half were killed, wounded, or sick. That evening there was no burial, for the first time since the siege began.

At nine o'clock the same evening Ungud returned with the following letter:

'*Mangalwar, August 4th.*

To: M. Gubbins, Esq.,

Dear Sir,

We march to-morrow morning for Lucknow, having been reinforced. We shall push on as speedily as possible. We hope to reach you in four days at furthest. You must aid us in every way, even to cutting your way out, if we can't force our way in. We are only a small Force.

B. Fraser Tytler, Lieut. Col.'

But this was not the latest news. Ungud had been captured by the enemy on his way from Havelock's camp and detained for some days. On being released he had retraced his steps to Mangalwar, where he learnt that, after beating the enemy for the second time at Bashiratganj, Havelock had found his communications threatened and had been forced to recross the Ganges and fall back on Cawnpore. Ungud added that the fresh troops that were making their way up country were due to reach Cawnpore by about the 20th August, and that as soon as they arrived Havelock would cross the river again and renew his efforts to relieve the garrison.

It was clear from Fraser Tytler's letter that he had no conception of the state of things at Lucknow, for, encumbered as they were with the women and children and the sick and wounded, it would have been madness for the garrison to leave their defences and engage in street fighting with the enemy's immensely superior numbers. As soon as the Brigadier had read the letter, Mr Gubbins pointed out how important it was that any reply should explain the position as clearly as possible, and suggested that he and Inglis should confer as to the terms of the despatch. Next day Inglis was courteous enough to bring the following draft himself to Gubbins' quarters:

'*Lucknow*, *August* 16*th*.

My dear General,

A note from Colonel Tytler to Mr Gubbins reached us last night, dated Mangalwar 4th inst., the latter paragraph of which is as follows: "You must aid us in every way, even to cutting your way out, if we cannot force our way in." It has caused me much uneasiness, as it is quite impossible with my weak and shattered Force that I can leave my defences. You must bear in mind how I am hampered, that I have upwards of 120 sick and wounded, and at least 220 women, and about 230 children, and no carriage of any description, besides sacrificing 23 lacs of Treasure, and about 30 guns of sorts.

In consequence of the news received, I shall soon put the Force on ½ rations unless I hear again from you. Our provisions will last us then till about the 10th September.

If you hope to save this Force, no time must be lost in pushing forward. We are daily being attacked by the Enemy, who are within a few yards of our defences. Their mines have already weakened our post, and I have every reason to believe they are carrying on others. Their 18-pounders are within 150 yards of some of our Batteries, and from their position and our inability to form working parties we cannot reply to them and consequently the damage done hourly is very great. My strength now in Europeans is 350, and about 300 natives, and the men dreadfully harassed and owing to part of the Residency having been brought down by roundshot many are without shelter. Our native force having been assured, on Colonel Tytler's authority, of your near approach some 25 days ago, are naturally losing confidence and if they leave us I do not see how the defences are to be manned. Did you receive a letter and plan from me from this man "Ungud"? Kindly answer this question.

Yours etc.,

J. Inglis, Brigadier.

To Brigadier-General Havelock,
Commanding relieving force.'

This despatch struck Gubbins as pessimistic, especially in its estimate of supplies, and he suggested writing more hopefully, lest Havelock should make fresh efforts before being adequately reinforced. But Inglis replied that he had consulted his staff, who concurred with his reading of the situation, and the same night Ungud took his letter out, unaltered.

Although the military had brushed Gubbins' objection aside it was not without substance. The remaining gun bullocks would obviously supply the meat ration till long after September 10th, and it was widely believed among the garrison that there were still large stores of grain. Mr Simon Martin, Deputy Commissioner of Lucknow, could have told the authorities, had they asked him, that Sir Henry Lawrence had ordered him to make provision for three thousand people for six months. Any confusion was probably due to the fact that before the siege supplies had been brought in by both the military and the civil departments. Lieutenant James, the head of the Commissariat, had been severely wounded at Chinhat; his native subordinates had almost all deserted; and, although Lawrence on his deathbed had expressly ordered that a general inventory should be taken, this had never been done. James was disabled throughout the siege and irritable from his wound, but he would not give up control, and the officers who worked under him were new to the department. Lieutenant Keir, who was in charge of the grain store, knew that there were large supplies, but the authorities never asked him for any figures.

The garrison were not suffering so much from shortage of food as from lack of variety. Scurvy was increasing, and every day men risked their lives to gather the leaves of a wild cruciferous plant which grew among the ruins and was highly prized as a vegetable. Bobbie Fayrer, who was living almost entirely on ground barley, was little better than a skeleton, and Herbert Dashwood was dangerously ill. Mrs Fayrer was weak and poorly from a choleraic attack. The women and children were now sleeping in Dr Fayrer's dining-room because the underground rooms were damp and infested by rats. The garrison as a whole was suffering great discomfort from flies, mosquitoes, bugs, and fleas. There was still a stench everywhere and, in spite of the Brigadier's orders, conditions in the graveyard were still so bad that one evening when Harris returned from his duties there he vomited continually for two hours.

The firing at Anderson's post was so heavy that the Indian servants refused to stay, all except one Madras boy, and he fell ill of fever. All ranks took turns to chop wood, light the fire, cook, and attend to sanitary arrangements, but when the cry 'Turn Out' was heard they had to leave their domestic duties, seize their muskets, and rush to their posts. There was constant fear that the place was undermined, and the enemy's shells and roundshot were continually destroying both shelter and personal property. One day, soon after a shell had burst inside the house, Signor Barsottelli went to look for his trunk and found that it had been blown to bits. He called the Madras boy and asked: 'Where is my trunk?' The boy went off to the corner where the trunk had always stood, and, after searching for it in vain, returned to Barsottelli in amazement and said: 'Trunk not got, sir.' Barsottelli pretended to be very angry, 'Not got a trunk, you rascal!' he said. 'Where is it?' One of the other men was considerate enough to show the boy the few splinters that were left. He was delighted with the explanation and told Barsottelli: 'Before, trunk got, sir—*now*,—not got—shell break him.'

During the heavy rains the grass had grown to a great height in the no-man's-land outside the defences, affording excellent cover to an approaching enemy; the sentries were therefore instructed to be more vigilant than ever, and special patrols were sent out from time to time. The rain had also beaten down or covered up with mud many of the obstructions outside the entrenchment such as abattis, small stakes, and crowsfeet.

The nights were long. Often the men sat up for hours waiting for an assault. One might be seen loading his piece by the glimmer of the lamp, while others looked to their pistols or refilled their pouches with ammunition. Presently one of the party would shoulder his musket and take his turn on sentry, while another lowered himself down the shaft of the countermine to listen for the enemy's picks. Then at last the sentry would shout that the enemy were advancing, and the cry 'Turn Out' would be followed by the rattle of musketry. The bullets whistled overhead, the grapeshot could be heard striking the parapet, and the roundshot crashed through the walls. Amid the din of artillery they could hear the enemy's bugles sounding the Advance, and the elephants trumpeting as they dragged the heavy guns into position. The garrison would wait patiently, withholding their fire and watching the long grass outside. Sometimes they mistook the glint of moonlight on flickering leaves for the turbans of the enemy. Then the men in the outposts would see little streaks of fire passing swiftly over their heads as their own mortars began to bombard the enemy, and, as the shells burst outside, the splinters would come whizzing back over their heads again.

Sometimes when all was quiet a dog would appear on top of the parapet, and the sentry, seeing something moving in the dark, would fire, wounding him and setting him yelping till all the dogs in earshot were barking too. They would all rush out to worry the injured one, who would bolt with the others after him, growling and yelping as they rushed through the palisade, until they woke the enemy, who fired their muskets in all directions, fearing that the Europeans were upon them, and abusing each other heartily for not being on the alert. The garrison would hear them shouting to one another in the vernacular:

'Don't you see they're coming? Look out!'

'Who are you to give me orders?'

'Well, do as you like; the Sahib log (people) will soon come and cut your head off.'

'Well, do you think they're likely to spare you more than me?'

The argument would grow hotter and hotter until the second speaker protested: 'Come, come, if you're going to threaten me, I shall run off to the hills.'

To this the first would retort: 'Do you think you'll be safer in the hills than anywhere else? Why, they'll chase you all over the face of the earth.'

They would end by calling each other cowards and falling off to sleep; and then perhaps all would be quiet until at dawn the mutineers sounded the Assembly and opened their morning cannonade.

In spite of the efforts that were being made to repair and reinforce the parapet at the Cawnpore battery, there were still many misgivings about its fate, and some of the garrison even took it as a personal disgrace that the guns had been silenced by the enemy. One night the Brigadier slept in the battery himself to give the men confidence.

On the 16th August the enemy were heard mining opposite the east end of the Sikh Square on the south face. A countermine was immediately begun, the Sikhs, who were admirable miners, receiving two rupees, or four shillings, in cash for each night's labour, which was generous enough pay to make the work popular. Next day, the countermine at Anderson's post having reached a length of thirty-six feet, the enemy's picks could be heard no longer, and the work was therefore suspended.

The sharpshooters were still making such good practice from the top of Johannes' house that the authorities at length determined to take the offensive underground and instructed Lieutenant Innes to make a survey with a view to blowing up the building. By climbing onto the roof of the Martinière house, and noting, as he crawled along, the positions of certain shot holes in the parapet, through which he took a number of bearings, he was able to calculate that Johannes' house was fifty feet long, forty feet distant from the wall of the Martinière, and thirty-four feet from the adjoining shops, which had been barricaded off on the 21st July, and in which the shaft of the mine was to be sunk. The gallery was to be driven out to a length of fifty feet, which would bring the end sixteen feet inside the face of Johannes' house, and branches were then to be dug to right and left, each twelve feet long, at the end of which there were to be short returns—like the serifs on the top of a capital T—to form convenient chambers for the charges. Innes' plan having been approved, the miners broke ground on the afternoon of the 17th August. The operation was kept secret, only men of the 32nd being employed, and every precaution being taken to avoid unnecessary noise. The roof was supported by casing where the gallery passed underneath the outside ditch.

At the Sikh Square in the early hours of the 18th August, the fiftieth day of the siege, mine and countermine were rapidly approaching one another. Lieutenant Hutchinson stopped the work, laid his charge, and began to tamp it. Suddenly there was a burst of firing overhead, and, just as he and his Sikhs had rushed up from the gallery, the enemy's mine went up. Evidently their charge had not been tamped, for the explosion spent most of its force along their own gallery and destroyed the shelter in which the shaft was sunk.

It had been reported that a second mine was being aimed at the Sikh Square, but the engineers had pronounced that what the garrison could hear was not the enemy's picks but the stamping of their own horses picketed in the inner court. Between five and six in the morning of the 18th August Lieutenant Mecham, 7th Oudh Irregular Infantry, and Captain Adolphe Orr, Oudh Military Police, were standing on the roof of a house at the corner of the square with two sentries, Band-Sergeant Curtain and Drummer Ford. There were none of the enemy in sight. Suddenly one of the sentries saw a man moving outside. Mecham fired at him but missed, and the shot was followed by an immense explosion. Mecham, Orr, and Ford were thrown into the air but came down among the wreckage on the inside of the wall, with nothing worse than bruises. Confused by the noise and smoke, Ford lost all sense of direction, and was just walking out into the enemy's arms when he was stopped by a shout from Captain Orr. Curtain was pitched into the road outside, where the enemy made short work of him; next day his headless trunk was lying by the road-side. Inside the house were six Eurasian drummers and one sepoy, all of whom were trapped in the ruins.

A great cloud of smoke and dust hung over the scene of the explosion, clearing away at last to reveal a practicable breach thirty feet long. The local garrison at once abandoned the outer square, taking cover behind the wall of the next court, so that there was nothing to defend the breach but their direct fire and the flanking fire from the roof of the Brigade Mess. The enemy were soon swarming in the buildings on the other side of the street, but were backward in following up their success. One of their leaders, a fine-looking officer of Irregular Cavalry, mounted the breach, waving his sword and calling on his men to follow him; but as they hung back he was hit by a bullet from the Brigade Mess and died inside the defences. Another officer took the lead, but when he too was shot the enemy gave up the attempt to storm and kept themselves safely under cover.

The whole garrison was called to arms; the general reserve, now reduced to eighteen men of the 84th Foot, was posted so as to command the breach from the right; and boxes, doors, planks, and tents were piled up to provide cover from the enemy's musketry. After desperate exertions—a house was pulled down to make way for them—a couple of 9-pounders, double-charged with grape, were brought to bear on the breach through embrasures swiftly improvised in a wall fifty yards away. Meanwhile the enemy had made a lodgment in an outhouse at the end of the lane that divided the Sikh Square from Mr Gubbins' compound, and had already begun to loophole the wall, so as to fire along the inside of the breach, when they were driven off by a 24-pounder howitzer at the inner end of the lane.

Meanwhile the breach was still gaping in the outer wall. The square was full of wounded horses, hit by shots from either side, and some of the men who had been trapped in the ruins could be seen still struggling to get free. The firing was so hot that it was hopeless to send out a rescue party, but a friend of one of the drummers was allowed to creep up and see what he could do. He came back with the news that one man at least was still living, though pinned down by a beam across his chest: he thought he could release him if he had a saw. Lieutenant Birch, A.D.C., who was in charge of the reserve, sent for one immediately, promising fifty rupees (five pounds) and an honourable mention to any man who could effect the rescue. As soon as the saw was brought the same man crept out again, but was observed by the enemy and driven back by their musketry in such haste that he left the saw behind.

Some of the garrison had abandoned their arms when the mine was sprung, and these were still lying inside the remains of the outer wall. The enemy now began to dig their way through, until presently their hands could be seen as they tried to pull the muskets and swords out through the holes; Birch had to fire his revolver five times at one of them before he could drive him away.

In the afternoon the Brigadier determined to

take possession of the breach. Heavy shutters were brought from the windows of the Residency building to be used, double, as shields against the enemy's musketry. Holding these before them, Inglis himself, Couper, Thornhill, of the Civil Service, Wilson, Hutchinson, and Birch advanced towards the outer wall down one side of the square, while several of the 84th filed down the other. On gaining the edge of the breach every man in succession set down his shutters, overlapping them with the next so that a barricade grew slowly from either side towards the middle. The six drummers and the sepoy were all dead by now; their bodies formed the foundation of the new defences. As soon as the two lines of shutters had met, the garrison re-occupied the outer square in force, and after dark fresh doors and planks were added to the barricade, which was then reinforced with earth and sandbags. During these operations one man was killed and several wounded, besides those that were buried by the mine. All the troops, both European and Indian, worked with a will throughout a long day under a burning sun.

Inglis was not content with regaining what he had lost, but made a sortie, as soon as the breach had been repaired, with Captain M'Cabe and a detachment of the 32nd. Crossing the road and making for the nearest house occupied by the enemy, they found a sentry posted at the door with a tulwar, or curved sword. Inglis' pistol misfired, but M'Cabe threw a hand-grenade at the man, who fled without waiting for it to burst. The enemy abandoned the house, which Captain Fulton then demolished with two barrels of powder. Several more buildings and also the shaft of a mine were destroyed before the enemy had recovered from their surprise, and by the end of the day the situation on the south face was slightly better than it had been before the mine was sprung.

That night a duplicate of Inglis' letter to Havelock of the 16th August was sent out with this addition: 'P.S. Since the above was written the enemy have sprung another mine which has given us a great deal of trouble and caused some loss. I trust that you will lose no time in coming to our assistance regardless of the statements contained in any letters which may reach you from Mr Gubbins. Military men are unanimous regarding our case.'

Next day Fulton, Hutchinson, and Lieutenant J. C. Anderson, Madras Engineers, led another sortie from the south face, covered by a party of Sikhs and Europeans in the Sikh Square. Further damage was done to the surrounding buildings, the enemy offering no resistance, and the Indians at Gubbins' post seized the opportunity of bringing in supplies of rafters, doors, and laths which had been loosened by the demolitions and which were invaluable for repairing the works. Inside the houses there were trenches which had apparently been dug as a protection against shell-fire; it was clear, however, that they had not proved effective, for there were pools of blood about the place as well as recent graves.

By now the garrison had learnt to make their sorties as destructive as possible to the enemy with the minimum of risk to themselves. They always attacked a passage or doorway from the left, since a man approaching from the right could not fire into the opening without presenting his whole body to any one lurking inside. Sometimes an officer and a sergeant went on ahead of the rest. If the door of the house to be demolished was open they threw in a hand-grenade, while if it was shut they drove a bayonet or screwed a gimlet into the wood, suspended a bag of powder, fired it with a short fuse, standing aside for the explosion, and then, as the door fell in, charged into the building followed by the rest of the party.

As soon as the house was cleared one of the engineers would arrive, generally Captain Fulton followed by a huge Sikh named Hookum Singh, who could carry a barrel of powder on his back with ease. If the house was near the entrenchment there was a danger that the explosion might damage the defences, but Fulton had a genius for this kind of work and was never at fault. Directly the train was laid word was passed to withdraw the escort, and all the men were ordered back to the entrenchment, except the sentries who were posted in case the enemy made a last minute rush. Then the order was given to withdraw the sentries, and Fulton was left alone. As soon as all the rest were under cover he fired the train and ran for his life; the explosion was sure to follow just as he had reached the entrenchment.

Private William Cooney, 32nd Foot, knew more about the enemy's movements than any man in the garrison, for he used to make sorties on his own account, followed by one of the loyal sepoys, who idolised him. One day the pair of them crawled into a battery, bayoneted four of the gunners, and went on to spike the guns. Time and again Cooney was put in the guardroom for disobeying orders, but they always let him out when there was any fighting to be done.

In the early morning of the 19th August Herbert Dashwood died. The little boy had seemed better the day before, but his fever had increased during the night and he had been gasping so painfully that they were almost glad when death put an end to his sufferings. Mrs Dashwood, who had lost her husband in the early days of the siege and who was expecting another child before long, washed the body herself and dressed it in a white nightgown. In the forenoon Charles Dashwood, her brother-in-law, came and sat with her beside the dead child. At eleven o'clock Mrs Harris took the body away, sewed it up in a clean white cloth, and gave it to her husband, who carried it over to the hospital to await the evening's burial. Mrs Dashwood had little time for mourning, since her other child, Ally, was dangerously ill with fever and dysentery.

On the evening of the 20th August a small body of the enemy crept up to the Baillie Guard, where they succeeded in piling wood and straw against the gate and setting them alight before being observed. The flames leapt up fiercely, but Lieutenant Aitken, 13th Native Infantry, forced open the gate, which was barricaded, under a heavy fire, and the Indian water-carriers were able to put out the blaze before any damage had been done. The walls flanking the gate were then loopholed in case the enemy should try that trick again.

On the same evening the gallery and chambers of the mine under Johannes' house were finished. During the night four charges of powder of a hundred pounds each were laid and tamped, and the powder-hose by which they were to be fired was laid along the gallery as far as the shaft. Just before daybreak on the 21st August the mine was ready to be fired, and arrangements had been completed for two sorties which were to be made to left and right as soon as it was sprung. The enemy were quiet, having apparently heard nothing of the mining, but when the garrison opened a brisk fire of musketry they awoke and beat to arms, swarming into Johannes' house and the neighbouring buildings, where their lights could be seen through the windows. Then, as soon as it was broad enough day for the sorties, the hose was fired from the shaft. It burned slowly, but in less than a minute a single shock was felt as the walls of Johannes' house opened outwards and collapsed.

In the confusion a detachment of fifty Europeans filed out of the entrenchment, splitting into two parties in the street outside. The first, under Lieutenant Browne, 32nd Foot, advanced to the nearest battery, where one of the enemy's artillerymen was sleeping on his gun. Browne, who was first into the battery, tried to shoot him with his revolver, but as it misfired the man woke up and ran away. One of the guns was spiked, but not with great success, since the vent was so enlarged that even double-spiking it did not suffice to put it out of action for more than four hours. The vent of the other gun was so enormous that spiking was out of the question.

The objective of the second party, under Fulton and M'Cabe, was the shop behind Johannes' house. On reaching the verandah and finding the place shut up, the two officers set their backs against the door and their feet against the verandah wall; at the third heave the frame of the door parted from the brickwork, and Fulton fell in head over heels, to find himself at the bottom of an eight-foot trench. M'Cabe and the rest burst in after him, and as soon as the house was cleared two barrels of powder were brought up and placed in position. Fulton had already ordered the rest of the party back to the entrenchment, and was just about to set light to the hose, when someone shouted from the lane outside that there was yet a wounded man to be taken in through the sally-port. Fulton waited for the word that all was clear, then fired the train and left the building, happy, as he wrote in his diary, to be the last out and the first in.

The enemy had not fought hand-to-hand but had fired from the neighbouring buildings at any man that chanced to expose himself. The casualties in the two sorties were only two killed, and one mortally, one dangerously, and one slightly wounded—not a heavy price to pay for the elimination of Johannes' house and shop. Lieutenant Innes, who had superintended the work in the mine for three days and nights without sleep, fell into a stupor as soon as the strain was over, and could not be roused for the next two days.

With so many military duties and fatigues to tax them, the garrison sometimes needed a sharp word to keep them up to the mark. On the 22nd August the following letter was sent to Captain Lowe, commanding the 32nd Foot:

'Sir,

I have been instructed by the Brigadier Commanding to call your attention to the careless and indifferent manner in which the soldiers of H.M.'s 32nd Foot perform their duties when on sentry. On several occasions the Brigadier has spoken to the men himself, and this morning he found an important post without a sentry and on inquiry he was told that the man had gone to the rear.

The Brigadier is fully sensible that the duties at present devolving on the men are fatiguing and harassing, but at a time when so much vigilance and alertness are required for the safety of the garrison it behoves every soldier to be most watchful, and therefore the Brigadier wishes you to speak personally on the subject to the men under your command.

I have the honour etc.
T. F. Wilson, Capt.
Offg. A.A. Genl.'

That evening the enemy were so quiet that Inglis thought it safe to take his wife and Mrs Case for a short walk past Ommanney's house. Although there was nothing to be seen beyond bare walls, they found it treat enough to be away from their own courtyard, which they were forbidden to leave without express permission.

The next day was Sunday. Mr Harris held a service at the Brigade Mess in the morning and at Dr Fayrer's house in the afternoon, administering Holy Communion at both places. Five newly made widows attended the afternoon service, among them Mrs Barbor and Mrs Polehampton, who were escorted from the Begam Kothi by Lieutenant Colonel Palmer. After this expedition the two ladies ventured more often outside their own quarters. One evening Palmer took them across to the Residency and they roamed all over the building. Mrs Polehampton visited the room that she and her husband had occupied for several weeks before the siege. It was in a state of ruin; part of the wall had fallen in, the floor was covered with bricks and mortar, and there were several roundshot strewn about; the large earthenware bath in the next room had been shattered. The ladies climbed onto the roof to view the surrounding country, which looked more beautiful than ever after the cramped and sordid quarters they were used to. Mrs Polehampton strained her eyes for a glimpse of the church in cantonments, thinking sadly of her own home which was hidden among the trees. But it was not considered safe for them up there and they were soon sent down.

On the 25th August Inglis sent out a further copy of his letter of the 16th with this addition: 'We have had no letters from you of a later date than the 4th inst. Since the 18th the enemy have placed more guns in position and harass us in all directions. We have too the most alarming reports of the disaffection and plots of our native troops inside who are wavering in their fidelity owing to your return across the Ganges.'

One of the reports referred to by the Brigadier had been made by an Indian to Mr Phillips of the Military Secretary's office. He declared that all the Indian troops in the garrison were parties to the following plot: first, the Sikhs were to enter the enclosure of Gubbins' post on the pretext of speaking to Mr Gubbins about an issue of pay; then, at a given signal, the Indian gunners at the same post were to turn their guns on the Europeans, while all the Indians in the garrison mutinied and the enemy made a general assault from outside. Gubbins himself, when asked by the Brigadier for his comments on this report, replied that, while the whole story was most improbable, it might be well to press Mr Phillips for the name of his informant, who should then be carefully examined, and to forbid the Sikh troopers to enter his own compound on any pretext; the authorities took the latter precaution.

The same day the meat rations of the Europeans were reduced, the men's by a quarter and the women's by a half. The rations of dal, a kind of lentil, were also cut down.

It was now the time of the Mohurram, and the Mohammedans among the investing forces were mourning clamorously for the blessed martyrs, Hasan and Husain. As they listened to the sound of drums and horns from the processions through the city, the garrison began to wonder if religious fervour would inspire another general assault.

On the 26th August Inglis went down to Gubbins' bastion to examine a new battery which had been thrown up within five or six hundred yards of the defences. Apparently the enemy's gunners observed that the bastion was full of people, for suddenly Inglis saw that they were about to fire. He called out 'Stoop!', bending down quickly himself. A 24-pound shot crashed through the parapet, covering his head with dust, but he jumped up at once and said: 'All right.' A sergeant standing beside him said: 'No, it's not all right, sir'; Lieutenant Webb, 32nd Foot, and an Indian sweeper were both lying dead on the ground. The bastion was evacuated for the time being and orders were sent for the nearest mortars to shell the enemy. The engineer and artillery officers reported that heavier metal than the

9-pounder in Gubbins' bastion would be needed to make an effective reply to the new battery, and advised that the south-west angle should be retrenched, the thickness of the parapet increased to sixteen feet, and the bastion armed with an 18-pounder. The work was put in hand at once and the new gun was mounted by the 31st August.

In the meantime the south-west corner would have been suffering severely from the enemy's cannonade but for the resource of Second Lieutenant Bonham, who had knocked together a rude piece of ordnance out of a mortar and a truck, to replace the 8-inch howitzer that had been lost at Chinhat. While the work was in progress at the bastion, 'The Ship', as it was called, was posted close to Gubbins' house, and with great pains Bonham contrived to score several hits on the enemy's battery, close to the embrasure, the shells bursting within the wall and doing considerable damage. Without completely silencing the enemy's guns, he was able to keep their fire within bounds until the new 18-pounder had been mounted. Later on a second mortar was adapted in the same way.

On the night of the 27th/28th August heavy rain flooded the countermine by the Brigade Mess, holding up the work for several hours. It was hoped that the enemy's miners would soon break through into the gallery, and next day the work was stopped again since it was found that the enemy ceased as soon as they heard the pick in the countermine.

During the following night a Hindu orderly and two dismounted troopers deserted from Gubbins' post, the orderly being in such a state of panic that Mr Gubbins believed he would have gone mad if he had stayed. Next day an Indian gunner deserted in broad daylight; a European sentry fired at him but missed.

That morning it was found that the enemy's mine opposite the Brigade Mess had been driven past the head of the countermine, which was therefore turned in the hope of striking the enemy's gallery in the flank. Fulton was down there digging by himself when suddenly he broke through. The enemy were no longer to be seen, but they had left behind a lantern, some oil, and a candle, which he took away. He then sent for powder, laid the charge about fifteen yards along the enemy's mine, and blew it up. The same day the pick was heard again outside Sago's post; a countermine was driven out from the salient angle and before long another was begun at the northern end.

From day to day the spirits of the garrison went up and down. There were rumours that gunfire and musketry could be heard in the distance, slowly drawing nearer, and hopes at the Post Office were raised to the highest pitch for two nights by the stamping of a pony, tormented by insects, which was amplified in a well until it sounded like a cannonade.

At midnight on the 28th/29th August Ungud returned with the following letter from Havelock:

'My dear Colonel,

I have your letter of the 16th inst. I can only say, do not negotiate, but rather perish sword in hand. Sir Colin Campbell, who came out at a day's notice to command, upon news arriving of General Anson's death, promises me fresh troops, and you will be my first care. The reinforcements may reach me in from twenty to twenty-five days, and I will prepare everything for a march on Lucknow.

Yours very sincerely,

H. Havelock, Br. Gen.

To Col. Inglis, H.M. 32nd Regt.'

Ungud had found it impossible to cross the Ganges at Cawnpore, where the northern bank was held by the mutineers, and had been forced to fetch a compass. He reported that the Nana Sahib, who was now at Fatehpur, had been defeated by Havelock at Bithur, nearly fifteen miles from Cawnpore, where, as the mutineers boasted, the sepoys of the 42nd Native Infantry had actually crossed bayonets with British troops; that the relieving forces were now assembling at Cawnpore; that the capture of Delhi by the British was expected within three weeks; and that the enemy, who declared the Indian troops inside the entrenchment to be in league with themselves, were preparing to make a general assault, eleven thousand strong, in the course of the next few days. Ungud added that it was easier to pass through the enemy's lines than to enter the entrenchment without being shot by the British sentries.

On the following night there were many more desertions. The outhouses near the racquet court on the west face were manned by a party of Christian drummers, Eurasians, most of whom had been forced to leave their wives and families in the city when the Residency was invested. Now eleven of them decamped, removing the barricade near one of the bullock sheds, and leaving their post undefended with the door standing open. They were followed by a number of Indian servants, one of whom carried off Captain Boileau's double-barrelled gun. In the morning several inscriptions were found on the wall: 'Because I have no opium.' It was rumoured that all the deserters were taken by the enemy at the iron bridge and shot later on.

On the 30th August Bonham had his collar-bone broken by a musket ball as he sat in the doorway of the Post Office. This was the third time he had been injured. He was greatly missed by the rest of the garrison, having distinguished himself by the excellence of his artillery practice, especially with the mortars and 'The Ship', and also by his gallant and gentle temper.

On the 31st August the enemy opened fire with two guns, one of which was a 32-pounder, from a new battery at the Clock Tower, less than a hundred and fifty yards from the Baillie Guard gate, and several of their roundshot crashed through the gate itself, smashing two wagons with which it was barricaded. Lieutenant Aitken and his men of the 13th Native Infantry began work at once on a sunken battery between the gate and the Treasury, designed by the engineers to mount an 18-pounder gun and a 24-pounder howitzer. The sepoys set to work with such enthusiasm that, though the task involved the exhumation of their own dead comrades, even the Brahmans among them did not scruple to dig out the putrid and defiling corpses. During the day the enemy miners were heard at work near the Financial post. It seemed that their gallery was being driven obliquely across the front of the position, and a countermine was run out in the hope of intercepting it. Early next morning the enemy could be heard very close; the countermine was therefore loaded and fired, the explosion breaking up the earth so thoroughly that the enemy's underground offensive could not be continued in that quarter.

The same morning Mrs Dashwood went into labour. Mrs Harris hurried into the men's quarters to wake Dr Partridge, and then ran to fetch a curtain, on which they carried Mrs Dashwood into another room, where the child was born almost at once. Mrs Harris went off again to borrow clothes for the baby, for the mother herself had none ready yet, and it was on her way back that she heard its first cry. It was a boy, the image of his father, as all who saw him at once remarked. Mrs Barwell sent in her nurse to wash and dress him, and afterwards Mrs Harris did what she could for both mother and child, though her hands were full enough with little Ally, who was too ill to be left for very long. Mr Harris tried all day in vain to find another nurse.

Before the siege began Mr Polehampton had befriended a young Indian who had learnt English at the Martinière College and wished to become a Christian. He was an orphan. The Hindus with whom he lived took a dislike to him when they discovered his sympathies, and at last the mistress of the house forbade him to eat with the rest of them. He therefore begged the chaplain to let him live somewhere in a corner of his compound, and Polehampton found a little room for him and employed him on clerical work and interpreting. The Babu, as he was called, was baptised just before the investment of the Residency. The chaplain told him to write to his brother in England if he and Mrs Polehampton should be killed in the troubles, and gave him fifty rupees (five pounds), which was all he would accept.

After Mrs Polehampton had left the hospital for the Begam Kothi, the Babu used to do all kinds of work for her, and even insisted on washing her clothes. He came in one day with his white clothing soaked with blood, looking faint but curiously happy. She asked what was the matter. He replied: 'I am very glad; I have been shot in the head.' Mrs Polehampton had already noticed that he was quite indifferent to his own safety, but it startled her to find him taking positive pleasure in being wounded. She sent him at once to the European hospital where he was examined at her request. The musket ball had only struck a glancing blow, and next morning the Babu came back a little weak from loss of blood but otherwise recovered.

Soon after this he determined to leave the Residency and see for himself what was going on outside. He proposed to disguise himself as a cooly and if possible to pay a visit to the Polehamptons' derelict house in cantonments. He said it was unlikely that he would be recognised, and promised to return within three days. Mrs Polehampton did her best to dissuade him, telling him that she never expected to see him again if once he left the entrenchment, and forbidding him to go without consulting Mr Harris. But his mind was made up. Before long he disappeared, leaving this note behind him:

'My dear Madam,

I have been to Mr Harris. He said to me some Christians have gone out, and he heard they are all killed; their blood scattered about the ground. I think myself to death as a dream. I am not the least frighted of it. If I die, I will see Mr Polehampton. Is it not a good thing for me? I hope God will protect me, if I put my trust in Him.'

They never saw him again. Mrs Polehampton had little doubt that he was killed at once, since many of the mutineers knew him well, having often seen him in the company of his English protectors. She had heard that all the servants who had deserted at the beginning of the siege had been done away with, as well as every Indian who was known to have been of any service to the Christians. But she was happy to think of the Babu's death, for he seemed to have been longing for the chance of testifying to his faith; and how soon, she thought—almost with envy—he had been granted his wish of rejoining his best friend and earthly master!

September opened with a drying wind, the sun being still powerful though the nights and mornings were becoming cooler; but just as the ground had begun to harden, the wind changed and the rain came down again.

On the first day of the month and the sixty-fourth of the siege, Inglis sent out a runner with the following despatch:

'*Lucknow, September* 1.

'My dear General,

'Your letter of the 24th July has duly reached me in reply to mine to you of the 16th ultimo. I regret your inability to advance at present to our relief, but in consequence of your communication I have reduced the rations and with this arrangement and our great diminution in numbers from casualties, I trust to be able to hold out from the 20th to 25th instant. Some stores we have been out of for the last 14 days, and many others will be expended before the above date. I must be frank and tell you my force is daily diminishing from the enemy's musketry fire and our defences are daily weaker; should the enemy make a really determined effort to storm the place I shall find it difficult to repulse them owing to my paucity in numbers, and the weak and harassed state of the force. Our losses since the commencement of hostilities here have been in Europeans only upwards of 300. We are continually harassed in countermining the enemy who have about 20 guns in position, many of them of large calibre.

'Any advance of yours towards this place will act beneficially in our favour and greatly inspirit the native part of my garrison who have up to this time behaved like faithful and good soldiers.

'If you can possibly communicate to me any intelligence of your intended advance pray do so by letter. Give the bearer the pass word 'Agra' and tell him to give it to me in person. Oblige me by forwarding a copy of this letter to the Governor General.

'I have prohibited the civil authorities from corresponding with your camp,

Yours sincerely,

J. Inglis, Brigadier.

To: General Havelock.'

It is doubtful whether the sanguine Mr Gubbins, at whom the prohibition was aimed, would have approved of the tone of this despatch, for in several directions there seemed to be now more room for hope. The elimination of Johannes' house had apparently damped the enemy, whose musketry had ever since been so much less effective that Captain Fulton had seized the opportunity to repair the works where they were damaged by the rains, to extend his system of 'listeners', or defensive mines, and to retrench the south-west angle of Gubbins' post, where conditions were not favourable for counter-mining. By now the engineers were convinced that the enemy's miners would never succeed in making another breach, though the local garrisons did not always share their confidence.

The enemy's gunners had still concentrated on Gubbins' post, both from the south and south-west and from the north, until all the upper rooms had to be vacated, their occupants being divided between the lower storeys of the same house, the Brigade Mess, Ommanney's house, and the Begam Kothi. The lower storeys were unpleasantly crowded, the rooms in which the women lived being small and low. The men slept in the porch, in the hall, which was not safe from roundshot, and on the table and floor in the dining-room. The enemy's shot was collected regularly and sent across to the magazine. One day a 21-pound shot was known to have entered the house but could not be accounted for, until, some days later, Chivers, Mrs Gubbins' maid, was sent upstairs to move a small trunk; surprised to find it so heavy, she unlocked it and found the shot resting on top of the other contents.

Day by day it became harder to find enough effective labour to countermine, repair the works, handle stores, shift guns when necessary, throw up barricades, and bury corpses. Not only had sickness and casualties reduced the numbers of the garrison, but those that were left were growing steadily less fit for prolonged exertion. As time went on a larger proportion of fatigue duties and mining operations was allotted to the Indian troops, who were less easily exhausted than the Europeans and worked with good will.

The dearth of tobacco was very trying to the Europeans, many of whom were now smoking tea-leaves, when they could get them, and leaves from the shrubs in the Residency grounds. There was still a constant stench on the west side of the position, where the offal from the slaughterhouses was thrown over the wall, and the flies were as thick and as odious as ever. There were rats and mosquitoes, too, to try the nerves, and the women and children were still suffering from the lack of servants and of coolies to pull the punkahs. They were left pretty much to themselves, for even the married women saw little of their husbands, who seemed to be for ever on duty or taking necessary sleep. Soap and candles were both becoming scarce, and in the evenings Mrs Bartrum used to sit by the light of a cotton wick dipped in oil for want of a better lamp. Mrs Inglis and Mrs Case found the only relief from the irksomeness of their confinement in listening to the cooing of the servants' doves, and in contemplating the green tree outside the door, from which a swing was hung for the children.

Many of the garrison were finding that the least

contusion left a large purple blotch—one of the classic symptoms of scurvy, known as ecchymosis, and caused by the extravasation of blood under the skin. Vokins, Inglis' servant, died on the 2nd September, having never rallied from the shock of losing his leg: indeed, all amputations were still proving fatal. The Brigadier found time to visit the hospital every day, and sometimes handed round cigars, with which the men were delighted.

Since the 30th May Mr Harris had been sleeping in his clothes to be ready for any emergency. Sometimes before burying the dead he helped to dig the grave himself, and often as he read the service his voice was drowned by a volley of musketry or a charge of grapeshot sweeping across the open. One night in the churchyard he found a private of the 32nd whose head had just been carried off by a roundshot, and buried him with the others there and then. Another night, when a Catholic and a Protestant were to be buried in the common grave, opinions differed as to which was which; fortunately the officer in charge of the burial party had the wit to make a summary decision.

In two months' fighting there had been so many hairsbreadth escapes that even the women and children had ceased to think about them. The personal effects of those who did not escape were always sold by auction: a man might be talking with his friend on such and such a day, and bidding for his boots before the week was out, or watching his other friends try on the dead man's coat, and chaffing them about the fit. Trade was so brisk that garments would sometimes be exposed for sale again before the last purchaser had had time to get them washed. Flannel shirts, which were always in demand, fetched prices of £3.10. and upwards. At the sale of Sir Henry Lawrence's effects bidding was reckless, since settlement was not to be made till after the next issue of pay, which few of the garrison counted on living to receive. Some of the prices were as follows:

Brandy—from £14 to £16 per dozen.
Beer—from £6 to £7 per dozen.
Sherry—£7 per dozen.
Two small tins of soup—£5.10.
Hermetically sealed hams—from £7 to £7.10 each.
A quart bottle of honey—£4.10.

Sugar might have commanded almost any price, but there was none for sale.

What little flour was left was being husbanded by the Commissariat, and wheat was issued instead, ground in handmills by the Indian servants and by all the boys who were over ten years of age. Most of the younger children were still suffering from the coarse food and insanitary conditions, and the evening of the 1st September saw the burial of no less than five babies. One or two children had been slightly wounded by musket balls. A boy of two or three, playing in the Residency grounds, was hit by a bullet which passed through his calf without damaging the bone; he was taken to the hospital, where they gave him lumps of sugar to keep him quiet while the wound was probed and dressed.

Mrs Dashwood and the new baby were doing well, though both a little restless. To the relief of Mrs Harris, the chaplain had discovered a nurse at last, the widow of a sergeant named Ryder who had been killed a few days before. Mrs Inglis' children were pretty well, though what the baby ate seemed to do him little good, and he grew thinner every day. Johnny never lost his rosy cheeks, which were greatly admired. He spent most of his time in the adjoining courtyard with the Sikhs, who were much attached to him and often gave him chapatties to eat when they had little enough for themselves. Mrs Inglis always encouraged this connection, thinking that if at last the enemy broke in it might be the means of saving the boy's life.

Whenever a spent bullet dropped in the courtyard while Johnny was indoors, he was sure to hear it and rush out to pick it up while it was still warm. One day when he had fallen down and covered himself with dust he remarked: 'They'll say I've been mining.' The children used to sleep through the heaviest cannonade but were very warlike in the daytime, constructing mimic batteries, and making balls of earth which they threw against the walls so that they burst like shells. Captain Anderson heard a little boy say to his friend: "You fire roundshot, and I'll return shell from my battery." Another, losing his temper with his playmates, shouted: 'I hope you may be *shot* by the enemy.' Others, playing with grapeshot instead of marbles, cried: "That's clean through his lungs,' or: 'That wants more elevation.'

The men found little time for reflection, and the women were perhaps less fortunate in having more leisure to dwell upon their troubles. Sometimes the continual strain and discomfort caused ill-temper and there was bickering among them, or 'pecking' as they called it; but on the whole they were less irritable than the men, who were nerved by the sight of their passive fortitude to be yet more active in their defence.

On the 2nd September, the following letter was addressed to Mr Gubbins, who was still chafing at his supersession:

'Sir,

'I am directed by Brigadier Inglis Commanding to acknowledge your letter No. 6 of this date to his address in which you express your regret that General Havelock and the Government of India should be deprived of your opinion regarding our position and also lament that your proposed despatch to General Havelock was not suffered to be forwarded to that officer.

1. In reply I am instructed to state that the Briga-

dier's letter of the 16th ultimo was shown to several officers of experience in this garrison whose unanimous opinion was that the Brigadier had underrated rather than overstated the gravity of our position. You are aware that your despatch was calculated to convey to General Havelock that there was no necessity whatever for his immediate advance.

2. Under the above circumstances the Brigadier is of opinion that both the General and the Government of India will agree that he was right in refusing to allow a despatch so calculated to mislead to be forwarded to that officer who has however been informed that you have been prohibited from corresponding with his camp.

I have the honour etc.

T. F. Wilson, Capt.

Offg. A.A. Genl.'

That morning the enemy's miners were at work within thirty feet of the Financial post, but fortunately they ran their gallery across a well-shaft, and the smoke rising from their lamps gave them away. The countermine was driven out to within two or three feet of the enemy, then loaded, tamped, and fired by Lieutenant Innes while their miners were still at work. That evening Lieutenant Birch, 59th Native Infantry, attached to the engineer department, who was a cousin of Inglis' aide-de-camp, went out after dusk with several other officers to examine the ruins on the north side for traces of mining. The sentries had been warned of what was afoot, but the guard was changed while the party was still outside, and one of the reliefs was not informed. The sentry saw Birch moving in the dark as he made his way back to the defences, and fired instantly. Birch fell with the bullet through his body. The men who carried him in tried to reassure him, but he smiled sadly and said: 'I know it's all over with me.' He died two hours later. His father, Lieutenant Colonel Birch, commanding the 41st Native Infantry, had been shot by one of his own men in the mutiny at Sitapur. He himself had been married only six months and left, as well as his widow who was with child, a young brother and sister who had both been dependant on him. The sentry who had fired the shot was held to have done his duty, since at night there was often no time to give the challenge, but it was long before he ceased fretting over the accident. The corporal who forgot to pass the word on lost his stripes.

Soon after this, Captain M'Cabe, on one of his nightly rounds, passed outside a post at which another Irishman was on sentry. For fear of accidents the men had all been warned that M'Cabe was on the prowl, and the sentry, recognising him, let him reach the post without so much as a challenge. M'Cabe said:

'Are you the sentry?'

'I am, sir.'

'And why the devil didn't you challenge me?'

'Because I knew it was you, sir, and that you would be coming this way.'

'You should have fired, sir,' said M'Cabe severely. 'You are not supposed to know anyone outside of your post, especially at night, sir.'

At this the sentry lost his temper and retorted: 'Then, by Jasus, the next time you come the same way at night, I'll accommodate you. I'll shoot you right enough.' M'Cabe went away and did not trouble him again.

By the 3rd September, although the sun was still powerful during the day, the mornings were so much cooler that there were fears for the health of the troops, many of whom were sleeping out in the trenches. A search was made for tents, but it was found that most of them had been used as screens and barricades and had been rotted away by the rain.

The enemy miners were at work again outside the Financial post. Much of the ground in that direction had already been broken up, and it seemed that they had therefore struck out at right angles to their old gallery and begun to work along parallel to the face of the defences, skirting the craters. Another countermine was driven out. On the evening of the 4th, when it had reached a length of twenty-two feet, the miners found brickwork—presumably the foundations of a wall outside the post—through which they cut their way.

The enemy miners could still be heard approaching. The engineer in charge believed that their gallery would strike the brickwork before meeting the countermine, and it occurred to him that, since they never seemed able to determine their position underground, they might perhaps mistake this obstruction for their objective, load their mine at once, and blow it up. It seemed that he was right, for as soon as they had reached the brick they ceased work, whereupon the engineer and his men dug their way quietly into the mine. There was a light at the far end by which they could see one of the miners still sitting in the gallery, but before he could be killed or captured someone sneezed, the light went out, and he was gone. Finding that the enemy still commanded the shaft, the engineer laid a double charge, so as to break up the ground thoroughly, and blew up the mine.

The same day the enemy's picks were heard opposite the middle of the Brigade Mess. A countermine having already been driven out from either side of the post, Lieutenant Hutchinson now began work on a listening gallery, parallel to the defences, which was to join up the two countermines about thirty feet from the shafts, thus intercepting the enemy's approach.

During the afternoon of the 4th September Major Bruere, commanding the 13th Native Infantry, was hit in the chest as he was trying to pick off one of the enemy's most noted sharpshooters from the roof of the Brigade Mess. He died almost at once, deeply regretted by the sepoys of his regiment. As many as could be spared from their posts followed him to the grave that night, and insisted on carrying the body themselves although to touch it meant ritual defilement. The sepoys had made such good progress with their new battery by the Baillie Guard gate that the 18-pounder was brought down and placed in position the same night. During the evening, the outer wall and the buildings on top of the Brigade Mess came down with a crash, having been shattered by the enemy's roundshot; no one was hurt, however, and some of the women and children still went on living in the inner rooms. After midnight one of the sentries at Gubbins' post reported sounds of mining. Mr Gubbins and Captain Edgell, the Military Secretary, went along to listen, but could hear nothing, though the sentry assured them that he had heard the sound of the pick.

At sunrise next morning, the 5th September, enemy forces estimated at eight thousand bayonets and five hundred sabres were seen in movement round about the position, and the garrison were called to arms to repel a general assault. First there came a severe cannonade and then, at ten o'clock, two mines were sprung. One was at Gubbins' post—the sentry had been right. The report was so tremendous and seemed so close, and the air was so darkened by smoke and falling fragments, that the garrison feared that the bastion on which they had spent so much labour had been destroyed. They were relieved to find as the air grew clearer that the crater was short of the defences. The enemy came boldly on and tried to scale the parapet by hooking a huge ladder with a double row of rungs onto the sole of an embrasure. On reaching the top they thrust in the muzzles of their muskets and fired, without shewing their faces, but were soon dislodged by the men of the 32nd, under Major Apthorp, with hand-grenades and musketry.

The second mine to be sprung was the one that had been reported at the Brigade Mess. This too fell short and only reached the countermine, which was empty at the time, the miners having just come up for their grog. 'No damage to us,' wrote Captain Fulton afterwards, 'and their own labour spoilt more effectually by their own act than it would have been an hour later by us.' The enemy attacked in force on this side also, but were repulsed with heavy loss.

Further assaults were delivered and repelled at the Slaughterhouse, Innes', Sago's, and the Financial posts. The Clock Tower battery opened fire on the Treasury post but was quickly silenced by Aitken's new 18-pounder. The sepoys were very proud of their battery and delighted with the gun, which they served themselves assisted by three artillerymen. 'We load it,' they said, 'and Aikeen Sahib fires it.'

In an hour or two the assault was over, though for some time the enemy maintained a heavy fusillade from the neighbouring houses. For many hours afterwards they could be seen carrying their dead and wounded across the bridges in carts. The garrison had lost only three sepoys killed and one European wounded, nor had they been unduly taxed to repel the enemy, who had fought with far less spirit than in the general assaults of the 20th July and the 10th August. It was observed that to-day for the first time the storming parties were largely composed of matchlockmen, the Talukdars' retainers, and it was therefore supposed that many of the mutineers had marched out to dispute Havelock's advance along the Cawnpore road.

In the evening an 18-pounder shot from a new battery on the far side of the river traversed the whole length of the hospital, which was crowded with patients, slightly wounding Lieutenant Charlton, of the 32nd, and a private of the same regiment as they lay in their beds. During the day Lieutenant Graham, 1st Oudh Irregular Cavalry, who was in bed with fever, shot himself through the head with his revolver during a fit of depression. He left a young widow who had been confined a few days before and who had already lost a child during the siege.

As September went on and the rain became less frequent, the pools of stagnant water in and about the entrenchment dried up, leaving such a stench that it was feared there would be more fever than ever. The live-stock was fast diminishing and supplies of rum and porter were running low. The enemy seemed to have no more stomach for fighting in the open but were still mining, though hampered by countermines and broken ground. Besides maintaining their constant desultory fire on the position, they would often accompany a furious cannonade and fusillade by shouting and bugling on every side, as if about to launch a general assault, so that the garrison were forced to turn out, whatever the time of day or night, and stand to their arms, however unlikely an attack might be. They would keep well under cover and fire a few rounds of shell in whatever direction the enemy seemed thickest. Perhaps the demonstration would last only half an hour, and there might be no casualties at all, but it was sound policy for the enemy to harass men who were already overworked.

Serious efforts were now made by the enemy's gunners to effect a breach, but were defeated by the use of Bonham's 'Ships.' It was fortunate for the garrison that few or no mortars could be brought against them, for the searching effect of vertical fire on such a position would have been disastrous. The enemy were still pitching logs of wood over the defences, some said from funnels in the ground, others from a 13-inch mortar which had been abandoned in the Machhi Bhawan.

In the early afternoon of the 6th September, Captain Fulton led out a party of sepoys from Innes' post to destroy a house which the enemy were loopholing for musketry. The sortie was made over the wall and down a ladder on the outside of the works. The house was occupied, two barrels of powder were placed in position, the train was laid, and the men were ordered back to the entrenchment. Fulton retreated as usual after firing the train, but found when he reached the ladder that some of the sepoys had been hanging back to gather wood, though the explosion was due at any moment. If the men were killed it would be entirely by their own fault, but he waited to chase them up the ladder and was only half way up himself when the charge exploded. Fulton and one of the sepoys were buried up to the waist in the wreckage of a wall not ten feet distant, and Fulton's arm was so badly hurt that at first the surgeon who examined it feared that it was broken.

On the 7th September, the seventieth day of the siege, there was great activity among the enemy, large numbers of whom were seen crossing and re-crossing the bridge of boats. In the forenoon a regiment of foot, with band playing and colours flying, and about a thousand matchlockmen, marched by in one direction, while during the afternoon about five thousand men went past in the other.

Next day the enemy's cannonade made a breach in the wall by the Martinière house wide enough for four or five men to pass abreast; but the post was soon secured by means of palisades and retrenchments.

On the morning of the 9th September the enemy's picks were heard at the Cawnpore Battery and the Sikh Square. At the former post, where the countermine had been ready loaded since the end of July, the charge was fired at ten o'clock, destroying the enemy's gallery and shattering the fronts of the houses on the far side of the street; the enemy beat to arms and opened a brisk fire on the position. At the Sikh Square two countermines were driven out; the enemy ceased work opposite one of the galleries but continued to approach the other.

Soon after dawn on the 11th September two sides of Innes' house collapsed after being steadily battered for days by an 18-pounder. The sentries were lucky enough to escape with their lives, and the garrison still held the ruins. At 10 A.M. the second countermine at the Sikh Square was fired, destroying the enemy's gallery and burying their miners, whose groans could be heard for some time after. The garrison were greatly exhausted by their labours underground. Later in the day Captain Fulton made another sortie which he described in his journal as follows: 'At 1 o'clock I went to a suspected spot and after failing, owing to my arm, to get on a cross wall to get out a bit to peep, I got a clever little corporal to go, and we discovered another mine under the church wall. We went down, broke into the house, the enemy bolted, leaving 1 sepoy's jacket, 3 pairs of shoes, and three baskets. They had progressed 25 feet. We destroyed the house with their works, with two barrels of powder. It is a great thing that we have no scarcity of powder, and they are such cowards outside.'

That evening the enemy threw in, probably from a howitzer, the most complicated projectile that had yet been seen. It was made of five hollow cylinders of iron, filled with incendiary composition and done up in a strong canvas cover; when it struck the ground the cover burst and the cylinders belched fire without any further explosion. Work was now resumed on the two batteries on the west face that had been left unfinished when the siege began.

That day both Mrs Inglis' boys had been so unwell that she began to be anxious, having noticed how few of the children rallied when once they had been seriously ill. During the night Johnny was delirious.

On the night of the 12th September one of the grass-cutters of the 7th Light Cavalry was found straying about inside the entrenchment, having just returned from the city. He said the enemy had received intelligence that Havelock's advanced guard had crossed the Ganges; that many of the mutineers had retired to their villages with their loot, leaving the Talukdars' matchlockmen and the city rabble to prosecute the siege; and that the whole population of Oudh was hostile to the British Government and disappointed by the failure of the mutineers to storm the Baillie Guard. The Brigadier cheered Mrs Inglis by speaking more hopefully than usual of the chances of relief.

The authorities were still haunted by fears for the loyalty of the Indian troops. Poorly fed and badly housed as they were, and often taking more than their share of the fatigues, most of them were still working and fighting staunchly; but there were constant rumours that if no relief were in sight by the end of the month they would give up hope and abandon the British cause.

The mutineers used to shout across the road to them, declaring that the Europeans had been beaten everywhere and that there was no hope of reinforcements; to which the loyal sepoys would reply: 'We have eaten the Company's salt—we cannot break faith with our masters, as you have done.' Beyond such taunts no correspondence with the enemy was ever discovered among the Hindustani sepoys, though many of the Sikh troopers had deserted, and it was known that those who remained had been tampered with from outside. Captain Hawes, Mr Gubbins' assistant in the Intelligence

Department, had actually heard a deserter proposing that the rest should join him, foretelling certain death if they remained, and promising them good pay and prospects if they came over to the mutineers. Some of the deserters used to pass in opium, which the Sikhs inside then sold at famine prices.

One night at the new Sheephouse battery Lieutenant Innes was told by an Indian officer that he and many others had little faith in Ungud's news, and did not believe that there was any British force approaching. Ungud, they were convinced, had trumped up all these tales in the hope of promotion and reward. Innes pointed out that the handwriting of Ungud's letters had been identified and that he had given particulars of regiments, and names of officers, which he could not possibly have known unless he had been in touch with Havelock's column; the Indian officer seemed to be impressed by these arguments, which Innes hoped he would pass on to his men. More incredulous still were the Sikh troopers, who declared that Ungud had never left the Residency at all, but had been hidden away by the authorities and trotted out from time to time with a faked despatch to keep the garrison in heart.

Since it was clear that the present enceinte of two thousand yards or over could not be defended without the help of the Indian troops, efforts were made to complete a system of retrenchments which could be held by the Europeans should they be forced to abandon all or part of the outer works. Further precautions were taken, such as keeping the Sikhs in a position commanded by some of the 32nd, but it was recognised that these were desperate remedies. When Mrs Inglis, shocked by the prospect of treachery, said she wished there were no natives in the place, the Brigadier replied: 'Do not say that; we could not hold the place without them—they outnumber us.'

Still, there might be no truth in the rumours after all. Except among the Sikh troopers there were yet no signs of disaffection. The Sikh and Hindustani infantrymen and the Pensioners, who had behaved admirably throughout the siege though many of them were old and infirm, had refused an issue of pay on the 1st September, having, as they said, no use for the money—which seemed to argue their fidelity.

The sepoys were not alone in believing that the case was desperate. When Innes spoke of their fears to one of the Europeans, a man of wide experience and undoubted courage, he agreed with the Indian officer. 'Havelock', he said, 'may come near, but how can he make his way against the large force hemming us in, through the streets or other routes which they are certainly barricading? Also he will probably have other forces to tackle; we hear nothing of Delhi. Ten to one, our small army there has been wiped out, and the enemy may pour down an army from there onto Havelock's, or any other

British troops that may be keeping the field here.' Such misgivings were not easily disposed of.

During the past weeks Gubbins' bastion had suffered so severely from the enemy's guns that Major Apthorp, who was now commanding there, had frequently asked for permission to silence them by a continuous cannonade. The authorities were still loath to supply the enemy with roundshot and would only allow an artillery officer to spend two hours in the bastion every day, firing one round every twenty minutes from the 18-pounder. This did not prevent the enemy from firing frequently into the bastion, damaging the embrasure, and knocking the musket-proof shutters to bits. At last Apthorp was given permission to take more strenuous measures. On the 14th September Second Lieutenant J. Alexander came down to the bastion and made good practice with the 18-pounder. In twenty rounds he shattered the enemy's embrasure and damaged the carriage of their 24-pounder, which went out of action and could be clearly seen with its muzzle in the air.

That afternoon Captain Fulton dined at Gubbins' post. For the past few weeks he had been in excellent spirits. Once, in the early days of the siege, when he was being shouted for on all sides day and night, and was worn out by exposure and lack of sleep, he had lain down and given up hope; but after rest and food he had returned to his conviction that nothing but sickness or starvation would reduce the Residency, and he had never despaired again. He was none the less awake to the danger when the enemy sprung their first mine, and entered into the struggle underground with the utmost zest and proficiency: now, with the rest of the engineers, he believed that his work had been successful and that the enemy's miners would not make another practicable breach. He was hoping, too, that the distinguished part he had played in the defence would be recognised, in spite of the prejudice he conceived that Inglis had against him, to the advantage of his wife and six children who were safe at Simla.

During dinner Mr Gubbins told him how Alexander had silenced the enemy's battery towards the south-west, and pointed out that their 'Garden' battery on the west side was still active. When dinner was over Fulton went out with Apthorp and some others to examine the effect of Alexander's twenty rounds. He could see with his glass that the enemy were at work on the damaged battery and, calling to Alexander to follow him, he went down into the bastion. As he reached the embrasure a 9-pound shot carried away the back of his head, leaving his face still on his neck, like a mask, untouched. When they laid him out on a bed in the hospital there was nothing to show how he had met his death.

The news was received on every hand with keen sorrow and dismay, for it was felt that this was the most serious loss since the death of Henry Lawrence. With his skill, activity, and daring, his shrewd, resolute face, and his kind and cheerful manner, Fulton had done more than any man to inspire the garrison and stiffen the defence. His duties devolved upon Lieutenant J. C. Anderson, an officer of merit who was hampered, however, by ill-health.

Lieutenant Innes wrote afterwards to Fulton's widow: 'He was the life of the defence, foremost in every danger, quickest to observe the enemy's movements, acutest in perception of their intentions, most fertile in resources, and prompt in action to frustrate them. You can imagine the difficulties he had to contend with—outside a numerous and deadly enemy, inside a pack of alarmists, everyone ready with a suggestion, and angry if it were not carried out, few men for fatigue duty, few tools and implements, no artificers, and a worthless commandant. He surmounted them all—forced the garrison into confidence until his word was law, planned every arrangement that succeeded—was, in fact, the guiding hand and master spirit of the place.'

The siege having now lasted eleven weeks, the appearance of the garrison was growing steadily more disreputable. One of the officers was wearing a floorcloth shirt, while a civilian had made himself a loose green coat out of a spare billiard-cloth. At the auctions of personal effects the normal scale of values was oddly inverted, for whereas a handsome uniform was knocked down for twenty-four shillings, a lot consisting of three very old flannel shirts fetched no less than ten guineas. Some of the men did not altogether dislike the hazardous life, for all its hardships, and there were civilians who seemed to enjoy swaggering about in red or green shirts, with their trousers tucked into their boots. Others cast their thoughts outside the defences: one evening Captain Anderson heard a rugged private of the 32nd say: 'I'm sure there'll be some wet eyes for me at home by this time—I was such a pet at *our* house.' One of his mates replied: 'What, Bill—you a pet? Queer folks, I think, as would make a pet of you.'

The women were denied even the simple pleasure of swaggering, and their passive rôle was almost uniformly dreary. Soap was selling at fourteen shillings for a small square piece. The Indian washermen charged as much as a pound for a dozen articles done without soap, unstarched, and unironed, and the ladies therefore did as much of their own washing as they could. The Inglis children were better now. Mrs Dashwood was up and about, little Ally was recovering, and the new baby was thriving; one day a spent bullet hit the tin he was being bathed in, but he only chuckled, according to Mrs Ryder. Not all the children were so fortunate: Mrs Soppitt, who had lost her baby from cholera early in the siege, wrote in her journal: 'Mrs Marriott nursing Katie, who is wasting away. Poor little orphan! At times, when seeing children gradually fading away, I feel thankful that my poor boy was spared slow death.'

Boils were almost universal and the least scratch was apt to become inflamed. There were still cholera, smallpox, dysentery, fever, and scurvy in the garrison, though none of these diseases had been so severe as might have been expected: Dr Fayrer said that in all his experience of India he had never known such a healthy September. There was little fare for the sick and wounded beyond gun-bullock beef, chapatties, and rum.

The number of artillerymen had been so reduced by casualties and sickness that, although they were assisted by volunteers, they were forced to run from one battery to another when there was a general assault, firing into the enemy wherever they were thickest, since there were not enough gunners to serve half the guns and mortars at the same time.

Soon after the middle of the month the beer and rum rations were reduced by half, and in a few days they ceased altogether. Coffee was sold at six shillings a pound, tea at sixteen shillings. Eggs could occasionally be bought at prices up to two shillings apiece, and a man whose wife was ill paid two pounds for a small fowl. Some of the women were half starving themselves so that their husbands and children might not go short. It was a great occasion at Fayrer's house when there was a quarter of mutton for dinner, as well as suet pudding with some patent sauce provided by Captain Weston. On the 15th September Mrs Soppitt made an important entry in her journal: 'Bought a bullock's heart at a fabulous price, 10/-. Mrs O[gilvie], wife of a doctor, who was a personal friend of General Outram, gave me a sheep's head.'

At 10 P.M. on the 16th September Inglis sent Ungud out again with a letter done up in a piece of quill. Most of these despatches were written partly in Greek character in case they fell into the hands of the enemy, an old dodge which had been practised in the Afghan war. The ladies used to wonder where the Indian runners carried the letters, since they wore so few clothes, to which the answer was that they were curiously secreted in the bearer's staff, sandals, hair, nose, mouth, or rectum. Ungud had now earned a thousand pounds and was promised another five hundred if he could make the double journey once again. Inglis' despatch read as follows:

'My dear General,

The last letter I received from you was dated the 24th ult. Since then I have received no news whatever from your camp, or of your movements, but am now daily expecting to receive intelligence of your advance in this direction.

Since the date of my last letter, the enemy have continued to persevere unceasingly in their efforts against this position and the firing has never ceased either day or night. They have brought about eighteen guns in position round us, many of them are 18-pounders.

On the 5th inst. they made a very determined attack after exploding two mines and succeeded almost in getting into one of our batteries, but were repulsed on all sides with heavy loss. Since the above date they have continued a cannonade and musketry fire, occasionally throwing in a shell or two.

My weekly losses continue very heavy both in officers and men. I shall be quite out of rum for the men in eight days, but we have been long on reduced rations, and I hope to be able to get on pretty well till about the 1st proximo. If you have not relieved us by that time, we shall have no meat left as I must keep some few bullocks to move my guns about the position. As it is I have had to kill nearly all the gun bullocks, as my men could not perform the hard work without animal food.

I am most anxious to hear of your advance to enable me to reassure our native soldiers.

There is a report, though from a source upon which I cannot implicitly rely, that Rajah Man Singh has just arrived in Lucknow, and has left part of his force outside the city. It is said that he is in our interests, and that he has taken the above step at the instigation of British Authority, but I cannot say for certain whether such is the case, or whether he is really in Lucknow at all, as all I have to go upon is bazaar rumour.

J. Inglis, Brigadier.

To General Havelock,
Commanding the Relieving Force,
Cawnpore.'

Rajah Man Singh of Shahganj had been playing a double game since the Mutiny began. After the troops had risen at Fyzabad he had sheltered a number of English fugitives for a time, but in the end had sent them on to Dinapore, protesting that he was afraid of the mutineers. When Lawrence offered him large rewards in return for open support, he sent friendly but evasive replies, declaring that he had not enough followers or guns to take the field. His name carried much weight in Oudh, where he was the acknowledged leader of the Hindu interest against the Mohammedans.

In the forenoon of the 18th September there was a partial eclipse of the sun, which seemed to have awed the enemy into quiet, for when Apthorp and Gubbins looked over the parapet not a shot was fired, nor was there anyone in sight outside. The Indians in the garrison said that the eclipse spelt famine.

At daylight on the 20th September two new batteries were observed which the enemy had nearly completed, one of them armed with a 32-pounder. The garrison opened on them with one of the 'Ships' and an 18-pounder, but though they succeeded in keeping down their fire they did little damage to the batteries themselves, which had been built with huge wooden beams and thick parapets of earth. Next day, however, when one of the 18-pounders by the Post Office opened on the 32-pounder battery, it played such havoc with the enemy's parapet that the gun was exposed and the garrison of the Financial Post were able to pick off two of the gunners. In the afternoon the enemy knocked down a large section of the wall of the Martinière post, killing a water-carrier, whose body fell down a well; it was soon recovered, but none of the Indians would use the well again.

The rain had returned and the weather was so much cooler that the 21st September was like a wet day in England. The enemy were heard mining by the Church again and another sortie was made to stop the work.

Next day Second Lieutenant Cunliffe, Bengal Artillery, died of fever, having previously been wounded. He and his brother, Charles Cunliffe, of the Civil Service, had been engaged to the two Miss Ommanney's, but Charles had been killed in June as he attempted to escape from the mutineers disguised as an Indian. Miss Ommanney would not believe the account of his death, which came from a native source, and throughout the siege she clung to the hope that in the end he would be found alive. Mr Ommanney had been killed early in the siege and his widow was an invalid.

At eleven o'clock that night Ungud entered the entrenchment breathless, having just been fired on by the enemy's pickets, and produced the following despatch:

'*To Brigadier Inglis.*

North Side of the River,
September 20th, 1857.

The army crossed the river yesterday and, all the material being over, marches to-morrow, and, under the blessing of God, will now relieve you. The rebels, we hear, purpose making a desperate assault on you as we approach the city, and will be on the watch in expectation of your weakening your garrison to make a diversion in our favour as we attack the city. I beg to warn you against being enticed too far from your works when you hear us engaged. Such diversion as you can make, without in any way risking your position, should only be attempted.

J. Outram.'

Ungud said to Inglis: 'Now I have got back three times, I will go no more, but live or die with you.' He reported that, so long as Havelock had been on the north side of the Ganges, Man Singh had stayed quietly in his fort at Shahganj, recruiting and organising his forces, but that when Havelock had retreated on Cawnpore he had concluded that the British cause was hopeless and joined the mutineers. Ungud added that the investing forces numbered fifteen thousand, while the relieving column consisted of five thousand Europeans and one thousand Sikhs. Delhi, he said, was still held by the mutineers.

Ungud handed one of the officers a private letter from a cousin who was marching up with Havelock. He wrote that there were many regiments on their way out from Home, where the excitement was intense, far greater than it had ever been during the Crimean War, that all was quiet in the Madras Presidency, and that there had only been a few local outbreaks on the Bombay side.

The Brigadier did not tell the whole garrison that help was to be expected in a few days, foreseeing possible delay and disappointment, but announced that relief within two weeks was certain. Even this guarded version of the news was enough to raise the spirits of both Europeans and Indians to the highest pitch, and the sick and wounded were greatly cheered by the prospect of security and change of air. Mrs Inglis heard the sound of distant guns, and every time they boomed they seemed to say: 'We are coming to save you. We are coming to save you.' Mrs Bartrum wondered whether her husband was serving with Havelock's force.

That night there was heavy rain, but by 3 A.M. on the 23rd it had ceased, and at 11 A.M. the sun came out and the clouds were blown away. The sound of guns could be clearly heard on the Cawnpore side, and by 2 P.M. the cannonade was heavier and nearer, five or six miles away perhaps. Throughout the day large bodies of enemy troops were in movement outside, with guns and ammunition waggons. At 5 P.M. a fresh cannonade was heard much nearer, it was thought within three miles, besides a straggling fire of musketry. The garrison were in wild excitement, and even the Indian troops were at last convinced that relief was on the way. Ungud danced about, snapping his fingers at each report and demanding of the Sikhs: 'Who is the liar now? Who has been inventing tales, and telling lies about Havelock Sahib, and Tytler Sahib, and Neill Sahib, and Barrow Sahib?' Flocks of birds, mostly crows, were flying over the Residency from the south. At nightfall the rain began again and the firing died away.

That night was unusually quiet. In the morning a large body of cavalry was seen moving through the city, and at 8.30 A.M. the guns could be heard again, but further off, it seemed, than yesterday. Ungud was silent and the spirits of the Indian troops began to flag. There was great activity among the mutineers, and the garrison, remembering the trenched and barricaded roads and the loopholed houses, began to think of the fighting that still lay ahead of Havelock and his men.

At 8 P.M. the enemy made a demonstration against the Cawnpore battery lasting half an hour, and there were further alarms at 1.30 and at 4 o'clock next morning; the whole garrison were under arms during the better part of the night. A great uproar could be heard in the city. At the

Cawnpore battery Captain Radcliffe, who had led the charge of the Volunteer Cavalry at Chinhat, was mortally wounded.

Early in the morning of the 25th September, the eighty-eighth day of the siege, the guns were heard again in the south, and by ten o'clock there was no doubt that they were drawing nearer. While the garrison were eagerly listening at Gubbins' post a sepoy suddenly climbed over the parapet, to the amazement of the sentry, who was about to cover him with his musket when he held out a letter. It was a despatch from Sir James Outram, dated the 16th September, written before he had crossed the Ganges and superseded by Ungud's letter of the 20th. The runner had no news of the relieving column except that, as was already guessed, it had reached the outskirts of the city. He was sent back at once with the following reply from the Brigadier:

'*Lucknow*, *25th Sept.*, 1857
11 *a.m.*

My dear General,

I have this instant received your letter of the 16th instant. Yours of the 20th brought by my own messenger, I had before received. I regret I am quite unable to leave my position to make a sortie on your approaching the City. Were I to attempt it, I should run the greatest risk of losing my post. The enemy sepoys and matchlockmen with guns, some of large calibre, are now moving through the streets in your direction. I will shell them to the utmost. We can reach from 16 to 1800 yards down the Cawnpore road on either side, as you approach us, and are much on the alert.

J. Inglis, Brigadier.
Commanding Oudh Field Force.

To Major General Sir J. Outram K.C.B., Commanding the Relieving Army.'

A little before noon the firing died away, but soon many of the people from the city were seen making their way north across the bridges with bundles on their heads. Before long they were joined by sepoys, matchlockmen, and troopers, camels, carts, and elephants, while some of the cavalry rode down to the bank, cut their martingales, and plunged into the river. The garrison opened fire on the fugitives with every gun and mortar that could be brought to bear upon their line of flight. The bridge of boats parted in the middle, leaving a struggling mass in the water and crowds on the southern bank waving desperately for boats from the other side. Many of the enemy stayed at their posts, however—enough to reply with what was perhaps the heaviest cannonade of the whole siege, and to maintain a constant fire from the surrounding loopholes.

In the early afternoon gunfire and musketry could be heard on the east side. It seemed that Havelock and Outram were making a wide sweep to the right to avoid street fighting, and orders were given for the flank of their advance to be shelled by mortars. The men crowded on the roofs inside the entrenchment, straining ears and eyes for the next sign of the relief. Mrs Inglis, who had been ordered by the Brigadier to stay under cover with the children, found it almost impossible to keep still.

At 4 P.M. the officers on lookout could distinguish European troops in action by the Moti Mahal, less than a mile along the river bank. At 5 o'clock the sharp rattle of musketry was heard in the streets, growing louder every minute. Havelock's men were now hidden by the buildings, but the enemy could be seen crowding the roofs and firing down on them. Another five minutes and a body of Europeans and Sikhs, headed by a handful of officers on horseback, could be seen making their way up a long street which led to the Baillie Guard gate.

It was heavy going, for the road was broken up by trenches, and the enemy maintained a biting cross-fire from the roofs and loopholes on either side. The men in the street were dropping fast, but there was little time to pick up the wounded. Those that were still on their feet charged up the road at the best pace they could make, shouting and firing as they ran, until their shouts were answered by the garrison, and the cheering rose from the roofs, the trenches, and the batteries, from the ruined houses that were still defended, and from the hospital itself where the sick and wounded crawled out of bed to greet the relieving column.

The Baillie Guard gate, broken and riddled with shot, was still barricaded and banked up with earth, but Outram, Havelock, and the rest entered through an embrasure, followed by a stream of Highlanders and Sikhs. Lieutenant Birch, struck by the unfamiliar sight of officers in uniform, sent an orderly for Inglis' sword, for the Brigadier had nothing but a brace of pistols in his belt and looked more like a pirate than a soldier.

Outram, who had been wounded in the arm, was distressed by the heavy losses in the streets and said he feared there might be as many as eight hundred killed. When the Brigadier asked him for orders he bowed and said:

'General Havelock commands to-day.'

Inglis remarked to Havelock: 'We hardly expected you in before to-morrow.'

'When I saw your battered gate,' said Havelock, 'I determined to be in before nightfall.'

The gate was soon thrown open to the men who were still thronging up the street in a victorious rout, tired and dusty but wearing a look of health which had long been strange to the garrison. Outram entered Fayrer's house, the doctor being an old friend, and the 78th Highlanders, the Ross-shire Buffs, surged into the compound and onto the verandah, shaking the ladies by the hand, picking up the children and passing them from one to another profoundly moved, exclaiming as they remembered Cawnpore: 'God bless you! We thought to have found only your bones.'

The ladies made haste to bring them water, while many of the men treated them to tots of rum which had been saved for the occasion. Tea, without milk or sugar, was served for the officers in the taik-hana. Then, as the first excitement died away, the thoughts of the relieving force turned to those that had fallen. Among many lesser names was that of Brigadier General Neill, whose vigorous action at Benares and Allahabad in June had paved the way for Havelock's victorious advance. While her mother helped to prepare refreshments, little Lavinia Casey stared up at Havelock himself, and wondered why the tears were running down the General's cheeks. When she asked her mother afterwards Mrs Casey told her that he had been saying over and over again: 'My brave soldiers! My brave soldiers!' as he mourned for the men that had been killed in the streets.

The new-comers were plied with anxious questions. Wives met the husbands they had given up for dead, while others heard for the first time that they were widows. Mrs Bartrum was not left long in suspense, for she learnt from the first officer she met that Dr Bartrum had accompanied the relieving force and had actually shared a litter with her informant on the previous night. Thanking God that he had come at last, she took her baby and ran out into the crowd to see if she could find her husband. She walked up and down the road inside the gate, scanning the face of every man that entered, but in vain. At length she was told that Bartrum was in the rear with the heavy guns and would not reach the entrenchment till to-morrow morning. She returned to her quarters, where she hushed the child to sleep with a light heart.

Meanwhile as dusk was falling Lieutenant Moorsom, 52nd Light Infantry, who was familiar with the city, was leading in a second column by a street which led along the side of the Farhat Bakhsh and Terhi Kothi palaces. The enemy disputed their advance with a galling fire, to which they replied with small-arms and artillery, but fortunately this road was not cut up so badly as the other. When the guns reached the Clock Tower the way was found to be blocked by the enemy's battery. Captain Maude, Royal Artillery, could see the light of a portfire being lowered onto the vent of a gun, and immediately a shower of caseshot came whistling about his ears. He led a party forward to capture the gun before the enemy could reload, but by the time they reached the battery it had been abandoned.

Lieutenant Aitken had meanwhile taken out a dozen of his sepoys from the Baillie Guard with picks and shovels to clear away the earthwork. Seeing dark faces in the dusk, the advancing Highlanders took them for mutineers and received them at the point of the bayonet. The sepoys made no resistance; three of them were wounded and one of them said in the vernacular as he fell: 'Never mind, it was fated. Victory to the Baillie Guard!' The others lay on the ground crying: 'Aikeen Sahib! Aikeen Sahib!' until their commandant rushed up and shouted: 'For God's sake, don't harm these poor fellows, they've saved all our lives!' The Highlanders grounded their arms just in time, before any of the Indians had been mortally hurt. The battery was quickly levelled, and both guns and wounded were brought into the entrenchment, while Aitken went on to occupy a courtyard in the Terhi Kothi.

By now the moon had risen in a clear sky. There were troops still moving in, but many bivouacked in the streets and the Terhi Kothi, while the rearguard, under Colonel Campbell, 90th Light Infantry, with the heavy guns and the men that had been wounded earlier in the day, were still at the Moti Mahal, where they had been left in the afternoon. During the night the streets were deserted by the enemy, but the opportunity was not taken to bring the rearguard in.

Dr Ogilvie, the Sanitary Commissioner, had been ordered to find how many carts would be needed to evacuate the non-combatants, and the garrison concluded that at last there was no need to stint. At the Brigade Mess, where several dozen of champagne had been hoarded against the relief, every man was free to eat and drink his fill. The officers of the relieving force were astonished to find the men they had relieved living, as they thought, in such good style, having looked to find them eating horse flesh or even rat.

Mrs Inglis was kept awake by the noise among the Sikhs in the courtyard next to her own. Although the sound of revelry was ungrateful to her on an occasion more fitting, as she thought, for solemn thankfulness, she could not grudge the men their pleasure after the stress and labour of the siege. Spirits rose higher and higher as the night wore on, and it was three o'clock in the morning when Mr Rees retired, after dancing to the pipes of the 78th Highlanders. One of the pipers related how he had been attacked in the street by an Indian trooper.

He had just fired his rifle; there was no time to use his bayonet; and he would have been cut down but for a happy idea. 'All at once,' he said, 'I seized my pipe, put it to my mouth, and gave forth a shrill tone, which so startled the fellow that he bolted like a shot, evidently imagining it was some infernal machine.'

While Outram and Colonel Robert Napier (afterwards Lord Napier of Magdala), his chief of staff, both of whom were wounded, stayed with Dr Fayrer, Havelock quartered himself at Ommanney's house. The local garrison treated him to beef cutlets and mock-turtle soup, with champagne, but he had little heart for food, having heard during the afternoon that his son Harry had been wounded in the arm, and having had no further word of him.

After their months of isolation it was long before the garrison tired of listening to the news from the world outside. Two days earlier Outram had heard that at last the Delhi force had stormed the Imperial City. The Punjab was safe, thanks to the vigour and resolution of John Lawrence and his lieutenants, while the combined tact and firmness of Colonel George Lawrence, brother of John and Henry, had kept Rajputana comparatively tranquil. Agra was safe too. There had been a massacre at Jhansi, but Simla and the other hill stations were quiet. Communication by post and telegraph between Cawnpore and Calcutta had been resumed.

Now the garrison learnt why their relief had been

so long delayed. They heard how, after winning one action after another against immense odds, Havelock had checked his advance on finding his effective strength reduced by casualties and disease to less than a thousand, and fallen back on his entrenched position at Cawnpore, which was already threatened. The mutiny at Dinapore, on his line of communications by the Ganges, had delayed the promised reinforcements for another month. The blue cap-covers that Ungud had described were worn by the Madras Fusileers, 'Neill's Bluecaps', and the square or diamond-shaped buttons belonged to the 78th Highlanders, whose bagpipes supplied the curious music that had impressed Aodhan Singh.

Ungud's story of the Cawnpore massacre was true. One of the four survivors of the slaughter on the river bank, Lieutenant Delafosse, 53rd Native Infantry, had come in with the column. Captain Evans, 17th Bombay Native Infantry, commanding the battery behind the churchyard, had lost his wife and two children, and Dr Darby's wife had been killed with her baby, to whom she had given birth behind a gun in Wheeler's entrenchment. A young bandsman of the 32nd named Syms was told that his mother, stepfather, sister, and brother had all been butchered: he made a vow that whenever he met the enemy again he would spare neither man, woman, nor child. Unfounded stories of torture and dishonour were repeated and believed, and the women thanked God for saving them and theirs from such a fate. Some of the garrison heard with savage delight of Neill's order of the 25th July: 'The Brigadier General has determined that every stain of that innocent blood shall be cleared up and wiped out, previous to their execution, by such of the miscreants as may be hereafter apprehended, who took an active share in the Mutiny, to be selected according to their rank, caste, and degree of guilt. Each miscreant, after sentence of death is pronounced upon him, will be taken down to the house in question, under a guard, and will be forced into clearing-up a small portion of the blood stains; the task will be made as revolting to his feelings as possible, and the Provost-Marshal will use the lash freely in forcing any one objecting to complete his task. After having the portion properly cleared up, the culprit is to be immediately hanged, and for this purpose a gallows will be erected close at hand.'

An ammunition waggon full of letters and newspapers addressed to residents of Lucknow had been left outside the city, and only a few odd letters found their way into the entrenchment. In the lane between Fayrer's house and the Post Office Lieutenant Innes met one of the Highlanders, who showed him a letter he had brought up from Cawnpore and asked him if he knew the owner. By a curious chance it was addressed to Innes himself.

That night Mrs Bartrum was so happy to think that she would see her husband in the morning that she could not sleep.

Next morning, the 26th September, Outram assumed command of both the garrison and the relieving force as general officer commanding the Dinapore and Cawnpore divisions. He had previously waived his military rank and accompanied the column in his civil capacity as Chief Commissioner of Oudh, and as a volunteer, rather than deprive Havelock of the honour of relieving Lucknow. He had retained some measure of control, however, and during the afternoon of the 25th September there had been a sharp difference of opinion between the two generals. On reaching the Chhattar Manzil, Outram had proposed halting for a few hours to let the rearguard come up with the heavy guns, the baggage, and the wounded, by which time he hoped to have occupied the palace and found a comparatively sheltered way into the Residency. Havelock, who understood him to suggest waiting all night, preferred to push on at once, fearing that the Residency might fall at the very moment that relief was at hand. He said: 'There is the street; we see the worst—we shall be slated, but we can push through and get it over.' At that Outram, always quick on the point of honour, replied with some heat: 'Let us go on, then, in God's name!' and led the advance himself. They were slated heavily and the rearguard was left behind. Outram asked himself afterwards whether he should not rather have said: 'Havelock, we have virtually reached the Residency, and I now resume.'

The wound Outram had received earlier in the day was not serious, the bullet having traversed the fleshy part of the upper arm without injuring the bone or any vessel of importance. In the morning Dr Fayrer found him wandering about with his coat in his hand. He showed his host the two bullet holes in the sleeve and said: 'Do you think Mrs Fayrer or one of the ladies could mend this for me?' Mrs Fayrer mended it herself, and the doctor gave the General a uniform cap to replace his own, which had been lost the day before. Neither Outram nor Napier would hear of having special dainties procured for them, but lived on the rations like the rest.

Mrs Bartrum rose at dawn that morning, and put her baby into the one clean dress she had been keeping throughout the siege for the day when his father should see him again. Taking him out, she met a man who had shared a tent with her husband on the march from Cawnpore, and who assured her that Dr Bartrum was on his way into the entrenchment, in the best of spirits at the thought of meeting his wife and child. Mrs Bartrum waited for some time, but as he did not appear she returned to her quarters to give the child his breakfast, and then sat beside the door to watch. She waited all that day.

There was still no news of the younger Havelock. Mr J. B. Thornhill, of the Civil Service, who had married General Havelock's niece, volunteered to go out to the Moti Mahal and bring in the wounded, including, as he hoped, his cousin by marriage whom he had never met. He went out along the river bank, skirting the palaces, the route being under fire at only two points, and started back with the wounded in doolies, or covered litters, and an escort of a hundred and fifty men. The convoy suffered little loss until Thornhill took a wrong turning to the left, which led them into an open square and through the same archway under which Neill had been shot the day before. The enemy closed in rapidly, opening a deadly fire of musketry at point blank range. Many of the escort were shot down at once, and most of the others pushed on for their lives. Two of the leading doolies, one of which was Havelock's, ran the gauntlet and reached the Residency safely, thanks to Private Henry Ward, 78th Highlanders, who stayed beside them all the way and would not let the bearers drop them. Some of the doolies in the rear were turned back in time by Assistant-Surgeon Bradshaw, 90th Light Infantry, and an apothecary, and taken in along the river bank. Thornhill himself got back alive but desperately wounded; he died a few days later.

Thirty or forty doolies were left in the street,

in the square, and in sheds along the sides of the square, the bearers having all been killed or wounded, or having run away. Dismounted enemy troopers entered the square, armed with swords, and a murderous fire was maintained from three sides at once. At about 10 A.M. Surgeon A. D. Home, 90th Light Infantry, took refuge with the remnant of the escort in a house which formed the right hand side of the archway. The party consisted of the doctor himself, two wounded officers, eight unwounded and three wounded men—fourteen in all. The enemy approached in force but were checked by Private Peter McManus, 5th Fusileers, who remained outside the door under cover of a pillar, keeping up a constant and effective fire. It was left to Dr Home, as both surgeon and the only unwounded officer, to direct and inspire the defence, and to tend the wounded, besides taking a hand with a rifle when the firing grew hot.

The enemy, whose numbers were steadily increasing, began to taunt them, asking again and again: 'Why don't you come out into the street?' One of their leaders called on his men to storm the house, declaring that there were only three of the Europeans left alive, but the fourteen wounded and unwounded men gave a hearty cheer to undeceive them while they barricaded the door as best they could. Seeing that the doolies were still exposed to the enemy's fire, Private John Ryan, Madras Fusileers, asked for a volunteer to bring in Captain

Arnold, of the same regiment, who was lying in one of the nearest. McManus came forward, though wounded in the foot, and the two men rushed out into the square. At first they tried to lift the dooly, but, finding it too heavy, they pulled Arnold out and carried him back into the house. Neither of them was hit though Arnold himself was wounded again in the thigh. A private also was brought in, but received a mortal wound while the men that were carrying him remained untouched.

Dr Home hoped that if they could hold out for another hour or two they would be relieved by the rearguard on its way into the Residency; but an hour passed away, during which three of the men were wounded, and still there was no sign of help. Private James Hollowell, 78th Highlanders, distinguished himself by killing the enemy's leader and encouraging his mates as he exposed himself freely and maintained a steady fire. After a time the firing died away, but soon they could hear a dull rolling noise in the street. As it grew louder Dr Home shouted: 'Now, men, now or never. Let us rush out and die in the open air, and not be killed like rats in a hole. They are bringing a gun on us.' It was not a gun, however, but a bullet-proof screen on wheels, by the help of which the enemy climbed onto the roof and set the house on fire.

After a quick discussion Dr Home and the others picked up the three most helpless of the wounded and, making a break for the open, dragged them across the square to one of the sheds. On the way two of the wounded were hit again, though the sound men did not get a scratch. It was now three in the afternoon: there were six men left who could bear arms, besides another four who were fit to stand sentry. From their previous position they had been able to cover some of the doolies in the square, but now the enemy came through the archway and began to butcher those of the wounded who were still alive, creeping up on the far side of the doolies and despatching them with their swords. Lieutenant Knight, 90th Light Infantry, had enough life left in him to spring out as they approached. The enemy fired a volley and two shots hit him in the leg, but in spite of his three wounds he distanced his pursuers and got back alive to the rearguard.

The enemy now dug holes in the roof of the shed, through which they began to fire down on the men inside. Home broke through the wall to look for some way of escape. The wounded begged to be shot if they had to be abandoned, for they could hear the cries of the men that were being slaughtered in the doolies. Home and another went through to reconnoitre. About fifty yards away they found a small mosque which appeared to be defensible, but before they were able to carry the wounded across they were seen and fired on. They therefore retreated to the shed, taking with them a pot of water, which afforded great relief to the wounded and to the men of the escort, who had been biting cartridges all day.

As it grew dark the enemy ceased fire, which was fortunate since Home and his men had only forty or fifty rounds left between them. Having arranged three reliefs of three sentries each they settled down to spend the night in the shed. The enemy could still be heard moving about the roof. There were dead men all around. Some of the wounded were delirious. The enemy had set fire to several doolies, and the moans of their occupants could be clearly heard, though the men in the shed did not speak of them to each other. They had long lost all hope of rescue and merely clung together in despair; there were moments when death would have come as a relief. At about 2 A.M. they heard firing close by, and a rush of the enemy above their heads. In a frenzy of joy they cried: 'Europeans! Europeans!', and with a loud cheer shouted again: 'Charge them! Charge them! Keep on your right!' But at once all was quiet, and soon they sank into apathy again.

A little before daylight Home roused himself and proposed that they should make a desperate effort to cut their way through to the Residency or to the rearguard. Creeping out in the shadow of the building, he found large numbers of the enemy gathered round a fire which was burning under the archway. Escape seemed hopeless in that direction, while if they tried to force their way back they would encounter those of the enemy who, as they supposed, had just defeated an effort to relieve them. Still, Home tried to persuade the others to make the attempt, since their case seemed hopeless if they stayed where they were, whereas one or two might be lucky if they went; but only two would agree to follow him, and rather than abandon the wounded Home resigned himself to stay.

Daybreak found them hopeless. There came a sound of distant firing, but they did not care any longer. It grew nearer: suddenly Ryan jumped up and shouted: 'Oh boys! Them's our own chaps!' Still they were not sure, until presently they heard the sharp crack of Enfield rifles. At that Home shouted: 'Men, cheer together!' There came an answering cheer and they shouted back which way to come. Then Lieutenant Moorsom appeared at the entrance of the shed, and before long they were safe in the shelter of the palaces. A party had been despatched in the early hours of the morning to capture the gateway—hence the firing they had heard—but the officer in charge had not known that Home and his men were in the square, and, judging the enemy to be too strong for him, had fallen back.

Meanwhile it had not been easy to extricate the rearguard, for the enemy had rallied after a night of inaction and were holding the Kaisarbagh Palace, opposite the Moti Mahal, in considerable force. On the morning after Outram's and Havelock's entrance two hundred and fifty men of the 5th Fusileers, under Major Simmons, and a detachment of Brasyer's Sikhs—the Sykeses, as the soldiers called them—under Captain Brasyer himself, guided by Lieutenant Moorsom, had marched out to reinforce Colonel Campbell and bring in the rearguard together with the heavy guns, about thirty ammunition waggons, and those of the wounded that had not been sent ahead with Thornhill's convoy. But the fire from the Kaisarbagh was so severe that all they could do was to occupy the buildings and enclosures between the Moti Mahal and the Chhattar Manzil and wait for further reinforcements.

Later in the day Colonel Napier, whose wound was not serious, volunteered to make a further effort. He took a hundred of the 32nd under Captain Lowe, a hundred of the 78th under Lieutenant Colonel Stisted, and some Indian troopers under Lieutenant Hardinge, 3rd Oudh Irregular Cavalry. He wished to take a couple of field guns, too, but Captain Olpherts, Bengal Artillery, whose men spoke of him lovingly as 'Hellfire Jack', objected and persuaded him to take instead a team of spare bullocks for the heavy guns, although Outram had given permission to destroy them if necessary. Olpherts accompanied the party at his own request, and Mr T. H. Kavanagh, the Superintendent of the Chief Commissioner's Office, went with them as guide. The way by the river was not fit for wheeled traffic, but there seemed to be a practicable road through the palaces. Leaving a detachment to maintain his communications, Napier joined hands with the rearguard with little loss, and as soon as it was dark sent in all the wounded and the camels, loaded with Enfield ammunition, along the river bank under the charge of Lieutenant Hardinge.

Meanwhile Olpherts had been bending all his courage and resource to save a 24-pounder which had been in action the day before, but had been silenced by the enemy's musketry and left out in the open. Private Thomas Duffy, Madras Fusileers, crept out in the dusk and attached a drag rope to the trail of the gun, which was then hauled under cover by a team of bullocks. During this operation Lieutenant Crump, Madras Artillery, was killed.

As the enemy were found to be so active it was resolved to withdraw at once instead of waiting for the early dawn as had been intended. Napier ordered his men to take off their white cap covers, which were too conspicuous in the dark, and to keep firing till the very last minute. He divided his small force into advanced and rear guards, with flankers of a hundred men each, and at 3 A.M. made his way out through a jungly garden, debouching into an open road while his rearguard were still firing from the original position. The enemy did not hear the jingling of the guns and waggons.

There was a check when the 24-pounder halted with its wheel jammed against a hedge of thorn. Napier feared that they might still be there by daylight, when they would certainly be shot to pieces, but as he hurried to the rear the gun moved slowly on again. They made their way safely through the enemy's posts, and were only observed and fired on when the column was already moving into the shelter of the Chhattar Manzil. The enemy then mounted the wall of a neighbouring enclosure and began firing on the troops below; but Captain M'Cabe and Lieutenant Colonel Purnell, 90th Light Infantry, with a party of volunteers, killed them almost to a man and occupied the enclosure. Then Napier pointed to the palace and said to his men: 'There are your barracks, go and rest yourselves.' They were glad enough to rest, and could hardly believe they had got through so easily, having keyed themselves up for some stiff fighting. Later on the whole of the Chhattar Manzil was cleared and the road was opened for the guns and waggons, which were brought into the Residency position during the next few days.

While the rearguard was still outside, various sorties were being made to extend the enceinte. On the morning of the 26th September Lieutenant Aitken, who had made a lodgment in the Terhi Kothi the night before, occupied the whole palace with a small detachment of the 13th Native Infantry. A hundred and fifty of the 32nd, under Captain Lowe, cleared the Captan Bazaar, between the entrenchment and the river, capturing a number of guns and spiking several mortars, but were unable to reach the iron bridge as they had hoped to do. Sam Lawrence distinguished himself by charging a 9-pounder gun just as the enemy were about to fire a second round of grape. The troops then worked round to the right, where they joined hands with Aitken at the Terhi Kothi and penetrated the next palace, the Farhat Bakhsh, or Ferret Box as it was afterwards known.

Harry Metcalfe went out with Lowe's sortie, accompanied by the lad Syms, who had lost so many of his people at Cawnpore. After they had been out for some time Metcalfe missed his friend and was told that he had rushed into one of the neighbouring houses. Thinking it strange that he had not come out again, Metcalfe went across to see what he was doing. He heard a scuffle inside, and, rushing in, found the lad struggling with a huge sepoy, who had gripped his musket and was cutting at him with his curved sword; Metcalfe was just in time to save him. Syms said: 'Oh, Harry, I'm a brute.'

'How's that, Jack?' asked Metcalfe.

'Oh, I said when I came out I would spare no one, and I fired at a young woman, and I'm afraid I killed her; and by so doing I've placed myself on a par with the Rebels.'

Metcalfe asked to see the body, and tried to cheer his friend by suggesting that the woman was not really dead. He was right, for they soon found that she had only fainted. Syms was overjoyed. They took her into the entrenchment, where her wound was dressed before she was sent about her business. Soon after this Syms was blown up by an accidental explosion and died in agony the same night, leaving two sisters in the garrison, one married to a colour sergeant and the other to a drum major.

All that day the place was in a turmoil as bullocks, camels, baggage, and wounded were brought into the entrenchment, besides the piles of loot that the soldiers and servants were fetching from the palaces and the bazaar. Ellicock, Inglis' orderly, said it was more like Donnybrook Fair than anything. General Neill's body was carried in on a gun-limber and buried after dusk, mourned by the whole of Havelock's force and especially his own regiment, the Madras Fusileers. The hospital was overflowing; many of the wounded were still lying outside with neither bed nor shelter. Those inside were little better off, for amputated arms and legs were lying everywhere, and the wards were so crowded and confused that little could be done to allay the pain and discomfort of the sufferers.

Councils of war were sitting all day at Fayrer's house and all kinds of rumours were about. Nobody knew whether Oudh would be evacuated altogether or whether the whole army was to remain at Lucknow and obtain provisions by force of arms. The joys and hopes of the previous night ebbed away as it became apparent that the situation was still critical. The garrison wondered which was more to be feared: the chance of starvation if the newcomers remained, or the hazards of a retreat through the city with the families and the sick and wounded.

That evening Mrs Bartrum climbed to the roof

of the Residency building with her baby in her arms. She looked down the road towards the gate but could not see her husband and returned to her room disappointed. Next morning she was still waiting, until at last she grew sick with suspense. In the afternoon, Dr Darby came in to see her. He looked into her face with a kind, sad expression. She said: 'How strange it is my husband is not come in!' 'Yes,' he said, 'it *is* strange.' Then he turned and went away. She thought: Something has happened which they do not like to tell me. Presently she heard that her husband had been killed down by the Moti Mahal, on his way to operate on a wounded man. Dr Bradshaw had said as they walked across the court: 'Bartrum, you are exposing yourself too much.' 'Oh, there's no danger,' he answered, and was instantly hit in the temple. He fell across Bradshaw, saying, 'It's all up with me,' and died at once. What became of his body was never known.

Mrs Polehampton came to sit with her, speaking little but offering a widow's sympathy. Mrs Bartrum tried to rouse herself for the sake of her boy, to whom she had been saying since the night of the relief: 'Papa is come; now baby will get quite well.' The child could not understand why his mother was so sad.

Havelock's relief, or rather reinforcement, had come none too soon, for although Fulton's genius had baffled the enemy's miners, there had still been the danger that the garrison might become fatally diminished by casualties, sickness, and desertion. At the beginning of the siege the total strength, including sick and wounded, had been 1720: by the 25th September it had shrunk to 979, of whom 577 were Europeans and 402 Indians. Of the 240 women, 3 had been killed and 11 had died, while of the 270 children, 54 were dead. The enemy's losses had, of course, been far heavier than the garrison's, but not enough to impair their overwhelming superiority in numbers, which were now being swelled by large bodies of mutineers escaped from Delhi.

Havelock had crossed the Ganges with 3179 of all arms. Major McIntyre, 78th Highlanders, had been left at the Alambagh, a garden house with a walled enclosure nearly two miles south of the city, with a detachment of 331 men, including sick and wounded, over 4,000 Indian camp-followers, and much cattle, the heavy baggage, commissariat, treasure, ordnance park, and store of small-arms ammunition. The total casualties of the relieving column on the 25th and 26th September had been 535, of which 196 were killed or missing—the same thing, since no quarter had been given. The remainder of the force, with a horde of Indian grooms, grass-cutters, bearers, drivers, and other camp-followers, was now quartered in either the original entrenchment or the new extended position.

Having fought his way into Lucknow, Outram was faced with a decision of the utmost difficulty and importance. His orders from Lord Canning, the Governor General, were to rescue the garrison even if this involved the evacuation of Oudh; but so long as the garrison were safe he might hold Lucknow if he could do so without depending upon early reinforcements. He had hoped that his approach would cause a reaction of the inhabitants against the mutineers, and that he could withdraw the garrison after forming a provisional government to hold the city until it could be reoccupied. Later he had proposed to withdraw the families and the sick and wounded, forage for fresh supplies, and leave Neill to hold Lucknow with three regiments. What he was most anxious to avoid was the complete evacuation of Oudh, which, he believed, would convince the inhabitants that British rule was gone for ever.

His hopes of a reaction were disappointed. By the night of the 25th most of the mutineers had fled, leaving the city rabble, the palace retainers, and the

Talukdars' men to maintain the siege; but on the morning of the 26th, when the rearguard was, for the time, cut off, and many of the wounded had been butchered, the remaining rebels sent the heads of the slain after their retreating allies and induced them to return. It was not long before the extended position was closely invested, and it was clear that any attempt of the garrison and the relieving force to cut their way out must be at best attended by heavy losses. For the present Outram had to be content with clearing the ground and exploring the possibilities of evacuation.

Meanwhile the survivors of the Indian troops in Inglis' garrison had been thanked on parade for their services and, with a few exceptions, promoted. Several were decorated with the Order of British India, and the Pensioners had their pensions doubled. The only Indian soldiers who received nothing were the Sikh troopers, who had been suspect throughout the siege. It was left to Government to reward the European troops in their own time, and some of the men were not best pleased at the thought of waiting for their due. They forgot that, whereas the Europeans had, after all, been fighting for their own hand, there had been little but the sentiment of loyalty to keep the Indians at their side, and they were heard to grumble: 'Damn those black fellows! There they go as usual, petted and rewarded, while we gets nothing.'

On the 27th September a sortie was made from the

Baillie Guard gate by detachments of the Madras Fusileers and the 32nd under Major Stephenson, of the former regiment, with a party of artillerymen, under Captain Evans, who were to burst any guns that might be captured. The object was the enemy's 'Garden' battery, opposite the south-east corner of the position. The experience of the old garrison was not drawn upon as it should have been, and after dashing forward without waiting for orders the troops lost their way. Several guns were taken, but the bursting party was late in coming up. The guns were to be destroyed by being charged with powder, tamped or plugged up with clay, and fired through the vent; but as the men had drunk the water that had been brought to moisten the clay, this could not be done. The sortie was withdrawn under a destructive fire from the surrounding houses, the Madras Fusileers losing four killed and seven wounded, and the 32nd, three killed and five wounded.

Major Stephenson's failure caused great disappointment. It was felt that the sortie should have been made on the night of the 25th, or during the 26th, while the enemy were still disorganised, and it was feared that they would take heart from their success. There was universal regret among the old garrison for the deaths of William Cooney, now a corporal, and his mate, Private Michael Smith, who had already distinguished themselves in so many sorties, and both of whom were killed during the retreat after displaying the utmost gallantry.

Cooney was on the sick list, having hurt his hand in a previous sortie when he and Smith had charged a battery by themselves, scaring the enemy away by shouting 'Right and left extend!' to suggest an attack in force; but to-day he had taken his arm out of its sling and joined the detachment, unwilling that Smith should go without him. When the bodies were brought in, Brigadier Inglis looked down at them and said: 'There lie two of the bravest men that ever wore a red coat.'

That afternoon the Dashwood baby, who was still thriving, was christened Arthur Frederick; Charlie Dashwood, his uncle, was a godfather and Mrs Harris stood proxy. Mrs Inglis had a copy of *Home News* lent her for two hours, and everybody read it eagerly although it was out of date. The garrison were still anxious and depressed. There were twenty-five funerals that night.

Next day the new position was extended towards the south from the Chhattar Manzil by Lieutenant Moorsom, with fifty men of the 90th and the 5th Fusileers. Outram despatched a letter to Major McIntyre at the Alambagh to say that he had not yet been able to spare the men to open communications, and might not be able to do so for another two or three days; in the meantime he assumed that McIntyre could hold his own. It was rumoured among the garrison that the entrenchment was to be strengthened, provisioned for three months, and held by part of the relieving force, while the 32nd and the rest of the old garrison were withdrawn. The enemy appeared in greater numbers every day. Outram kept his anxieties to himself and was as genial as ever, but Mr Money, his secretary, saw him one night in the small hours kneeling on his bed with his head on the pillow, wrestling with his problems in prayer.

On the 29th September there were three more sorties, which had been carefully planned by Lieutenant J. C. Anderson after the failure of the 27th. The first column under Captain Shute, 64th Foot, advancing from Innes' post, succeeded in destroying the 24-pounder near Hill's shop that had done so much damage in the earlier days of the siege. Two mortars were spiked and several guns of small calibre dismounted. It was hoped that this column might reach the iron bridge, but the attempt failed and, chiefly owing to lack of support, ten men were killed and twenty-three wounded, one of them mortally.

The second sortie, under Major Apthorp and Lieutenant Hardinge, was made from the Sikh Square, and worked across to the right, covered by musketry from Gubbins' post. Several houses were cleared and demolished, two mine shafts were destroyed, and a number of guns, including the 'Lane Gun' which had wrecked the upper storey of Gubbins' house, were burst or taken into the entrenchment. Mr Gubbins, who was covering the sortie from the top of Grant's bastion with a party of the 32nd, noticed that the enemy were making an active resistance from the ground floor of a mosque, and pointed out to Lieutenant Maitland, Royal Artillery, what great execution would be done if he could only knock down the minarets. Maitland had a 9-pounder placed in position, and in three rounds at four hundred yards' range both the minarets were brought down in ruins on the enemy's heads. By 11 A.M. Major Apthorp's party had regained the entrenchment with the loss of four killed and eleven wounded.

The third column left the Brigade Mess and worked round to the left. It was led by Captain M'Cabe and Major Simmons, 5th Fusileers. Inglis had protested against the selection of M'Cabe for this dangerous duty on the grounds that he had led enough sorties already, but Outram had insisted that he should go. The party filed out at daybreak, and after forming up under cover of a wall they rushed an 18-pounder which was posted behind a breastwork eighty yards from the Brigade Mess. The gunners fired two rounds as they came up and then abandoned the gun. While a building further to the left was being attacked, Captain M'Cabe was shot through the lungs, a mortal wound.

The ground floor of the building was quickly occupied, but some of the enemy still held out in the upper storey. A couple of ladders were brought up and placed against the windows, Harry Metcalfe being first up one of them, while Tom Carroll, a tall private of the Grenadier Company, ran up the other. Metcalfe climbed through his window to find the room, as he thought, deserted. He was looking round to see if the enemy had left any food behind, when he came upon a huge chest and, peeping under the lid, found three mutineers squatting inside. He shot one and bayoneted the second, but the third leapt at him and laid hold of his musket by the muzzle with one hand, so that he could not use his bayonet, and chopped at him with his curved sword in the other. Little Metcalfe defended himself as best he could by pushing up the butt of his musket to protect his head as he tried to close with the sepoy. He received a stroke which nearly severed his left thumb, and it would have gone hard with him had not the tall grenadier rushed in from the next room and buried the hammer of his musket in the Indian's skull. Metcalfe was covered with blood, and Carroll, looking him up and down, gave a great horse-laugh and shouted: 'You little swab, you were very near being done for.' He was astonished when Metcalfe showed him the contents of the chest.

A picket was left in the house while the main body occupied some further buildings, at the last of which Major Simmons was killed at the head of his men. By now the 18-pounder outside the Cawnpore battery was in sight, and Anderson sent to the entrenchment for the reserve, asking that it might be accompanied by an officer of rank to take command. But Outram, who had been watching the operation with Havelock from the Brigade Mess, sent back word that, unless a further advance could be made without the prospect of heavy loss, the party should retire after destroying the houses they had occupied. Anderson decided that Outram's stipulation would not allow him to advance, and after expending thirteen barrels of powder in the work of demolition, the party regained the entrenchment at 9.30 A.M. with the loss of two killed and nine wounded, one mortally.

By means of the two latter sorties the ground was cleared along the south face to the extent of three hundred yards, which made things far more comfortable for the defence. Great sorrow was felt for the deaths of Captain M'Cabe, who had been one of Inglis' most trusted officers throughout the siege, and of Major Simmons. Outram was disappointed by the failure of the first sortie to reach the iron bridge, for he had hoped to open communications in that direction. Being still acutely anxious about provisions, he recalled Colonel Napier, who was strengthening the defences at the Chhattar Manzil, to organise a prolonged sortie down the Cawnpore road.

On the 30th September several of the enemy's mines were examined and destroyed. It was stated by Outram in despatches that six galleries were ready for loading, the firing of which might have sealed the fate of the garrison if relief had come a day later; but he was mistaken, for in fact they were all far short of the defences. One of them was directed against the Redan battery, but was so widely out of bearing that it would have passed the apex of the work at a considerable distance.

The same day Outram wrote to Sir Colin Campbell, the Commander in Chief, as follows: 'Our present prospects have now to be considered. It was the urgent desire of the Government that the garrison should be relieved, and the women and children, amounting to upwards of 470 souls, withdrawn. . . .

'In considering the heavy loss at which we forced our way through the enemy, it was evident there could be no possible hope of carrying off the sick, wounded, and women and children (amounting to not less than 1,500 souls, including those of both forces). Want of carriage alone rendered the transport through five miles of disputed suburb an impossibility.

'There remained but two alternatives: one to reinforce the Lucknow Garrison with 300 men, and, leaving everything behind, to retire immediately with the remains of the infantry upon the Alambagh, thereby leaving the garrison in a worse state than we found it, by the addition to the numbers they had previously to feed, of the great amount of our wounded, and of the 300 soldiers, who would barely have sufficed to afford the additional protection that would have been required—without adding such strength as would have enabled them to make an active defence, to repel attacks by sorties, or to prevent the enemy occupying the whole of their old positions. At the same time, it would have been impossible for any smaller force than the remainder of our troops, diminished by those 300 men, to have any hope of making good their way back; and that not without very serious loss. I therefore adopted the second alternative, as the only mode of offering reasonable hope of securing the safety of this force, to retain sufficient strength to enforce supplies of provisions should they not be open to us voluntarily, and to maintain ourselves, even on reduced rations, until reinforcements advance to our relief. . . .

'Since my decision has been made, I have received a letter from the Alambagh, in which it is stated that they are in great want of provisions, but from returns of what they have, it is clear that they are not aware of their resources, which were sufficient for some days. I have, therefore, ordered back the cavalry to join them in the night by a circuitous route, with conditional orders to withdraw to Cawnpore, or to maintain their position, as may be found most practicable. Their only difficulty is provisions, as they are placed in a fortified enclosure, defended by two of our heavy guns, and two 9-pounders, besides other guns taken from the enemy, 250 European soldiers, and a number of convalescents fit to bear arms.'

This despatch was to be taken out by the cavalry under Captain Barrow, who had made a name for himself by his leading of Havelock's Volunteer Cavalry; Lieutenant Hardinge was to act as guide. It was felt by those that were to take part, as well as those that were to be left behind, that this was a desperate undertaking, for the moon was so bright that the enemy could see every movement. At 10 P.M. the cavalry set out along the river, but before long they were met by such a heavy fire from ahead and from the other bank that Barrow and Hardinge called a halt. The enemy bugled, howled, and beat their drums. Two men and two horses were wounded, one of the men being saved from severe injury by a couple of biscuits in his pocket which were hard enough to deflect the ball. It was soon agreed that there was no hope of breaking through, and the cavalry were ordered back to the entrenchment, much to their relief.

The siege had now lasted for three months.

The 1st October saw the opening of Colonel Napier's operations on the Cawnpore road. Outram had placed at his disposal detachments amounting in all to over five hundred men, with two engineer officers, five experienced miners of the 32nd, and a party of artillerymen with the means of bursting guns. Napier's dispositions were so effective that the garrison were at once impressed by his judgment and ability. On the first day several buildings were occupied outside the south-east angle; but night fell before the column reached its objective, the enemy's battery in the garden of Phillips' house, and Napier therefore decided to secure his position and defer the assault till the following morning, in spite of the eagerness of the troops to go ahead.

During their advance the men were just about to shoot a filthy creature who was seen emerging from a dry well, when he was recognised as a private of the Madras Fusileers. He had lost touch with the others in the sortie of the 27th September and, finding himself cut off from the entrenchment, had hidden in the well. His only food was a handful of tea-leaves and biscuits which he chanced to be carrying in his pocket, and his company the dead body of an Indian. The atmosphere was sickening, but it was only at night that he dared to creep out for fresh air. He was almost despairing when he heard the shouting up above, and showed himself in the hope of being rescued.

Next day Napier let the men have their breakfast and arranged for artillery support from the entrenchment, before reopening the attack. The enemy's fire was severe, but a detachment was sent round by the Cawnpore road to turn their flank, and before long the battery was taken, two 9-pounders and one 6-pounder being burst, while Phillips' house was blown up by a party under Lieutenant Innes. Outram attributed the capture of the battery with the loss of only two killed and eleven wounded to the excellence of Napier's dispositions. It was remarked that Mr Kavanagh, the volunteer who had acted as guide at the Moti Mahal, was always to the fore in these operations; he was, in fact, discontented with his life as a clerk in a Government office and welcomed the chance of distinguishing himself.

In spite of their diminished numbers the men of the 32nd were always told off to lead the sorties. Inglis objected that they were being overworked, but Outram insisted that their superior knowledge of the ground must not be thrown away.

The temper of the European troops was dangerously inflamed by the memory of Cawnpore. Many of those who had marched up-country with Havelock had seen the Nana's human shambles for themselves and, seeing, had vowed never to give quarter to a mutineer. Indeed, they were so prone to take every dark face for an enemy's that it was thought well to distinguish the loyal sepoys who took part in the sorties by means of a red armlet. On the 2nd October several peaceful traders met their death to the tune of Cawnpore, including an aged man, who tried to hide under his wife's petticoat and for whom Kavanagh pleaded in vain. When one of the mutineers was taken and begged for mercy his captor retorted: 'You black rascal, do you think we are going to carry your ugly face all over the face of the blessed earth?' and ran him through with his bayonet. Another man was asked on his return to the entrenchment what luck he had had in the sortie, and replied: 'Damned the hap'orth we got, sir, but an ould cock and a hen—oh yes, we *did* get a sepoy or two.' The rest of the garrison laughed to see the men returning with fowls, ducks, and turkeys spitted on their bayonets or dangling from their belts.

On the 2nd October Outram had decided that, owing to the danger of starvation, the 90th Light Infantry was to be left to reinforce the old garrison while the rest tried to cut their way out again. A sortie was to be made with the declared object of bringing in cattle, but instead of returning to the entrenchment the column was to make its way back to the Alambagh and so to Cawnpore. Inglis faced the prospect of being left alone again with a good heart.

Outram sent out a runner with the following message to Captain Bruce, who was in charge of the Intelligence Department at Cawnpore: 'Oblige me by conveying the following message to Brigadier Wilson: I request you to prepare a detachment of not less than 300 Europeans, and two guns, to advance to the relief of the retiring column; send rockets with the detachment to give us notice of its position when we are supposed to be in the vicinity. An experienced officer to command. . . .

'Draw from Fatehpur, Allahabad, and Benares, all men that can be spared to be sent to Cawnpore with all practicable despatch.

'Request the authorities at Agra to make known to the General at Delhi the urgent necessity there is for reinforcements being pushed on to Cawnpore as speedily as possible, without which the Lucknow garrison cannot be withdrawn.

'Delhi having fallen, it is to be hoped, at least, one strong brigade may be spared from there, and another may be completed by the troops from the eastward.

'Telegraph to the Commander-in-Chief that the insurgents are too strong to admit of withdrawing, besides this garrison, the sick, wounded, women, and children, amounting to upwards of 1,000. . . .

'Telegraph to the Governor-General: My hopes of

a reaction in the city are disappointed; the insurgent sepoys have inspired such terror among all classes, and maintain so strict a watch beyond our pickets, that we have not been able to communicate with one single inhabitant of Lucknow since our arrival. Nothing but a strong demonstration of our power will be of any avail.'

Outram also drafted a farewell order to be issued after his departure. It began as follows: 'The interests of the Lucknow garrison requiring that Major-General Outram should leave them for a brief period, the Major-General tenders to Brigadier Inglis and his gallant troops an affectionate adieu, and his most heartfelt wishes for their prosperity.' After explaining why he was at present unable to withdraw the garrison, and voicing his hopes for the future, he concluded: 'The Major-General has reinforced the Garrison to the full extent deemed necessary by Brigadier Inglis; and with every confidence in the ability of that gallant officer and his glorious Garrison to maintain themselves in their present position, the Major-General bids them each, and all, a hearty God's-speed.

'It would have afforded the Major-General very sincere pleasure to have been at liberty to have communicated to the assembled troops in person the message which he leaves to Brigadier Inglis to communicate to them. But the movement requisite to effect a junction with the Alambagh detachment, is one of great delicacy and peril; and its success depends in a great measure on the Major-General's intentions not being perceived until the moment of their execution.' But this order was never issued.

On the 3rd, 4th, and 5th October the operations along the Cawnpore road were continued, house after house being occupied on either side, but on the 6th further advance was found to be barred by a mosque, held by the enemy in great force, which might have cost more to reduce than it was worth. Outram decided against making the attempt; indeed, there was now no need to waste more life in this direction since he had determined on the evening of the 4th to maintain his position with the entire force. The change of plan was due to more accurate information as to the supplies of food. Both Havelock and Outram had, of course, accepted and acted upon the information given in Inglis' despatches, and though on their entrance they had found the state of the garrison less desperate than they had expected, they had still believed in the imminent danger of starvation. But on his return from the Chhattar Manzil Napier looked into the matter for himself, and soon found that there were ample supplies for the whole force for some time to come, though it was not easy to calculate the exact amount owing to the hurried manner in which the stores had been laid in. The Commissariat officers had no knowledge of the statements made by Inglis, nor had they been required to make returns of the stores under their charge.

On the 7th October Outram wrote to Captain Bruce as follows: 'Our whole force is now besieged by the enemy, who have increased in number and audacity, which leads me to think the Delhi mutineers must now be here. Our position is more untenable than that of the previous garrison, because we are obliged to occupy the neighbouring palaces outside the entrenchment to accommodate the Europeans, which positions the enemy are able to mine from cover of neighbouring buildings. Still no communication with the town, and little prospect of procuring provisions; the neighbouring streets, into which we have made sorties at much cost of life, containing nothing. We have grain, and gun-bullocks, and horses, on which we may subsist a month I hope, but nothing else. No hospital stores, and but little medicine. . . .'

The troops that had been working down the Cawnpore road were now withdrawn to the near side of Phillips' garden, the houses they had occupied being demolished, and the 78th Highlanders were left to hold a position outside the old entrenchment known as Lockhart's post after its commandant. Doorways were made to connect the three main buildings on this site, loopholes were cut in the walls, and all the outlets were strongly barricaded. The new position, which included the south bank of the river, the Terhi Kothi, Farhat Bakhsh, and Chhattar Manzil palaces, and the gaol, was now consolidated under Havelock's command, while Inglis remained in charge of the old entrenchment. The whole enceinte was strictly invested by the enemy, but the capture of their nearest batteries, the demolition of so many of the houses that had been used for musketry, and the widening of the neutral ground outside the works, had brought much relief to the defence. There was now no shortage of labour, and the garrison, reinforced by some of the Madras Fusileers and assisted by the Indian camp-followers, began to reconstruct the Cawnpore battery, to complete the batteries on the west face, and to fortify the mound outside Innes' post with a system of zigzag trenches which commanded the southern end of the iron bridge.

The enemy were now reserving their offensive efforts for the palaces. On the 3rd October they sprung a mine near the garden post, west of the Chhattar Manzil. The explosion was short of the wall, but on the 5th they sprung another mine which was more successful. They attempted to storm the breach but were soon repulsed by a brisk fusillade from the men of the 90th. They then set fire to one of the garden gates but failed again to force an entrance. Later on, this post was strengthened by a system of trenches.

On the 6th October the enemy succeeded in blowing up a picket in a house near the Chhattar Manzil, and in the confusion that followed they forced their way into the palace, from which they were ejected with the loss, it was believed, of over four hundred.

The possession of the neighbouring buildings was disputed for several days, but at last the enemy were driven out of a mosque from which they had been harassing the outlying pickets, and the position was consolidated. They were not long in attacking Lockhart's post, where they sprung a mine which did little damage to the defences but caused the death of one of the garrison in the countermine. This death should not have occurred: the men on duty knew that the enemy were at work and observed the smoke from the train immediately before the explosion, but instead of leaving the countermine at once they sent a message to the officer in charge and stayed where they were.

Now that the perimeter had been so widely extended it was not quite so difficult for the Indian runners to make their way to the Alambagh and back with despatches rolled up in quills or bamboo sticks, and once they had got so far the rest of the way to Cawnpore was comparatively safe. All communication with the Governor General and the Commander-in-Chief was carried on through Captain Bruce. Outram was still anxious about the garrison of the Alambagh, who would soon be in straits for provisions, and on the 7th October he wrote to Major McIntyre: '. . . Bhowanee Deen, the bearer, a pensioned zemindar [landholder] will do his best to procure you supplies, but *arrange with him* to introduce what he gets in such a way as to make it appear that *you looted his carts* on passing near your post. Otherwise you would get no second supply. He might be instructed to bring his carts into the vicinity of the Alambagh, when you would creep out and rush upon him with a cheer, and pretend to plunder, taking him and the banians [dealers] with him (to whom the grain belongs) prisoners, and, when out of observation, paying them most liberally in hard cash, from the public treasury, five rupees for every rupee's worth of supplies, and sending them off again with the carts *after dark*, with instructions to repeat the experiment. It is obviously necessary to manage it so that our friends must appear victims.'

The same evening, however, Outram's anxiety was relieved, for McIntyre sent word that a convoy of Commissariat carts, with an escort of two hundred and seventy men and two guns, had come up from Cawnpore without mishap.

Sunday the 4th October had been appointed by the Governor General as a day of humiliation and prayer throughout the whole of India. A special service was held at noon at the Brigade Mess, where there was a large congregation, nearly all of whom communicated. Another service was held at Fayrer's house at three o'clock. Mrs Germon and some of her friends appeared in the clean dresses they had been saving up to celebrate the relief of the Residency. During the day Captain Germon took his wife to see the Judicial post, at which he had commanded since the beginning of the siege. She was shocked to see a mere mass of ruins, surrounded by a bamboo stockade, and was more thankful than ever that he was still alive. Now that the defences had been extended she was able to visit her husband in his own quarters, whereas till now it had been so dangerous to move about inside the entrenchment that he had always come across to her.

The old garrison took a delight in walking out of the entrenchment where it was now sheltered by the new defences and remarking how different the works looked from outside. Captain Sanders, commanding at the Financial post, wrote: 'When it was in my power to go outside the line of defences, and look at my house, I was really struck dumb with astonishment at the enemy's want of pluck. You might have driven a buggy into the compound, and the verandah wall was so damaged that I walked over it with the greatest ease.' The enemy had not lacked industry, however, and the garrison were amazed to see how much labour they had expended on their lines. Many of the batteries were surrounded by trenches twenty feet deep and three feet wide, in which there were ladders placed at intervals, presumably to enable the sentries to go down and listen for the sound of the pick.

Captain Spurgin, Madras Fusileers, who had brought in Neill's body on the 26th September, wrote as follows: 'We are now living in a part of the Palace of Lucknow, but such a scene of filth, mixed up with costly things, it is impossible to imagine. The finest china of the latest pattern from Bond Street, or some other fashionable tradespeople, used by the soldiers of the force, cookboys, or anyone. Cookboys sitting on damask stools, cooking the men's dinners; shawls and ornaments all kicking about, no one being at the trouble to carry them for want of the means; and all this mixed up with the dead bodies of sepoys, horses, camels, until the stench is so great we can hardly sit—and no one to move all this filth. The men are all fighting, clearing the town, and the natives, with their abominable caste, refusing to touch a single thing.' The flies were as numerous and repulsive as ever.

After the palaces were captured the soldiers went round hawking china and all sorts of useful and valuable loot. Mrs Harris was glad of the chance to buy seven pairs of stockings, which she had badly needed. Among the plunder were jewels, shawls, rolls of silk, swords and daggers richly chased, books, pictures, clocks, telescopes, and pistols; but soon all except the crockery was declared to be prize, and agents were appointed to collect it.

Now that more labour was available the general organisation inside the entrenchment was much improved. The magazine was put in order, the spare shot and shell being collected, gauged, and piled. All the spare small-arms, too, were collected and large supplies of ammunition were prepared. Many of the relieving force had been armed with the Enfield rifle, which they had found so effective in the field that they were loath to revert to the old Brown Bess percussion musket for lack of rifle cartridges. A manufactory of Enfield ammunition was therefore established under Major North, 60th Rifles, assisted by Lieutenant Sewell, of the old garrison, who fortunately possessed a bullet mould. For close work, however, there were many who still preferred the smoothbore musket, since they found it quicker to load. While these military improvements were being made, Dr Ogilvie was given enough labour to overhaul the sanitary arrangements, and gradually the filth and carcases were cleared away from the neighbourhood of the entrenchment and the palaces. The buried treasure was exhumed and placed in charge of the civil authorities.

The recent increase of sick and wounded had taxed the resources of the medical department. Two large tents were pitched near the hospital, a room in the Begam Kothi was turned over to wounded officers, and further accommodation was provided in the inner Sikh Square. Old tents were cut up for bedding, and plentiful supplies of linen were brought in from the palaces, but there was a serious shortage of medical stores; there was little or no chloroform; milk, arrowroot, sago, and tapioca were scarce; and in spite of increased accommodation the wards were overcrowded. Mortality was high. Many of the wounds became gangrenous, and sometimes a trivial injury would go on sloughing till the patient died. The odds on death following the amputation of a limb were still overwhelming.

Now that the nearest of the enemy's batteries were out of action the upper storey of Gubbins' house was occupied again. Mr Gubbins took advantage of this to bring several officers across from the hospital, where they were making little progress, and give them a chance to recover in healthier conditions. Among them were Lieutenant Colonel Fraser Tytler, the younger Havelock, and Bonham, inventor of 'The Ship'. Both Outram and Havelock were frequent visitors in the wards, and a number of the women made their way to the hospital every day, braving stray bullets, to bathe the heads of the sufferers or read the Bible to the dying. Some of them cut their hair short lest it should fall down as they bent over the beds. There was little complaint from the patients; on one of Outram's visits a soldier who had come up with the relieving column smiled at him and said: 'We've saved them, sir.'

Gradually conditions in the hospital were improved. It was now safe to reopen the upper storey, which was occupied by the 32nd and the artillerymen of the old garrison. It was a welcome change to men who had been lying in the stench and semi-darkness down below to have fresh air through the windows and a view of the country across the river. The lower wards, which were given up to the sick and wounded of the relieving force, were still crowded, but fortunately it was found that the doors and windows need not now be so closely barricaded, and in any case the weather was growing cooler.

On the 2nd October rations were reduced all round. The daily issue for the European troops was now as follows:

12 oz. meat, about half of which was bone.
1 lb. ground wheat.
4 oz. rice.
1½ oz. salt.

The European women received:

6 oz. meat, including bone.
12 oz. ground wheat.
1½ oz. rice.
1 oz. grain.
½ oz. salt.

The Indian troops had their rations cut severely, while the camp-followers now received only:

1 lb. wheat.
2 oz. grain.
¼ oz. salt.

The beef was provided by the gun-bullocks and was pretty tough; a marrow bone was a great luxury. Some of the wheat had been allowed to become damp and mouldy, and was believed to cause diarrhoea and dysentery. No bakers had come in with Havelock's force and the Europeans still found the chapatties irritating to the bowels. The lack of green food was being felt more and more. Scurvy was increasing, and the least contusion might cause extensive ecchymosis: an officer who came to consult Dr Fayrer one day had been scared to find that his legs had turned blue after simply jumping down from a low wall. The rations never quite satisfied either the men or the women. One day when Outram was making his morning rounds, he passed a group of men who were eating their breakfast and remarked: 'I am very sorry, my men, to be obliged to reduce your rations.' One of them replied cheerfully: 'I shouldn't mind at all, General, if my appetite were not so uncommonly good.'

Some of the Lucknow residents had still their private stores. Mrs Inglis had enough arrowroot left for her own party, and was even able to give some away. She still had candles, too, though they had to be used very sparingly. Before leaving Cawnpore, Brigadier General Neill had prepared a box of comforts, such as sago, arrowroot, candles, and wine, for those of the ladies whom he knew. Captain Spurgin brought the box into the entrenchment and distributed the contents, some arrowroot and sago falling to the share of Mrs Case. The Madras Fusileers had clubbed together to provide a similar box, but this had been left at the Alambagh with the heavy baggage.

The troops engaged in sorties were always hoping to find food in the houses they occupied; indeed his friends said of Sam Lawrence, the burly commandant of the Redan, that this was his motive in volunteering for such dangerous service. Harry Metcalfe was lucky enough, one day, to find himself alone in a yard with some game fowl, two of which he was able to capture before his mates arrived. He also found some flour in a shed and emptied it into a puggaree which he unwound from his cap. A corporal named King saw what he was doing and said: 'Harry, you'd better throw away that flour.'

'Why, George?' asked Metcalfe.

'It might be poisoned, Harry, you know.'

'Poison here or poison there, George.' said Metcalfe, 'I'll stick to it. I might as well die of poison as die of hunger.'

On his return Metcalfe refused the most princely offers for his fowls, one of which he gave to Mrs Harris, and the other to a lady whose children he was sorry for because he knew they had been brought up, before the siege, with every luxury. The flour was made into a rude kind of bread, which Metcalfe thought the sweetest he had ever tasted. Now that rations had been reduced again he could not feed the dog Bustle, and decided, reluctantly, to give him back to Mr Harris, who somehow found means to keep him.

Though abstemious by habit the Indian servants and camp-followers found their rations very scanty, yet they worked well and bore their hardships with unvarying patience. Many of the servants showed an admirable devotion to their masters. Fraser Tytler, for instance, had his horse shot under him when entering the city, and was severely wounded later in the day; but his groom, left without orders, ran the gauntlet of the streets with the saddle and holsters on his head, and brought them safe into the entrenchment. He was most solicitous in nursing his master, and often crept out at night, at the risk of being shot by the sentries, to gather wild herbs for a kind of salad which seemed to be an antidote to gangrene.

The enemy still harassed the defenders by bursts

of firing in the night, accompanied by shouting and the sounding of shrill, discordant horns. They hoisted chapatties at the end of long poles, taunting the garrison, whom they knew to be straitened for victuals, and assuring them that they had but a few days left to live. They themselves were so short of roundshot that they once fired a smoothing-iron into the entrenchment, and so short of ball ammunition that they cut up the telegraph wires into slugs. The line was made of 3/8″ iron rods—such a heavy gauge being chosen, it was popularly supposed, because the monkeys used to swing on the wires and break them—and these improvised slugs answered their purpose at short ranges, inflicting the most ugly wounds. More was known of what was going on outside now that Outram had organised a new Intelligence Department; it was reported that the boy king of Oudh was the merest puppet and that the power was in the hands of the sepoys, who elected their own officers and, if they chose, degraded them again.

After his prolonged efforts to relieve the Residency Havelock was much exhausted, both in body and mind. For some years his health had been precarious, but in March of the same year he had written from Persia, where he was commanding a division under Outram: 'Harry and I have kept our health so far; I am sixty-two, but I think can campaign as merrily as in 1846. The recoil on the constitution may however be more severe.' The recoil had come at last. He found that now he could not face the hardships of a siege so easily as in 1842, when he had been one of the 'illustrious garrison' of Jalalabad, and the doctors told him he would have little hope of pulling through but for the excellent sherry sent across by Mr Gubbins. Fortunately his duties were not heavy since the defence of the palaces devolved chiefly on his engineers; indeed, once his morning rounds were over, there was little for him to do, and he spent much of his time reading books from Gubbins' library.

He was a small, stiff, upright man, with handsome features, a tanned complexion, and grey hair, whiskers, and beard which were already turning white. They had laughed at him in Calcutta, where he always wore his sword and medals in society, and on his appointment to command the Movable Column to relieve Cawnpore he had been sneered at as a fossil general, only fit to be made into pipeclay. He was a student of the art of war to the point of pedantry, but the campaign that had ended at the Baillie Guard gate had proved him a practitioner too. His men admired his coolness and decision in the field, but he was too hard on them to be loved. They thought that if only he would swear from time to time, when things went wrong, it would be more comfortable for them all, but Havelock never swore. He was an ardent Baptist, a rigid moralist, and a constant student of the Bible, without being a fanatic; he had a vein of grim humour, liked society, and would not always refuse a glass of wine. He was ready in retort, grandiloquent in harangue, Napoleonic in despatches. In spite of his ordinary reserve he had great powers of conciliation when he chose to use them.

Outram was only fifty-four, nearly eight years younger than Havelock, and his opposite in many respects. He, too, was a handsome man, but dark, thick-set, and asthmatical, with purple veins in his face, a broad and open forehead, and a penetrating and expressive eye. A devout churchman, he was not, however, so much occupied as Havelock with religion. His genial humour and care for the comfort of his men commanded the readiest affection. Havelock's perfect disregard of danger was less natural than acquired, whereas Outram had been born with the mad daring that, in his younger days, had enabled him to dominate the wild men of Khandesh. The Bayard of India, as Charles Napier had dubbed him, was always sensitive on the point of honour, and often quick in temper, though as quick to regret a rough word after it was spoken. His first thought on receiving good news was always to pass it on to the troops, himself, as soon as possible. He was a heavy smoker who gave away cheroots by the handful. The old garrison could not but admire him when they noticed that, while most of the relieving force had not yet acquired their own indifference to the enemy's fire, Outram never ducked to musket-ball or roundshot.

After the excitement of Havelock's entrance the families were beginning to settle down again to the monotony of the siege. The few newspapers that had been brought in were eagerly sought, and even the advertisements were welcome, speaking as they did of the quiet routine of Calcutta life. Mrs Bartrum had been relieved of the heaviest of her work by her husband's two servants, who had brought in his horse and a few of his personal belongings, but she still had enough to do. Now that the weather was becoming cooler she was making warm clothes for her boy, whose health seemed to be improving. All she hoped for now was to rear him and take him back safe to England, where he would be loved for his father's sake; for herself, she cared little how long relief might be in coming. She took the boy out into the fresh air every day, though there was still some danger of being hit by a stray shot. One evening her Indian bearer was wounded close beside her, the ball glancing across the child's leg.

Mrs Polehampton and Mrs Gall spent their days at the hospital, Mrs Barbor not being strong enough to take up the work again. Every evening as soon as it was dark Mrs Polehampton went across to the churchyard, where she spent an hour sitting by her husband's grave. There were often bullets flying over her head, and several shells burst close beside her, but she was never hit.

On the night of the 9th October, the siege having now lasted a hundred and two days, Mr Gubbins was roused by Mr Money, Outram's secretary, with the news that the whole of Delhi was now in British hands, that the last of the Moguls and his Begam had been captured, and that in spite of the heavy losses of the Delhi force a column had already marched for Oudh under Brigadier Greathed. The runner who had brought in the despatch reported that the Alambagh was not strictly invested, and that the garrison were able to obtain supplies from the countryside. It was now rumoured that Man Singh, who was known to have thrown in his lot with the mutineers, had offered to escort the women and children from the Residency to a place of safety, but with the memory of Cawnpore fresh in their minds they would have been sorry to entrust themselves to his care. Next day Captain Bruce sent word that Greathed had engaged and routed a body of mutineers on his way down from Delhi.

On the same day the following paragraph appeared in Outram's Divisional Orders: 'The Major General [Havelock] commanding the Field Force is requested to take the strictest measures to prevent the men of the different Brigades from going outside the pickets on any pretence. The bodies of five men belonging to the Artillery, who had gone out, it is supposed in search of liquor, two days ago, were found without their heads.'

On the 11th October Outram wrote to Captain Bruce that the Alambagh must on no account be evacuated, as its occupation was essential to the safety of the force in Lucknow. He concluded: 'By the strictest scrutiny it is ascertained that at our present rate (three-quarters rations for Europeans, and half for natives) our grain, allowing it to be all good, will last only till the 6th of November; our meat not so long. Rice will be out in four days. Unless, therefore, the Delhi troops come speedily to our aid, we must starve. Promulgate the news of the approach of the Delhi force as publicly as possible. Urge Greathed to push on with all possible despatch.'

The enemy's miners were now hard at work trying to breach the walls of the palaces, while the garrison were digging an immense system of countermines under the supervision of Captain Crommelin, Bengal Engineers. Although the soil was for the most part light and sandy, it was still found possible to dispense with casing and supports. There was now some fear of powder running short, and it was therefore usual to break into the enemy's mines and drive the workmen out, instead of blowing them up. As time went on the enemy became so cautious that they often fired the charge long before they were underneath their objective.

Many of Havelock's men who had given ample proof that they feared nothing in the field found the underground warfare a serious test of their mettle. In the early days of October one of them who had ventured down a mine for the first time returned in disorder, having been scared out of the gallery by a harmless fall of earth. The officer in charge asked him: 'What did you think?—That the enemy were coming at you?'

'I suppose so.'

'Well, no one knows better than you that if you think the enemy are there, you should go at them and not back from them.'

'Quite so, sir, but I didn't think at all; down below is very different from up above.'

A day or two later a noted wit appeared at mess, having just returned from his first descent, with a studied expression of dismay, and began to describe the terrors of mining. When some of the others chaffed him he offered to place a bottle of brandy at the far end of a gallery and bet ten pounds that no one who had not been down before would bring the bottle out. The bet found no takers, though before long most members of the mess had become familiar with the work.

One day Lieutenant Innes was told that mysterious sounds had been detected from a countermine at the Chhattar Manzil. On going down to listen he heard the sound of a gentle scraping, evidently very close. He told the sergeant to stop at the next bend in the gallery and to post a chain of men, one at each turn from there to the shaft, in case of accidents, while he himself waited at the point to which the sound seemed nearest. The scraping could still be heard at intervals. After a little Innes chanced to turn his head, and noticed a speck of light on the other side of his own gallery. Since he himself was sitting in the dark, it was clear that a tiny beam must be coming from the enemy's mine, and after a close scrutiny he found the hole, which was, however, too small for him to see through. He waited patiently while the cautious scraping continued. Soon it stopped, and there was a sound of whispering, followed by more scraping. Then, as he saw the hole beginning to grow larger, Innes broke down the thin partition of earth. The miners put out the light and ran for their lives, followed by several revolver shots from Innes, who went after them with the sergeant but could not catch them. The enemy then began firing down the shaft, and, thinking that they were about to be blown up, poured down skinful after skinful of water to drown the powder. Innes and his men replied with shouts of laughter and abuse. In the end it was decided to hold the gallery as a listener.

Mr Kavanagh, the volunteer who had done so well as a guide to the sorties, was appointed Assistant Field Engineer with several others. At first he found it nervous work, but after a number of successful brushes with the enemy he discovered that courage and resolution were even more at a premium below than above ground. Crawling about in the mines proved so hard upon his clothes that he fetched some coarse canvas from one of the palaces and made himself a suit of dungarees.

One day the enemy broke into a gallery in which he was waiting for them. After mortally wounding one of the miners with a pistol shot, he also hit a sepoy who came down to see what was the matter. Kavanagh then crept into the enemy's gallery, where he lay listening to the commotion up above and taunting them in the vernacular, until they began to fire down the shaft. As soon as the smoke had driven him back to his own gallery, the enemy recovered their wounded, but Kavanagh soon returned with a couple of Sikhs and began abusing them again. He charged them with ingratitude, cruelty to women and children, and cowardice, and told them that they and their families would soon be ruined.

'Why,' he asked, 'have you mutinied, and what can you expect from the atrocities you have perpetrated?'

'We are fighting,' they answered, 'for our religion, which you meant to destroy.'

'In what manner have we threatened your faith?'

'By giving us greased cartridges.'

Kavanagh explained that this was a mistake. They

seemed to be impressed by his arguments, but soon one of their own officers came up and ordered them to fire, and afterwards they began to fill up the shaft with earth. When Outram heard about this parley he startled some of his visitors by telling them that, since the articles of war condemned a man to death for conferring with the enemy, Kavanagh was to be hanged.

By now the mornings and evenings were becoming pleasantly cool, and the nights were sometimes too keen for the comfort of the troops, though it was still hot in the middle of the day. The general standard of health seemed to be improving with the change in the weather. The men were still fretted by the lack of tobacco, and tried to stifle the craving by smoking tea-leaves and leaves from the trees and shrubs. As the siege dragged on both men and women became more and more tired of the continual diet of sinewy beef and chapatties. 'What a luxury it will be', wrote Ensign Inglis, 63rd Native Infantry, 'to get bread, butter, eggs, fish, milk, fruit, vegetables, etc., again. How jolly to be able to get a ride again, to be able to come in and go out, to go to bed and get up again whenever you like; to sleep in pyjamahs [loose trousers] and night shirt, without boots and stockings on etc.' On the 15th October one of the masters of the Martinière College surprised the boys by producing a plum-cake in honour of his own birthday. The same day Mrs Soppitt wrote in her diary: 'Mrs Ogilvie gave us a glass of sherry. The first I have tasted for months. Quite a treat. Seems to put a little life into one. People are becoming generous with brighter prospects before them.'

One Sunday a large flock of sparrows alighted on a clump of bamboos in Fayrer's compound. Dr Fayrer was still weak from an attack of fever, but this was too good a chance to miss: he took his shot gun and killed a hundred and fifty of them. They were curried and pronounced delicious, though Mrs Germon could not bring herself to touch them.

The relieving force had reached the Residency with what they had on their backs, the baggage having been left at the Alambagh, and they were now as hard put to it for clothes as the original garrison. An old shirt of Captain Fulton's, covered with mud from the mines, fetched £4 10s. at an auction. One day Mr Money bought Outram a coat of distinctive pattern at the sale of Mr Ommanney's effects, and was only just in time to stop the new owner from wearing it on a visit of condolence to the late owner's widow.

In the absence of soap many of the garrison were verminous. Most of the officers had their hair cropped short, and made their servants swill them with buckets of water and scrub them down as if they were horses. One day an elegant subaltern, fresh from England, who had kept himself uncommonly spruce, observed that all the officers of another corps had had their heads shaved. When he enquired why they answered gravely: 'Pediculina.' He raised his eyebrows in sympathy, apparently taking it for some kind of brain fever or choleraic attack. At last they told him what it meant. 'Beastly!' he said, and suggested that they had only themselves to thank for their condition. At that someone shouted: 'Come! Fetch a rake, and let's draw his covert.' A comb was brought, the covert was drawn then and there, and a find was made, at which the exquisite ruefully joined in the laugh against himself.

After the failure of the cavalry to reach the Alambagh it had been suggested that all the horses should be turned out of the position. It was decided, however, to keep them as long as possible, and efforts were made to eke out the fodder by occasional raids on the standing crops across the river, and by sending out the Indian grass-cutters every night to forage, a service from which many of them never returned. Some of the horses died, but a number lived on, though, of course, they fell off deplorably.

On the 16th October Outram wrote to Brigadier Wilson, commanding at Cawnpore, as follows: 'The commissary has just informed me that after the strictest scrutiny, he finds that our attah [ground wheat] and bullocks (we have nothing else) will last only till 18th proximo, on half rations for natives, and three-quarters for Europeans. No possibility of our obtaining supplies unless previously relieved.

The Delhi column must push on to Alambagh. Spare no cost in sending express to Greathed, urging his immediate advance, and let there be no delay in bringing troops up from Allahabad. . . .'

On the 17th October the enemy sprung a mine under one of the outposts at the Farhat Bakhsh, killing three men. The same day they blew up part of the wall of the garden post beyond the Chhattar Manzil and advanced towards the breach with colours flying; but when their leaders had been shot down they retreated, leaving twelve of their number dead. From the loopholes of a building on the south side of this post the garrison could still see the doolies in which the wounded had been butchered on the 26th September.

On the 20th October a runner brought in despatches from Captain Bruce at Cawnpore with further news of Rajah Man Singh. He had written to Bruce, enclosing a letter for Outram, explaining that he had been forced by circumstances to take up arms against the British Government, and did not wish to be associated with the rebels. Bruce's reply had concluded as follows: 'I have written to-day to General Outram, who is now in the Lucknow Residency, and in the meantime if you are really friendly to the British Government, you are desired at once to withdraw all your men from Lucknow and communicate with the Chief Commissioner [Outram]. I have sent to tell your Vakil [agent] that if he likes to come in and see me, he will meet with no injury.' The agent had come in to say that Man Singh was willing to do as Bruce required, and had then left for Lucknow.

Great hopes were aroused by the prospect of Man Singh's defection from the rebel cause, but nothing more was seen of his agent. On the 24th October Inglis told his wife that all prospect of coming to terms with the Rajah was at an end, and that the garrison could only await the arrival of the second relieving force; meanwhile rations were to be reduced again. It seemed, however, that Man Singh was still hedging, for next day he sent in another message for Outram. The garrison took the keenest interest in the news of Man Singh, the Delhi Column, and the troops that were advancing up country, and it was hoped that the Residency would be relieved by about the 7th November.

On the 26th October Major North wrote in his journal: 'Most truly can each individually exclaim with the Psalmist: "My bones look out and stare upon me."' The quotation was inspired by the reduction of rations that Inglis had foretold. The European troops were now to receive half a pound of meat, half a pound of wheat, a little rice, and half an ounce of salt. The total numbers returned by the Commissariat on the 21st October had been as follows:

European men - - -	2396
,, women - - -	243
,, children - -	227
Indian troops - - -	755
,, camp-followers - -	2706
,, servants - - -	611
Total -	6938

On the 26th October Captain Bruce sent word that Greathed's column had routed a rebel force at Agra, and was due to reach Cawnpore by the 1st

November, Colonel Hope Grant of the 9th Lancers being now in command. It was hoped that a force of six thousand men would be concentrated at Cawnpore by the 10th November and would reach the Residency by the 15th. It was also reported that a large convoy of supplies had arrived at the Alambagh. On the night of the 27th October news came through from Bruce that Hope Grant's column had arrived on the previous day. The siege had now lasted a hundred and twenty days.

It was still difficult to find bearers for private communications, but Lieutenant Moorsom was fortunate enough to get the following letter smuggled through the enemy's lines:

'*Lucknow*, *27th October*.

My Dearest Mother,

All right physically and mentally, brain, body and limbs, to date. We relieved Lucknow from its instant peril, and are now ourselves occupying a more extended position in the town, blockaded with the garrison. Write to Inglis's, Gubbins', and Couper's people, if possible, to say that they and theirs are all well. We have grub, abundant ammunition, good quarters, plenty of fighting men, stout hearts, and our God on our side; on the other, our enemy numerous, but cowardly, with a scarcity of iron and lead for guns. Had we not many women and children, and sick and wounded, we could walk out of the town at any time.

As it is, we can hold our own, and steadily make small advances until reinforcements arrive. I tried once before to ease your anxieties by writing, but the messenger was compelled to throw away his despatches before falling into the hands of the enemy.

This goes through the beleaguering host, so you will, I hope, see the necessity for my writing no more fully. Mother mine! don't deem me "down among the dead men" until you hear it on the best authority; and with very dearest love to all,

Believe me your truly affectionate son,

W. R. Moorsom.'

It was now understood that the mutinous Gwalior Contingent, who had hitherto been kept out of harm's way by the diplomacy of Maharajah Sindhia, had accepted the offer of Tantia Topi, one of the Nana Sahib's retainers, to lead them against the British, and were marching in from the west to join hands with the Nana and the mutineers from Dinapore. In view of this threat to Cawnpore it was clear that the Commander-in-Chief, Sir Colin Campbell, could only make the relief of the Residency his first object by risking the communications of the relieving force, whereas, if he first struck a swift and crushing blow at the Gwalior Contingent and their allies, he would be able to extricate the Lucknow garrison at his leisure.

With this dilemma in his mind Outram wrote to

Bruce as follows on the 28th October: 'I received last night, by the hands of Kanauji Lal, your letters of the 24th and 25th, with duplicate of that of the 16th (neither the original nor Bussarut have come).

'Kanauji has certainly proved himself most zealous and able, has richly earned reward, and shall assuredly obtain it. Having such faith in him, I purpose sending a plan and further instructions to the officer commanding the relieving force by him to-night, if ready in time.

'If not ready to send by him, I hope it may safely reach Alambagh by other means, there to await the arrival of Colonel Grant, or whoever may be in command of the force. I shall not detain Kanauji beyond to-night, being anxious to prevent the force being hurried from Cawnpore to Alambagh. The latter post, having now been amply supplied with food, and sufficiently strengthened to defy attack, is no longer a source of anxiety; and however desirable it may be to support me here, I cannot but feel that it is still more important that the Gwalior rebels (said to be preparing to cross into the Doab) should be first disposed of. I would therefore urge on Brigadier Wilson, to whom I beg you will communicate this as if addressed to himself, that I consider that the Delhi column, strengthened to the utmost by all other troops that can be spared from Cawnpore, should in the first instance be employed against the Gwalior rebels, should they attempt to cross into the Doab [the country between the Jumna and the

Ganges], or be tangible to assault elsewhere within reasonable distance. We can manage to screw on, if absolutely necessary, till near the end of November on further reduced rations. Only the longer we remain the less physical strength we shall have to aid our friends when they do advance, and the fewer guns shall we be able to move out in co-operation.

'But it is so obviously to the advantage of the State that the Gwalior rebels should be first effectually destroyed, that our relief should be a secondary consideration. I trust, therefore, that Brigadier Wilson will furnish Colonel Grant with every possible aid to effect that object before sending him here. . . . Telegraph the substance of the above to the Commander-in-Chief, so much as relates to the advisability of taking measures to guard against the invasion of the Doab by the Gwalior mutineers.'

On the 30th October Outram wrote to Major McIntyre at the Alambagh, enclosing a plan of the city and its environs accompanied by detailed suggestions for the route to be taken by the relieving force. He was naturally anxious lest this important packet, which was hidden in the runner's bamboo staff, should be taken by the enemy, and he asked McIntyre to hoist a flag as soon as it arrived. It was proposed that, instead of marching straight into the city by the Charbagh bridge as Havelock's force had done, the second relieving column should take a wide sweep to the right by the Dilkusha, and then work round by the Martinière College and the Sikandarbagh, keeping to the open as far as possible. Outram added: 'You will, I suppose, leave all the heavy baggage at Alambagh, bringing only light carts, elephants, camels, and pony or bullock carriages, to the Dilkusha. But I beg you will bring the kits of the European troops here; for the cold weather is coming on, and they have neither greatcoats nor bedding.

'When you advance from the Dilkusha, I hope you will be able to bring on with you a few days' supply of rum, tobacco, and tea, for the Europeans (who have been so long without these luxuries), and gram [chick-pea] for our horses. Other supplies, which are less pressing, we can obtain when an escort can go back to the Dilkusha for more. . . .'

Next day McIntyre's flag was seen to be flying, whereupon one of the garrison suggested speaking to the Alambagh by semaphore. Although the distance was about three and a half miles as the crow flies, and there was often a low haze over the city, the authorities decided to make the attempt. Particulars of the semaphore system were found under the heading 'Telegraph' in the *Penny Cyclopaedia* in Mr Gubbins' library, and on the 31st October Outram concluded a despatch to McIntyre as follows: 'I enclose a plan for telegraphic communication; your share of which Sibley [McIntyre's second-in-command] will, I hope, be able to construct, as I know he is a great mechanic. Ours will,

I hope, be ready in a couple of days, and you will be able to make it out from the top of your house. A second set of apparatus should be got ready to send with the relieving column, for the purpose of being placed on the top of the Martinière.

'The evening before the day on which we purpose telegraphing to you, a bonfire will be lit on the highest point of our position (the Residency roof), to enable you to know exactly our whereabouts. A similar illumination on the top of the Alambagh will be proof to us that our signal has succeeded.

'We shall signal at twelve, noon, of each day, the time best suited; for the enemy annoy us least at this hour, and our signallers consequently will incur less danger.

'Even should our signals fail from your being too far from us, still do not delay in having two sets of telegraphic apparatus prepared; for so soon as we establish one set of apparatus at the Martinière, and yours also is ready, the signals will be carried on without difficulty.'

The siege was now in its fifth month, and the very knowledge that relief was at hand seemed to make the days drag more tediously than ever. The enemy kept their distance, playing at long bowls, as the garrison said, and there were neither sorties to be made nor assaults to be repelled. On the 1st November Captain Sanders wrote: 'The garrison, they say, is to go to Cawnpore. I shall be glad of the change, for I am getting tired of this kind of work, and a vegetable diet is absolutely necessary for the perfect recovery of our health, which has been failing latterly. The sick and wounded will bless the day that sees them out of it. Visions of fresh butter, milk, and eggs have been floating before me for the last three months. What would I give for a dish of Devonshire cream!' On the 2nd November Mrs Soppitt wrote in her journal: 'Mrs Ogilvie gave me a cup of coffee and a glass of liqueur. Such a treat in these hard times.' Mr Gubbins noted that Havelock was looking pale and thin.

Mrs Bartrum's little boy was growing stronger every day, and his mother used to think how happy his recovery would have made his father. The child was not yet two years old, but he had a sad, elderly look. His chief amusement was calling to the monkeys on the roofs, who sometimes came down to pick up scraps. Like many others Mrs Bartrum was driven to using 'basin', a preparation of grain which was ground into a paste with water, in place of soap; but food was so scarce that sometimes she hardly knew whether to use the grain to wash with or to eat.

On the 4th November Charles Dashwood was sitting sketching in the Residency garden when he was severely wounded in the feet by a roundshot. Both legs were amputated below the knee, but the surgeons held out little hope of his recovery. This was a cruel blow to Mrs Dashwood, who had come to rely on her brother-in-law since losing her husband from cholera. When she went to see him in the evening he knew her but seemed very low. Next day he was better, and there was a faint hope that he might live to see England again.

On the 6th November it was reported that the Delhi column were already on the way up to the Alambagh, that Sir Colin himself had arrived at Cawnpore, and that he was expected to reach the Alambagh on the 10th at latest, with a force of 5,100 bayonets, 600 sabres, and 36 guns, including three 8-inch howitzers and three 32-pounders. On the strength of this news some of the garrison drank their last bottle of wine and smoked their last cheroot. It was also reported that the Gwalior Contingent were still advancing on Cawnpore, but apparently Sir Colin had determined to relieve the Residency at all hazards, disregarding the threat to his rear. Inglis guessed that the women and children and sick and wounded would be evacuated at once. The siege had now lasted a hundred and thirty days.

The weather was rapidly becoming colder. Those who possessed warm clothing brought it out, but most of the troops had only summer kit and went cold as well as hungry. Havelock's men were instructed to cut holes in the native quilts that were to be found in the palaces and wear them poncho-fashion when on sentry. The weather naturally sharpened their appetites: one day some of the Madras Fusileers killed and ate Mrs Couper's milch goat and two kids belonging to Mrs Inglis. More than once a ravenous soldier dashed into somebody's kitchen, snatched up a chapatti, slammed down a rupee, and ran away.

Meanwhile there was no sign of the semaphore at the Alambagh. It was guessed that the despatch of the 31st October had miscarried, and on the 7th November Outram sent a further letter to McIntyre, repeating his general instructions and enclosing a fresh code. He added: 'I have requested the officer commanding the relieving force to light a beacon fire on the top of the Alambagh at 8 P.M., on the evening before advancing to Dilkusha. To prevent mistakes, a salvo of four or more guns should be fired *twice*. I have requested him to fire a similar salvo three times (five minutes' interval) at 2 P.M. on the day of his arrival at Alambagh.

'You ask me to write in the English character; so would the enemy wish me to do. As the only security against their understanding what we write in case our letters fall into their hands, the Greek character *must* be used.'

On the night of the 8th November Kanauji Lal came in with despatches from Cawnpore. Hearing next morning of his arrival, Mr Kavanagh, who was still at large in spite of Outram's threat, resolved to broach a scheme which had been forming in his mind since he had chanced to see the plans of the city being prepared for the relieving force. Remembering what difficulties Havelock's column had encountered, although both Outram and Moorsom were familiar with the city, and believing that the enemy were now in even greater strength, Kavanagh thought it would be helpful if someone who knew the ground made his way out to the Alambagh to guide the column in. Outram's plans and proposals applied to one route only, and might be of little use if the chances of war forced Sir Colin to find another way.

Kavanagh therefore went to see Kanauji Lal, who was to return that night, and told him that he thought of going with him in disguise. The runner replied that the risk of taking a companion, let alone a European, was too great, but Kavanagh would not accept his refusal and at last persuaded him to consider the plan. At first Kanauji Lal suggested leaving the entrenchment by different ways and meeting outside the city, but he agreed that this was out of the question on finding that Kavanagh's knowledge of the city byways was not complete, and that his Hindustani, though fluent, was not faultless.

Knowing that any chance of success depended on the runner's assistance, Kavanagh had sounded him before making up his own mind. Now he went away to a quiet corner to think the matter out. He was so amazed at the daring of his own conception that at first he was unable to compose his thoughts. During the past few months he had risked his life often enough in action, but to contemplate death in cold blood made his heart beat faster, and the tears ran down his cheeks as he sat there with his head in his hands. The violence of his emotion brought its own relief, but finding himself still incapable of a calm decision he joined some of his friends and deliberated as he talked. By two o'clock he was resolved to volunteer for the service.

He made his offer to Colonel Napier, who replied with a smile that the thing was impossible, but thought it only fair to pass him on to Outram. Kavanagh explained why he had volunteered and asked Outram to balance the advantage to be gained by success against the risk of a single life. The proposal could not but appeal to the Bayard of India, who admitted that Kavanagh's services as guide might be invaluable, and that he was tempted to accept his offer but feared that the risk was prohibitive. Kavanagh pleaded so earnestly, however, that at last Outram agreed to let him go so long as he could find an adequate disguise; but even after laying before him his plans for the relief he insisted that Kavanagh was not in any way committed, and might yet draw back from the attempt. While Kavanagh was making his final decision the following despatch was prepared:

Sir,

I σενδ un σκετch du γρουνδ ιντερυενινγ βετωην αλυμ βαγ et cette ποσιτιον et βεγ à συγεστ θη φολοωινγ μοδε d'οπερατιονς as that whereby vous may εφεκτ une jυνκτιον avec nous avec le λεαστ διφικυλτη. φρομ αλυμ βαγ πασινγ ρουνδ le σουθερν φασε de l'ενκλοσυρε et βετωην les υιλαγες de ὑσhτνυγρ et πορωα et προσηδινγ αλμοστ δυε εαστ pour αβουτ trois μιλες ουερ un λευελ κουντρη de γρας λανδ et κυλτιυατιον avec un σhαλοω jhηλ à κροςς σhορτλη après ληυινγ αλυμ βαγ (προβαβλη pas plus θαν ανκλε δηπ νοω et νο οβστακλε aux γυνς) vous will αριυε οποσιτε à la υιλαγε de jαμαιτα sur votre λεφτ—σλαντινγ παστ wh pour αβουτ une μιλε à νορθ εαστ vous αριυε à la διλκυσhαρ παλασε—rien mais le παρκ ωαλ ιντερυενινγ αβουτ ειτ φητ ἱ, wh est βροκεν δοων dans μανη πλασες et κουλδ βη νοκεδ δοων ανηωhερε par a κουπλε δες πιονηρς. Le παλασε ἁυινγ λαργε ωινδοως en ευροπεαν στιλε n'est pas λικελη être δεφενδεδ, mais ιφ σο, a φευ κανον σhοτ wd σοον εμτη ιτ et ινδηδ j'αντισιπατε λιτλε οp νο οποσιτιον à votre οκυπατιον de διλκυσhαp παλασε et παpκ οp des νειγhβουpινγ μαpτινιèpε or βιβιαποpε maisons shd vous θινκ νεσεσαpη, l'ενεμη's τpωπς βεινγ chηφλη sur θις σιδε du καναλ. L'υνιον jακ όιστεδ au τοπ de la παλασε et un pοyαλ σαλυτε φpομ υος γυνς à δpαω notre ατεντιον το ιτ, shd vous άυε άδ νο πpευιους φιpινγ wd ινφοpμ nous de votre αpιυαλ et notre υνιον wh nous wd θεν όιστ sur la chυτp μαν3ιλ παλασε (διστανт deux à trois μιλες) will show vous que nous sommes ινφοpμεδ. A la διλκυσhαp vous avez un οπεν μαιδαν pour ενκαμπμεντ οφ νηpλη une μιλε βετωην le παλασε & un δηπ καναλ βετωην vous et la ville, les βpιδγες sur wh sont βpοκεν δοων. Par ενκαμπινγ avec votre φpοντ to θη καναλ avec vos γυνς en votre φpοντ ετ φλανκς vous wd κηπ δοων ανη φιpε wh l'ενεμη cd βpινγ αγαινστ vous φpομ λε ville σιδε pour ils ont ονλη sept op huit γυνς en διφεpεντ ποσιτιονς sur cette σιδε de la γοομτη γυαpδινγ les διφεpεντ ήγpεσσες τοωαpδς la διλκυσhαp φpομ νοτpε ποσιτιον wh sont οφ διφεpεντ καλιβpε et σο βαδλη φουνδ εν καpιαγες ils wd have σομε διφικυλτη ιν τακινγ θεμ αωαι à τυpν αγαινστ vous et ιφ ιλς διδ pεμουε θεμ πουp θατ πυpποσε it wd φασιλιτατε notre δαsh ουτ à μητ vous quand vous δο αδυανσε à θις σιδε du καναλ where however ils ne sont pas λικελη à στανδ εξποσεδ as ils θεν wd be à ατακ φpομ φpοντ et pεαp. Under κουεp de vos γυνς vous n'aurez pas de διφικυλτη εν σλοπινγ πασαγες pour votre αρτιλερη δοων votre σιδε ιντο le καναλ et υπ νοτρε σιδε δυρινγ θη φιρστ νιτε ρεαδη à κρος ερλη νεξτ μορνινγ. φυρθερ δελαι, je pense, w[d] be ιμπολιτικ, as it w[d] give l'ενεμη τιμε à βρινγ γυνς φρομ διστακτ πλασες. λεστ μεσενγερς sh[d] μισκαρη votre σιγναλ pour ιντενδινγ à κροςς le καναλ ιν θη μορνινγ might be τροις γυνς φολοωεδ par trois ροκετς la nuit βεφορε, après une ρεκοναισανσε άδ σατισφιεδ vous de la φησιβιλιτη de πρεπαρινγ les σλοπες δυρινγ λα νυιτ. Les βανκς du καναλ sont φρομ vingt à vingt cinq φητ ί, περαπς λεςς τοωαρδς votre droit avec λιτλε ορ νο eau et σουνδ βοτομ. Vous w[d] οφ κουρσε άυε παρτης en οκυπατιον de la διλκυσhαρ παλασε, et après πασινγ le καναλ en σομε des πρινσιπαλ βυιλδινγς κομν· votre λινε de κομ[ν]· mais nous sh[d] μητ vous άλφ ωαι avec un πρετη στρονγ κολυμν d'ευροπεανς et γυνς et w[d] θεν αρανγε τογεθερ le μοδε de μαινταινινγ la κομ[ν]· βετωην votre καμπ sur le καναλ et notre εντρενchμεντ. Vous w[d] περαπς άλτ deux trois jours à αλυμ βαγ et may κοντριυε à donner nous νοτισε du jour de votre αδυανσε. Of course tous les τρωπς à αλυμ βαγ seront υνδερ vos κομανδ et un petit γυαρδ ινκλυδινγ λες κονυαλεσεντς will συφισε à μαινταιν θατ πλασε, θυς πλασινγ σομε cinq ou σιξ cents ευροπεανς à votre διςποσαλ—βεσιδες γυνς.

True Copy. J. Outram.

George Couper,
Secy. Chief Comr.

On leaving headquarters Kavanagh returned to his own room, where he lay on his bed with his back to Mrs Kavanagh, who was busy giving the children their scanty dinner, and whom he dared not face lest she should notice his agitation. She offered him a chapatti but he replied that he was too tired to eat. He lay there thinking of his happy married life, and of the chances that it would soon be coming to an end, until at last, overcome by his feelings, he was fain to hurry out with the excuse that he was wanted in the mines. He went and hid himself in a cellar by the Terhi Kothi, where he tortured himself with the thought of what would become of his family if he were killed. In tears again, he decided to withdraw; but on his way back he turned into the manufactory where Major North and Lieutenant Sewell were preparing Enfield ammunition, and when he left them, after talking for a quarter of an hour about the prospects of relief, he had finally made up his mind to go.

Next he made discreet inquiries for brown dye, without success. He then borrowed separate articles of clothing from different Indians, to avoid any suspicion of his object, and took them home in a bundle. He remained with his family, perfectly composed, until six o'clock, when he kissed them all round and left, saying that he was off to the mines again, and might not be back till late next morning. He carried the bundle to a small room by the slaughterhouse, where Mr Queiros, another volunteer, helped to dress him in a white muslin shirt, yellow silk jacket, tight trousers with a white cummerbund round his waist, a cream turban, a sheet of yellow chintz over his shoulders, native shoes, and a shield and curved sword. Kavanagh then coloured his face, neck, hands, and wrists with lampblack and oil, since he could get nothing better. He was tickled to see how ugly his face looked in the glass, and at the same time uneasy because the colour seemed unnatural. The chances of detection were great, since he was a tall, square-shouldered, large-limbed man with distinctly European eyes and features, reddish or auburn hair, and still lighter moustache and beard. His only hope lay in keeping in the shadow and letting darkness help out his disguise. When Kanauji Lal joined them he was much amused by the changed appearance of the sahib.

Crossing to headquarters Kavanagh walked into the house without taking off his shoes, and sat down in the same room as some of the officers. Such assurance caused quite a stir, for though the staff knew Kavanagh by sight they all took him for an Indian, and even Outram did not recognise him for a time. Kavanagh welcomed this as the happy omen that was wanted to give him confidence. Outram himself put the finishing touches to his make-up amid shouts of laughter from the rest; the turban was carefully adjusted; a pair of wide pyjamahs was given him to cover the tight trousers; and Captain Sitwell, Outram's aide-de-camp, presented him with a small double-barrelled pistol with which to shoot himself should he be taken and threatened, as was likely, with slow death or mutilation. It was arranged that if he ever reached the Alambagh a flag should be hoisted on McIntyre's semaphore. At half-past eight it was time to go, and the laughter ceased as Outram, Napier, and the others pressed Kavanagh's hand and wished him God-speed. He went out with Kanauji Lal and Lieutenant Hardinge, who came as far as the picket on the river bank to pass them out.

The night was dark and there was nothing to show the way but the stars and a few lights flickering across the water. The two men stripped and began to ford the river, which was less than five feet deep and about a hundred yards wide. The shock of the cold water and the nearness of the enemy's lines so daunted Kavanagh that, if his guide had been within arm's length, he would very likely have pulled him back and abandoned the attempt; but as Kanauji Lal was wading on ahead Kavanagh went after him and soon they had reached the opposite bank. They crept along a ditch to a grove of trees beside a pond, where they stopped to dress. A man came down to the pool to wash but did not see them. At this Kavanagh's courage began to rise, and as they moved on and passed a group of huts he remarked to a matchlockman that the night was cold. 'It is very cold,' said the other, 'in fact it *is* a cold night.' Kavanagh replied that it would be still colder by and by, and they passed on towards the iron bridge, where they were questioned by an Indian officer commanding a picket. Kanauji Lal came boldly forward, so that Kavanagh might lurk in the shadow, and soon satisfied the officer that they had come from the Mariaon cantonments and were bound for their homes in the city. They went on by the north bank of the river as far as the stone bridge, passing unregarded through a crowd of sepoys and matchlockmen, and notables in palanquins, whose escorts carried too many torches for Kavanagh's comfort. Crossing the bridge, where the sentry was examining a very shabby Indian, they entered the main street of the city, which was neither so crowded nor so well lit as it had been in time of peace. They were jostled by several armed men, who did not speak to them however, and passed a guard of seven sepoys dallying with some women of the town. Kanauji Lal wished to leave the main thoroughfare and steal out by the darker alleys, but Kavanagh insisted that their best hope lay in courting enquiry. At last they reached the outskirts of the city, and after a perfunctory challenge from the watchmen they struck out into the open country.

It was now five months since Kavanagh had been outside the city and his spirits soared as he smelt the green fields about him. He found a carrot by the roadside and ate it with delight. So far as they could see they were in a wooded country, planted with flowering shrubs and fruit trees. They walked on happily for several miles until they found themselves in the Dilkusha Park, far away to the north-east of the Alambagh. It was now about midnight. They came upon an aged peasant watching his crops outside a village, and asked if he would show them the way, but he said he was too old and lame. When Kavanagh required another villager more peremptorily to guide them, he ran away screaming until all the dogs began to bark, and the two men were forced to run, though Kavanagh's feet were painfully chafed by his unaccustomed shoes. The ground was now broken by frequent ravines, and often the way was barred by garden walls, but at last they came to another village. Entering a hut, Kavanagh groped in the dark until he touched a soft thigh; a woman started up, but when he whispered to her to be quiet she awoke her mother without disturbance, and the good-natured creatures set the travellers on their way.

At about two o'clock they stumbled on an enemy picket, but after the simplest of questions the sepoys let them go and gave them their direction. Kanauji Lal now proposed that instead of trying to enter the Alambagh, which was surrounded by the enemy, they should push on to Sir Colin's camp further down the Cawnpore road: Kavanagh agreed, though he was already tired and his feet were hurting cruelly.

The moon was now rising and they could see their way clear before them. At about three o'clock they reached a grove of mangoes, where there was a fellow singing at the top of his voice. Taking fright at the sound of their footsteps, he called out a guard of twenty-five sepoys, who began asking questions all at once. This was too much for Kanauji Lal, who lost heart for the first time and threw away his despatch; but Kavanagh, whose packet was still safe in his turban, told them they had terrified his companion, and begged them to deal gently with two poor travellers, who were making for a village near Bani to inform a friend that his brother had been killed at Lucknow. The sepoys seemed much relieved to find their visitors so harmless, and showed them which way to go.

After another half-hour's walking they lost themselves in a swamp. Sometimes the water came up to their waists, sometimes to their necks, and the mud clung to their heels and the reeds to their garments as they forced their way through. Where the water was deepest, Kavanagh, being the taller, had to help Kanauji Lal. Sometimes they thought they would never get out. Kavanagh swore at the water, the mud, the reeds, and the mutineers, while the guide, who took things more easily, was amused at the vehemence of the sahib. Soon all the colour was washed off Kavanagh's hands, and he knew that it might cost him his life if the same thing happened to his face. When at last they reached dry land he was so tired that he insisted on resting for a quarter of an hour, though the guide wished to push on at once.

They started off again, passing unseen between two of the enemy's pickets, and after accosting some more villagers, arrived at the corner of another grove at about four o'clock in the morning. Kavanagh, who was now dead beat, lay down to sleep for an hour. Kanauji Lal begged him not to take the risk. Kavanagh, who thought him over-anxious, asked him to enter the grove and see if he could find anyone to tell them where they were. The guide had not gone far when they were both startled by an Indian voice delivering the challenge: 'Hoo cum dar?' Kavanagh could hear Kanauji Lal adroitly framing his reply so as to discover whether these were friends or enemies before committing himself; but as soon as the guard turned out they knew that they had reached the British lines. Kanauji Lal was under suspicion until Kavanagh came up and greeted the Sikh officer in charge of the picket, who told off two of his troopers to escort them to the advanced guard. On the way they met an officer of the 9th Lancers, who took Kavanagh to his tent and gave him dry stockings and trousers and a glass of brandy. He felt better for the drink, but was still so dazed by the rapid alternation of hope and fear that he found it hard to grasp that he was safe.

The sun was rising in a clear sky as Kavanagh approached the tent of the Commander-in-Chief. At the doorway he met a spare, muscular, elderly man with tousled hair, a seamed forehead, and piercing eyes. Kavanagh asked for Sir Colin Campbell. 'I am

Sir Colin,' said the other brusquely, 'and who are you?'

Pulling off his turban Kavanagh took out Outram's note of introduction from the folds. 'This, sir,' he said, 'will explain who I am and from whence I came.'

Sir Colin read the letter, only pausing from time to time to glance sharply into Kavanagh's face. 'Is it true?' he asked.

'I hope, sir, you do not doubt the authenticity of the note?'

'No, I do not. But it is surprising. How did you do it?'

But Kavanagh was too tired to tell his story then and there, and only asked to be put to bed. After arranging for the flag to be hoisted at the Alambagh, he was taken off to a tent, which was carefully darkened for his comfort. As soon as he was alone he knelt down to thank God for his escape, nor did he forget how much he owed to the courage and address of Kanauji Lal. He could not sleep, but lay there comparing himself with the heroes of antiquity and wondering whether his name, too, would go down in history to edify his country's youth. He hoped that the ladies of Lucknow would remember him as a true knight who had ventured much to save them, and he was relieved to think that now some provision must surely be made for his wife and children should he fall as he guided Sir Colin and his troops to the rescue.

Between ten and eleven he sat down to breakfast with the Commander-in-Chief and his staff: there was bread and butter, eggs and bacon, Scottish marmalade, and coffee—with milk and sugar. He told his story between the mouthfuls. Afterwards Sir Colin took him aside to discuss Outram's proposals for the advance, enjoining him to say nothing about plans for the relief to anyone else in the camp.

At the Residency meanwhile there was great anxiety for Kavanagh, whose wife had not yet been told of his attempt. They were now in touch with the Alambagh by semaphore, and on the morning of the 10th November Outram had the message sent: 'Has Kavanagh arrived?' The reply was: 'Unintelligible.' About midday, however, the signal flag was sighted, and Mrs Kavanagh was told what her husband had achieved. When Mr Rees called to congratulate her he found her much put about, being vexed and happy at the same time.

At two P.M. the whole garrison were listening for the salvo from the Alambagh which would indicate the arrival of the relieving force, but either the signal was never given or Outram's instructions were not strictly followed, for though gunfire was heard in that direction no one knew what to make of it. But at eight o'clock that night, in answer to a beacon on the Residency roof, a blue light was displayed at the Alambagh, and Outram was satisfied that Sir Colin was at hand.

By the 9th November Charles Dashwood had taken a turn for the worse and, though Dr Boyd would not pronounce his case to be hopeless, Mrs Harris wrote in her diary: 'It will indeed be wonderful if he lives, for not a single case of amputation during the siege has recovered.'

On the 12th November Colonel Campbell of the 90th died, his leg having been amputated the day before. Mrs Inglis had taken him in on the 26th September and made him more comfortable than he would have been in the hospital, but he had been attacked by fever and his wound had not done well. On the same day a little white hen, which Brigadier Inglis had bought for ten shillings earlier in the siege, stopped laying. The bird had been tied by the leg so that it might hop about outside the door, picking up what it could, and just before Campbell had become seriously ill they had decided to kill and eat it, since it refused to lay. Then one morning Johnny Inglis ran in and said: 'Oh, mamma, the white hen has laid an egg!' This rare delicacy was given to the sick man, and the hen went on producing one egg a day until he died. After that it never laid another, but no one had the heart to kill it.

That day the semaphores were very active. It was signalled from the Alambagh that the Commander-in-Chief intended to advance on the Dilkusha on the 14th. Outram's dispositions for joining hands with Sir Colin to the east of the Chhattar Manzil were now complete. Two batteries had been posted in the advanced garden, and mines had been driven under the walls to unmask the guns when it was time to open fire. Mines had also been driven under a neighbouring building, the Hiran Khana. That evening an order was circulated that neither officers nor men must leave their posts by day or night until the relief should be effected. The garrison believed the order to be due to a rumour that the enemy, and especially the mutineers from Delhi, had sworn to make a last assault and kill every European in the place before Sir Colin arrived. Next day it was signalled from the Alambagh that the army would advance without fail on the following morning.

During the forenoon of the 14th November the sound of heavy firing was heard to the south-east, and the smoke of the guns could be seen from the Residency roof. By the evening it was clear that Sir Colin was in possession of the Dilkusha, and after dark there were beacons on both the Dilkusha and the Martinière. The enemy still seemed in good heart, however, and maintained a continual fusillade throughout the night.

On the 15th November the garrison expected Sir

Colin to make a further advance, but were disappointed. It was Brigadier Inglis' birthday, and Mrs Inglis decided to mark the occasion by asking Captain Barrow to dinner and having a fruit pie. The children were delighted, for they had not seen such a thing as that for the last four months. Johnny caught sight of Captain Barrow outside and ran after him, shouting: 'Come to dinner; we've got a pudding.'

About noon that day a body of the enemy's irregulars, both horse and foot, were seen to cross the bridge of boats from the north and advance towards the Martinière, followed by a second force, with artillery, from the Kaisarbagh. They were lost to sight among the woods, but before long the British guns opened fire from the north side of the Martinière, and soon the enemy were retreating faster than they had advanced. In the evening a semaphore was erected on the Martinière, and just before dark the signal 'Advance to-morrow' was received. That night Sir Colin's mortars were bombarding the buildings on his left—a pretty sight for the garrison, who watched the shells soaring like balls of fire with long bright tails, or sometimes bursting in the air and lighting up all the eastern sky.

On the morning of the 16th November, the siege having now lasted a hundred and forty days, the garrison were crowding the roofs to watch Sir Colin's advance. By ten o'clock the firing on his right showed him to be taking a more northerly route than Outram had suggested, and presently the troops had reached the Sikandarbagh, an enclosure over a hundred yards square with massive brick walls twenty feet high, loopholed and flanked by bastions at the corners. Sir Colin's guns opened fire on the walls, and after a check the gleam of bayonets could be seen as the troops forced their way in. The tide rolled on to the Shah Najaf tomb and the Kadam Rasul mosque, but the garrison's view was sadly obscured by trees and smoke. From the Chhattar Manzil Mr Gubbins could see men in kilts and feather bonnets, the 93rd (Sutherland) Highlanders, the Thin Red Line of Balaclava.

Early in the afternoon Captain Maude's 8-inch mortars in the garden beyond the Chhattar Manzil opened on the neighbouring buildings, and word was given to unmask the batteries by blowing up the wall. But the mines had been loaded on the night of the 13th, and owing to the delay the powder had become damp; the explosions were consequently weak, leaving two breaches to the right, with a length of wall still standing in between, while to the left the fabric was cracked and shaken but still erect. The enemy at once opened fire on the breaches from the Kaisarbagh. 'Hellfire Jack' Olpherts' guns were turned on the walls from the inside, the shot flying through the brickwork as if it were a sheet of paper, leaving round holes behind, until it began to crumble and fall.

At 3.15 P.M. the mines were sprung under the

Hiran Khana, one of which was successful in making a breach. At 3.30 Havelock, who was in charge of these operations, gave word to sound the Advance, and the note of the bugle was followed by cheers from the columns of assault, for the men were glad to be at work in the open again.

In a few minutes both the steam-engine house and the Hiran Khana were occupied, in spite of the severe fire from the Kaisarbagh, and there was nothing of importance but the old 32nd Mess House and the Moti Mahal palace between the garrison and the relieving force. That night a new battery was thrown up in advance of the steam-engine house. The 8-inch howitzer and two heavy guns with which it was armed had to be man-handled, for the last of the bullocks were to be killed on the following day.

By 9.30 on the morning of the 17th November, Sir Colin's heavy guns were in action in the direction of the Shah Najaf, and the Mess House was bombarded by rockets from the relieving force and by shells from either side. By about 3 P.M., the musketry from the Mess House being silenced, the building was occupied and a regimental colour appeared on the roof; it was shot down by the enemy and replaced; shot down, replaced, and shot down again; and propped up a third time on its broken staff.

Soon both Indian and European troops were running the gauntlet of the fire from the Kaisarbagh to attack the Moti Mahal, and after sapping their way in they drove out some hundred of the enemy, who ran down to the river for their lives. In the palace Captain Garnet Wolseley (better known as Sir Garnet Wolseley—'all Sir Garnet'—or Lord Wolseley) ran into a detachment of his own regiment, the 90th, who had just made a sortie from the Chhattar Manzil, and cheer after cheer passed down the road as the relieving force learned that they had now joined hands with the garrison.

Outram, Havelock, Napier, and their staff were waiting at the steam-engine house when a queer, tall figure in breeches, long jackboots, a quilted cotton tunic, and a felt sun-helmet came running up breathless. For the moment they were at a loss, then someone shouted: 'It's Kavanagh! Three cheers for him! He's the first to relieve us!' It was a proud moment for Kavanagh, the uncovenanted clerk, when so many distinguished people pressed round him with congratulations.

'Are you willing, Sir James,' he asked Outram, 'to join the Commander-in-Chief at once? The road is clear, but there is that fire from the palace to be encountered.'

'Never mind it,' replied Outram, turning to his staff and telling them to follow. They all reached the Moti Mahal without mishap, though Outram himself was too heavy and asthmatical to force the pace. In a courtyard of the palace a shell fell close to Havelock, ricochetted against a wall, and burst almost at his feet. He was knocked down but otherwise untouched. In the passage from the Moti Mahal to the Mess House several of the staff were wounded, among them Napier and the younger Havelock, who was hit in the same arm as before. As soon as Kavanagh had Outram safe under cover he went off to find Sir Colin and said: 'Sir James Outram is waiting, sir, to see you.'

'The devil he is! Where is he? Where has he come from?'

'I have fetched him, Sir Colin, from the Residency, and he is standing yonder.'

'Well done! Lead the way!'

When Kavanagh had introduced the two generals Sir Colin said: 'I am delighted to meet you, Sir James, and I congratulate you on the successful defence of Lucknow.'

He dismounted as Outram, in his turn, congratulated him on the relief, and they shook hands cordially. Then Sir Colin said: 'Are you prepared, Sir James, to quit the Residency in two hours? Time is precious.'

Outram was startled and replied: 'It is impossible, Sir Colin.'

'Nothing is impossible, sir!' snapped Campbell.

'If you will permit me', said Outram deliberately, 'to explain the reasons for considering it impracticable, you will, Sir Colin, be well satisfied that it cannot be done.'

'Very well, Sir James, we'll discuss this as early as possible.'

Meanwhile Havelock had been recognised in the Moti Mahal by some of the 53rd, his old regiment, who gave him a cheer. His eyes filled with tears and he addressed them as follows: 'Soldiers, I am happy to see you. Soldiers, I am happy to think you have got into this place with a smaller loss than I had.' Brigadier General Hope Grant, who was commanding the relieving force under the general supervision of the Commander-in-Chief, asked Havelock what he supposed their losses to have been. Havelock said he had heard about eighty, and was grieved when Hope Grant told him that the figures were more like forty-three officers and four hundred and fifty men killed and wounded. Hope Grant then took him to Sir Colin, who addressed him as Sir Henry Havelock. It cheered him to know that he had been granted the K.C.B., but First Lieutenant Fred Roberts, Bengal Artillery (Lord Roberts in later years), who now saw him for the first time, thought he looked worn and ill. After a brief conversation with the Commander-in-Chief he returned to the Residency with the others. On the way back they took to their heels across the open space, but Havelock soon began to tire. Turning to Captain Dodgson, his Assistant-Adjutant-General, he said: 'I can do no more, Dodgson, I can do no more.' Dodgson gave him his arm, and they walked slowly on together, with the enemy's musket-balls knocking up the harmless dust around them.

Back in the entrenchment Kavanagh, whose

exploit had been described in generous terms by Sir Colin, was hailed with unstinted admiration everywhere but at home, where his wife at first reproached him for his rashness.

It was like old times for the garrison to see officers in smart uniform, on fresh, well-conditioned mounts, and there was a pleasant novelty in the appearance of the 'Shannon' Naval Brigade, commanded by Captain William Peel, R.N., third son of Sir Robert Peel, who had already made a name for himself ashore in the Crimea. The 'Shannons' were ready to go anywhere and fight anybody, and regarded the campaign as a highly sporting event. The army was inclined to pet them; whatever they asked for they were given, and if ever they were in liquor they were handed over to their own people without unnecessary fuss. They wore their ordinary uniform, their straw hats being fitted with white cotton covers and curtains for the neck. The Indians who saw them were deeply impressed and described them to their friends as men four feet high and four feet wide, of enormous strength, who carried 24-pounder cannon on their shoulders.

Lieutenant Roberts and another staff officer were given permission to accompany Havelock and Outram back to the Residency. They stopped by one of the batteries at the Chhattar Manzil, watching the gunners' attempts to silence the enemy's artillery across the river, and chatting with the men, who were eager to hear their news. Olpherts was in command, but in his torn and dirty summer clothing, with his face thin, worn, and grimed with smoke, they could not at first distinguish him from his men.

Tobacco and rum were the ruling topics wherever the rank and file of the garrison were in touch with Sir Colin's men. Captain Wolseley had brought up a supply of tobacco, which he distributed among the officers and men of the 90th. He had also had a keg of rum conveyed as far as the Mess House, where it had been left when he was told off to command a storming party. Night was already falling when he started back with volunteers to fetch it, and it took him several hours to make his way back again with the rum to the Farhat Bakhsh, where he was told that his brother officers were to be found. Putting his head through the door of a summer-house he saw a number of men sitting inside, none of whom he recognised. As he withdrew, however, one of them shouted: 'Why, it's Wolseley,' and it dawned upon him that he knew them well enough, but had not allowed for the effect of the siege on their appearance.

During the afternoon two strange officers walked through the courtyard outside Mrs Inglis' room, leading their horses, and asked for the Brigadier. One of them was Colonel Berkeley, who was to take command of the 32nd Foot—a sad reminder to Mrs Case of her husband, whose ambition it had always been to command the regiment.

In the evening Inglis announced that the whole garrison and all the non-combatants were to evacuate the Residency position on the following night and retire on Cawnpore. Sir Colin's decision was ill received by the garrison. Often as they had longed to see the last of them, they were now loth to abandon the defences they had held for a hundred and forty days, against such odds, with so much labour and blood. The prospect of evacuation was a black one for the sick and wounded. It was said that no baggage could be taken away, so the ladies began fitting their clothes with extra pockets to carry their personal treasures.

Sir Colin had undertaken the relief of Lucknow with between five and six thousand men of all arms, about a fifth of whom were now employed in keeping open his communications at the Alambagh and the Dilkusha. To extricate the garrison and the non-combatants he had little over four thousand men against the enemy's thirty, forty, or fifty thousand. His line of retreat to the Dilkusha, which was four and a half miles long, must be secured by a chain of posts on either side, and sheltered if possible from the fire of the enemy in the Kaisarbagh and across the river. A successful attack on his rear during evacuation might spell complete disaster.

On the 18th November a breaching fire was opened on the walls of the Kaisarbagh from the guns in the Residency advanced posts and from Peel's 24-pounders, which had been placed in battery on the west side of the Moti Mahal. A flying sap, or covered way, was made between the steam-engine house and Martin's house, near the Moti Mahal; short cuts were opened up through the buildings; and screens were fitted at exposed corners so that though the passers-by were within range of the enemy they could not be seen. Guns were posted at the Moti Mahal, and picked marksmen at the Shah Najaf, to silence the enemy's fire from across the river.

Both Outram and Havelock were anxious that Sir Colin should follow up his success by an immediate assault on the Kaisarbagh, which was the enemy's chief remaining stronghold. Outram believed that once this had fallen the city could be held by twelve hundred men. Hope Grant and other senior officers were also in favour of the assault, while Inglis volunteered to maintain his old position with one more regiment so long as the non-combatants could be taken off his hands; but Sir Colin, who was short of both men and ammunition, preferred to mask the city by a movable division outside, as had recently been done at Delhi. Outram's opinion carried weight, however, since, as Chief Commissioner of Oudh, he was concerned with the effect upon local opinion of abandoning the city. Sir Colin therefore informed the Governor General of the issue by telegraph, the line to Calcutta having now been re-established, and asked him for instructions. Canning replied as follows: 'I have received your message of yesterday. The one step to be avoided is, a total withdrawal of the British forces from Oudh. Your proposal to leave a strong movable division, with heavy artillery, outside the city, and so to hold the city in check, will answer every purpose of policy.'

On the 18th November the artillerymen were

busy destroying the ex-King's guns that had been brought in before the siege—a tedious job, since they had already been spiked and could not be burst until the spikes had been drilled out of the vents. Some of the men were told off to collect vehicles, but all the carriages they could find were half rotten with exposure and riddled with bullet holes. The non-combatants had been granted twenty-four hours' grace to prepare for the retirement, and as it was now understood that a limited amount of baggage might be taken, the women were sorting their possessions and bundling up the most valuable items; but of course those whose homes had been in Lucknow had to face the loss of almost all their property.

Mrs Polehampton had had a headstone carved for her husband's grave by a stonecutter whom she had found in the ranks of the 90th; and Mrs Barbor had made a little sketch of the churchyard, showing the grave, for her to take away. She filled a large pocket with her favourites among the chaplain's sermons, and sewed his gown, surplice, hood, and stole, together with her dead baby's clothes, into a pillow. She was hoping to save the harmonium, which had been presented by the 32nd Foot, and had been lying unharmed in the church throughout the siege. Mrs Bartrum's heart failed her at the thought of walking to the Dilkusha carrying her boy. Dr Darby, who had been so kind to them both, had just been wounded, and it was feared that he would not recover; but another doctor, who had arrived with the relieving force, promised to find her a dooly.

The garrison had already received some benefit from Sir Colin's arrival: not only had they been provided with bread, butter, oranges, and rum, but several cartloads of letters and newspapers had been brought in, the first that most of them had received for the better part of six months.

Early in the morning of the 19th November Lieutenant Roberts, who was Hope Grant's Deputy Assistant Quartermaster General, was sent to inform Outram that arrangements for the withdrawal of the families were now complete, and that conveyances would be sent along as soon as they arrived from the Dilkusha. Outram questioned Roberts about the route, asking if he had noticed whether the openings in the walls were large enough for the guns, carts, and carriages to pass. Roberts replied that, while he had not given them close attention, he fancied they were on the small side. To his dismay Colonel Napier, who was lying on a couch at the far end of the room, having been wounded on the 17th, asked him indignantly whether he had measured the openings. Roberts replied that he had not, and Napier went on: 'You had better wait to give your opinion until you know what you are talking about; those openings were made by my orders, and I am quite sure they are the necessary size.' Roberts felt badly snubbed, though Outram good-naturedly pointed out that he had not volunteered his opinion, but merely answered a question; he proved to be right about the openings.

At noon the same day the women and children began to leave the entrenchment, some in carts, carriages, and doolies, but many more on foot. Captain Wolseley and his men, who were on picket duty by the road, felt a little dashed when the women they had nerved themselves to save, cost what it might, passed them without offering a single gracious word, and seemed too wretched to do anything but grumble. The rigours of the siege had told so much on their appearance that Captain Peel's coxswain was flatly disappointed, and said they looked a rough lot. The sailors found the children more attractive, and picked them up and petted them whenever they had the chance. Mrs Case's carriage, which had been damaged by roundshot as well as musket-balls, was drawn by coolies, the children riding while the women walked, escorted by Lieutenant Birch. When there was any danger from the enemy's musketry Birch carried the children and the women ran. The little white hen had not been left behind.

Mr and Mrs Harris rode in a carriage drawn by a pair of half-starved horses, who stopped dead every five minutes, generally at the most dangerous corners. Once the enemy's fire was so hot that the chaplain and his wife got out and ran, and two coolies who were pushing the carriage from behind were hit. The dog Bustle was safely brought away, only to be lost on the road.

Mrs Germon had a pony to ride, but was so bloated that she could hardly mount. She had put on three of every kind of undergarment, a pink flannel dressing-gown, and a plaid jacket, with a cloth dress and jacket over all. She wore a bustle, too, into which she had stitched her Honiton lace wedding dress, her veil, and two large shawls, while her inner pockets were stuffed with jewellery, her journal, and various other papers. She had tied a cashmere shawl round her waist and wore a worsted cap and hat. Her husband and Captain Weston roared with laughter as they helped her into the saddle, though Captain Germon sobered up when they came to say good-bye at the Baillie Guard gate.

From the Sikandarbagh onwards the road was deep in sand and somewhat exposed, and it was therefore decided that the families should wait there till nightfall and then be sent on to the Dilkusha in doolies. Sir Colin met them in person at the Sikandarbagh, where he spoke very civilly to Mrs Inglis about the dear creatures, as he called them, though she felt that he was wishing them far away. His staff and various other officers were handing round wine, biscuits, tea, and bread-and-butter. Hope Grant noticed that many of the women seemed strangely sorry to have left the Residency, though the children were more alive to the main chance: he heard a little girl say to her mother: 'Oh,

Mamma, there's a loaf of bread upon the table. I'm certain of it; I saw it with my own eyes.'

Hope Grant asked a delicate looking lady if he could fetch her anything. She replied: 'Oh yes; if you could procure me a piece of cheese, I should be so thankful—it is for a poor sick lady.' It struck him as an odd remedy, and he answered that as it was getting dark it might be difficult to find; but she assured him that a certain Captain Ximines would give him some. He discovered the Captain at length, and received a large portion of strong, greasy-looking cheese, done up in a bit of newspaper. It seemed a come-down for the divisional commander of the force that had saved the garrison of Lucknow to be wandering about with this offensive parcel, but Hope Grant was a good-natured fellow and took it, if with reluctance. It was some time before he could find the lady again, and he was just about to throw the stuff away when she came up and claimed it.

Three days before, nearly two thousand mutineers had been trapped in the Sikandarbagh, where they had been shot down and bayoneted without hope of quarter, while Sir Colin's troops shouted: 'Cawnpore! Revenge for Cawnpore!' Mrs Inglis did not see the bodies, many of which had had some kind of burial, but it sickened her to think of them so near.

The journey in the dark to the Dilkusha was broken by a number of alarms and halts. After she had been moving for some time Mrs Bartrum noticed that the tramp of the dooly-bearers behind was no longer to be heard. She looked out to find that she and her baby were alone with her own bearers in an open plain. The men said they had lost their way, and it flashed into her mind that they were going to take her over to the enemy. She sprang out with the child in her arms, and ran away screaming until she heard answering voices and met a party of British soldiers. They told her that they too were lost and feared that they were near the enemy's pickets. 'However,' they said, 'don't get into the dooly again, and we'll do our best for you, poor girl.' She found it heavy going through the deep sand with the boy in her arms, but the men were kind and helped her as well as they could. Suddenly there was a noise among the trees, and the men said: 'Oh God, it's all up with us: we're done for now.' Then they placed her in the middle and whispered: 'Don't scream, and we may be able to creep on presently.'

Mrs Bartrum was stiff with terror and could only clutch the child more tightly as she prayed for help, but having heard nothing more they soon moved on again. It was three o'clock in the morning when at last they reached the Dilkusha. Mrs Bartrum was so exhausted that she sat down and cried, until a friendly officer found her and took her to a large tent, where she was given a cup of tea for herself and milk for the baby; afterwards they lay down on the ground and slept.

The evacuation of the sick and wounded was

begun on the evening of the 19th November, and though the medical staff did all they could for their comfort many of them died on the way. Charles Dashwood was much worse for the journey. The younger Havelock, whose second wound was doing well, stopped his dooly by Ommanney's house to take leave of his father, whom he found reading Macaulay's History by lamplight. The General had written cheerfully that day to the new Lady Havelock, but next morning he was suffering from dysentery, which yielded at first to treatment but later became more acute. On the 21st November he was taken to the Dilkusha by dooly after dark, and though he suffered from the motion he seemed better for the change.

The arrival of the families had caused the utmost confusion at the Dilkusha, but gradually they were made more comfortable and began to feel the benefit of the pure air and the fresh, plentiful food. There were more letters from home, many of them written in the apprehension that those whom they were addressed to would never live to read them. Mrs Bartrum received several letters from her dead husband. The dog Bustle turned up again one morning, to the delight of Mr and Mrs Harris.

Charles Dashwood died on the 22nd November. Not long before the end Mrs Harris went with Mrs Dashwood into the tent where he was lying. He did not know his sister-in-law, but once, when Mr Harris was reading the commendatory prayer, he opened his eyes and seemed for a moment to be struggling to speak. Dr Darby died the same day. Havelock's disorder did not seem to be dangerous, but he told those about him that he did not think he would recover.

Meanwhile the entrenchment was being cleared of everything that was considered worth the carriage. The enemy were so harassed by the breaching-fire at the Kaisarbagh that they did not observe the withdrawal of the guns from the old position. All the treasure, including what was left of the ex-King's jewels, was removed, as well as the large supplies of wheat that still remained to witness the forethought of Sir Henry Lawrence. The place was strewn with all sorts of clothes and household gear which the families had left behind them, and to which both soldiers and civilians were helping themselves freely.

It so angered the garrison to think that, after all, the enemy would overrun the place and loot it, that they would have preferred to blow up all the houses as they retired; but this would have wrecked the concerted plans of Outram and Major General Mansfield, Sir Colin's Chief of Staff, which required the routine of the defence to be maintained as long as possible. It was not till the afternoon of the 22nd November that the bulk of the Europeans were informed that they were marching out that night, and the news was withheld from the Indian troops till the very last minute, though of course they had already guessed what was to come. The old pensioners who had served so loyally throughout the siege were sadly disappointed. As natives of Oudh they had hoped to return in triumph to their own villages, instead of leaving the country, as they feared, for ever, with the prospect of long marches for which most of them were unfitted by infirmity or age.

It was planned that each exterior line should retire through its supports, as if a gigantic sock, with its open top at the Dilkusha and its toe at the farthest corner of the Residency, were being pulled inside out. Thus the old garrison would retire first, then Havelock's force in the palaces, passing through the advanced posts of Sir Colin's command at the Moti Mahal and the Mess House; these would fall back next, followed by the detachments at the Shah Najaf, and all in turn would pass the last line of infantry and artillery, under Sir Colin in person, which was waiting by the Sikandarbagh with guns loaded and portfires lighted to crush the enemy if they dared to follow up the retreating pickets. The operation was one of extreme delicacy, which would depend for success on silence and perfect liaison between the adjoining posts.

The retreat began at midnight, the lights being left burning in the entrenchment for the enemy to see. Inglis and Outram stood with Captain Wilson, Lieutenant Barwell, the Brigade Major, and Lieutenant Birch, watching each separate garrison march out in turn. There should have been fourteen, but when the last had gone by some said that only thirteen had passed, and Birch was therefore sent back to Innes' post, the extreme point of the position, to make sure that they were all withdrawn. The unaccustomed quiet and the loneliness of the place struck coldly on his nerves, but he had to go on. There was no one there. When he had returned and reported to the two Generals, they bared their heads to the Baillie Guard in honour of the long defence, and then Outram waved his hand to Inglis to go first; but Inglis stood his ground, claiming it as his right to come behind. Outram smiled and held out his hand. 'Let us go out together,' he said; so they shook hands and walked side by side down the slope that led away from the battered gate.

Behind them came the staff, both Wilson and Birch having determined to be last man out. The hardships of the siege had told more heavily on Wilson; Birch sent him rolling down the slope with a charge he had learnt on the playing fields of Harrow, and was himself the last, as he thought, to leave the entrenchment.

The retreat of the old garrison was covered by the 78th Highlanders from Lockhart's post. Outram said to them: 'Soldiers, you had the honour of leading the advance into Lucknow, and for that reason you have been selected to form the rearguard on leaving.' They were ordered to break step lest the regular tramp of their feet should arouse the enemy's suspicions.

The retreat continued through the Terhi Kothi, the Farhat Bakhsh, and Chhattar Manzil palaces, and still the enemy were quiet. Outram's men passed silently through Sir Colin's posts and down a narrow lane, taking up their positions at last in front of the Dilkusha. As soon as the lane was clear the most advanced posts of Sir Colin's force began to fall back. Suddenly there came a burst of firing from the Kaisarbagh, and for a moment it was feared that the enemy had observed the retreat and were about to sally out in force. Fortunately one of the Naval Brigade's rocket carts was still available, and after a few Congreve rockets had been sent into the Kaisarbagh the enemy there ceased fire. They were still firing into the Residency, however, and it was not till long after daylight that they found the place was empty.

Birch was not the last man out. Captain Waterman, 13th Native Infantry, had fallen asleep at the Brigade Mess after his name had been called, and awoke at two o'clock to find himself alone. He went to every outpost in turn, but they were all deserted. Panic seized him; he ran out of the gate and through the palaces, which were silent too, and when at last he came up with the rearguard the shock had unhinged his mind.

Next morning the following appeared in General Orders:

1. 'The Commander-in-Chief has reason to be thankful to the force he conducted for the relief of the garrison of Lucknow.

2. Hastily assembled, fatigued by forced marches, but animated by a common feeling of determination to accomplish the duty before them, all ranks of this force have compensated for their small number, in the execution of a most difficult duty, by unceasing exertions.

3. From the morning of the 16th till last night, the whole force has been one outlying picket, never out of fire, and covering an immense extent of ground, to permit the garrison to retire scathless and in safety, covered by the whole of the relieving force.

4. That ground was won by fighting as hard as it ever fell to the lot of the Commander-in-Chief to witness, it being necessary to bring up the same men over and over again to fresh attacks; and it is with the greatest gratification that His Excellency declares he never saw men behave better.

5. The storming of the Sikandarbagh and the Shah Najaf has never been surpassed in daring, and the success of it was most brilliant and complete.

6. The movement of retreat of last night, by which the final rescue of the garrison was effected, was a model of discipline and exactness. The consequence was that the enemy was completely deceived, and the force retired by a narrow, tortuous lane, the only line of retreat open, in the face of 50,000 enemies, without molestation.

7. The Commander-in-Chief offers his sincere thanks to Major General Sir James Outram, G.C.B.,

for the happy manner in which he planned and carried out his arrangements for the evacuation of the Residency of Lucknow.'

That morning Sir Colin had the old garrison paraded, Europeans, Eurasians, and Indians. They looked a queer lot. The 32nd Foot had lost 85 of all ranks at Cawnpore; their strength before the defeat at Chinhat had been 650; that engagement had reduced them to 535; and on the 17th November they only numbered 357, including sick and wounded. Their strength on the parade of the 23rd November was about 250. Sir Colin looked them up and down and said to Inglis: 'On my honour, Brigadier, you have a motley crowd to command, and more like an invalid depot than the once fine regiment who fought with me in the Punjab and on the North-West Frontier. But never mind, men,' he added, 'you have nobly done your duty, and when we get back to Cawnpore you shall have a rest to recruit yourselves.'

After the evacuation Captain Sanders wrote as follows: 'We are out of Lucknow, which place we left on the 22nd. The feeling of liberty is delightful, after being so long cooped up, and it feels so strange being free from the "ping" of the bullets; but it is excessively cold sleeping in the open air without a greatcoat, and very hot during the day. The enemy have not molested us. We evacuated the entrenchment without the loss of a man. If it were not for the disgrace, I should be very happy; as it is, I hope to be back again before many months are over.'

Early on the 23rd November Mr Gubbins went to Havelock's tent to inquire after the General. Inside he found an aide-de-camp and the doctor, who whispered that he was worse and pointed to the dooly in which he was lying. The curtain on Gubbins' side had been dropped, but he went round and saw the younger Havelock sitting on the ground on the other side, his wounded arm in a sling, tending his father with the sound one. Gubbins withdrew sadly, since there was nothing he could say or do. Havelock himself declared that his case was hopeless, and looked forward to the hour of death, confident in the merits of his Redeemer. He said more than once: 'I die happy and contented.' After years of disappointment, his life-long prayer to command in a successful action had been granted, again and again. He had turned the tide of war when flowing most strongly against British arms; the people he had fought for had been saved at last; and he himself had lived to be honoured by his countrymen and Queen.

Outram went to see him in the evening. Havelock spoke to him with the tenderest affection, telling him how happy it made him to look back on their service together, which had never been marred by any kind of discord, nor embittered by an angry word. He said too: 'I have for forty years so ruled my life, that when death came I might face it without fear.'

He slept little that night. Next morning, the

24th November, he seemed better, but at eight o'clock he took a turn for the worse, and at half past nine he died quietly, in the hope of the life to come. Soon after his death the column began the march to the Alambagh. Havelock's body was carried down in the dooly and buried there, his grave being marked by a mound of earth and the letter H carved on a mango tree close by. Campbell, Inglis and many more gathered round to see the last of him, but not Outram, who had been left at the Dilkusha to bring up the rear.

The long stream of men and cattle, doolies, guns, carts and carriages moved slowly towards Cawnpore in a cloud of dust, the enemy offering no resistance. There was great confusion when they camped at the Alambagh on the night of the 24th November. Mrs Inglis' baggage cart was missing, but luckily she found a flock of goats and was given some milk for the baby. Later in the evening Inglis, who had commanded the advanced guard during the day's march, went foraging for her in the camp of the 9th Lancers and returned with Hope Grant, laden with bread, cold beef, and bottled beer. Mrs Polehampton had been lent a bullock cart for her harmonium, which had been too big for the camel that had brought it down to the Dilkusha, and had tumbled off several times on the way. Mrs Bartrum's little boy was looking better for the change, but she was not yet happy about his health.

On the 25th and 26th November the convoy halted while Outram brought in the rear division and prepared to defend the Alambagh with about 4,000 men of all arms, 25 guns and howitzers, and 10 mortars, thus holding the Lucknow rebels in check until Sir Colin should return with sufficient force to reduce the city and reconquer Oudh. Mr Gubbins had a last look at the old position from the top of the Alambagh house. Through the glasses the enemy could be clearly seen crowding the roof of the Residency building, where they had already smashed the semaphore.

At eleven o'clock on the morning of the 27th November the march was resumed. Most of the country was swampy or under water, and all the heavier traffic had to keep on the narrow road. The column was some twelve miles long, and, since the next camp was to be not more than fifteen miles away, the head was nearly there before the tail had started. The women and children and the sick and wounded suffered much from the jolting and the long delays.

Sir Colin was becoming every hour more anxious for the safety of his communications. He had left Major General Windham, known since Sebastopol as 'the hero of the Redan', to hold Cawnpore with a force that had been cut to the bone, in the hope that he himself would return from Lucknow before Tantia Topi's threat should develop; but the extrication of the garrison had taken longer than he had foreseen, and it was now ten days since there had been any news of Windham, good or bad. The officer commanding the post at the Bani bridge reported that he had heard heavy firing on the Cawnpore side all that day and the day before. It was on the cards that Windham might have been overwhelmed by sheer numbers, and if so it was a certainty that Tantia Topi would destroy the bridge of boats across the Ganges and cut off the convoy from the Grand Trunk Road.

On the 28th November the march began at 7 A.M. and as the day went on the guns at Cawnpore could be plainly heard. At noon an Indian runner emerged from behind a hedge with a small note written in Greek character, marked 'Most Urgent', and addressed to 'General Sir Colin Campbell, or any officer commanding troops on the Lucknow road'. It was dated the 26th and said that there had been severe fighting, that the enemy were in great force with many guns, and that Windham might have to abandon the town and retire into his entrenchment. It ended with an urgent request for help, and was soon followed by two more letters, the second reporting that Windham's force was now shut up in the entrenchment, and that the bridge was threatened.

The column marched on doggedly. There was severe suffering among the sick and wounded, and the troops were tired and footsore. As the miles passed the cannonade became louder and louder. Late in the evening camp was pitched within a few miles of the bridgehead, after a march of nearly twenty-five miles. Sir Colin and some of his staff had ridden on ahead and seen with profound relief that the bridge was still safe, though there were flames and smoke rising from the city and cantonments on the other side. Sir Colin crossed over to confer with Windham, returning after dark. Next morning the troops began the crossing, supported by artillery massed on the river bank, and before the day was out the line of communication down country was secure. It was saddening for the women, who only asked for peace and safety, to hear the din of war again so soon.

At three in the afternoon the convoy began to cross, and it was nine o'clock on the following evening before Inglis brought the rearguard over. The women were thrown into alarm by a burst of musketry from the entrenchment, but the crossing was made in safety in spite of the enemy's desultory cannonade and their attempts to burn the bridge with flaming rafts. Mrs Soppitt's baby was born in a buggy on the way over, under the care of Dr Brydon, the Afghan survivor. Cawnpore looked sinister in the moonlight with its ruined bungalows and fallen or shattered trees.

The next few days were spent in expediting the removal of the convoy to Allahabad, for Sir Colin was burning to see the last of the non-combatants and to take the offensive against Tantia Topi, who was still in possession of the town. The stores of clothing that had been prepared for the comfort of the refugees had been burnt by the rebels, but the families made themselves as comfortable as they could in tents or barracks. The children enjoyed the pleasant weather, playing with their dolls, or the knotted handkerchiefs that passed for dolls, or such simple toys as empty sardine-tins dragged along the ground with string.

The house where the Nana Sahib had butchered the women and children was now in the hands of the enemy, but many of those who had been through the siege at Lucknow examined the remains of Wheeler's open entrenchment, and saw that their own sufferings of a hundred and forty days could not compare with the horrors of a defence which had lasted only twenty. The place was still littered with shreds of clothing, fragments of letters, torn books, and sheets of music. Mrs Harris picked up a leaf from the Bible which she kept as a relic, and Dr Fayrer found the flyleaf of a song, 'The Last Man', by Thomas Campbell, which began: 'All worldly shapes shall melt in gloom.'

On the night of the 3rd December the convoy set out on the long and tedious journey to the coast. Inglis remained at Cawnpore, having succeeded to Windham's command. There was still too much fighting ahead for the men of the 32nd to have their promised rest, but Harry Metcalfe had been given leave to visit Mr and Mrs Harris and the dog Bustle the afternoon before they left. On the 7th December the convoy reached Allahabad, where the survivors were received with cheers and provided with every comfort, and had nothing to do but enjoy the quiet and the safety as they waited for the steamers to take them down stream to Calcutta.

On Christmas Day Mrs Inglis gave a dinner to

the women and children of the 32nd, but it was not a festive party since of the seventeen women who were there every one was a widow, while every child had lost either its father or its mother, or both. Father Adeodatus, the saintly old priest who had hoped to lay his bones in St Mary's, Lucknow, had been carried down in a dooly and died on the 9th December, just thirty-five years after he had set sail for India from Leghorn. Mrs Soppitt's baby lived and was christened Ada, and Mrs Dashwood's little boy survived as well. When at last the refugees reached Calcutta there was more trouble to come, for some of them were wrecked on the way to England and escaped with little but their lives.

On the 19th January, on the way down to Calcutta in the river steamer, Mrs Bartrum wrote: 'We seem to be very slowly proceeding on our homeward journey, and it will be months before I reach England if I go round the Cape, which I must, for my child's sake, for he is still extremely weak, and he is so precious to me that I could not lose him now.' While she and Mrs Polehampton were waiting in Calcutta for their passage home the boy was steadily declining, but Mrs Bartrum would not believe that she was going to lose him. By the 10th February he was gravely ill, and at half past one next morning Mrs Bartrum called Mrs Polehampton in great distress. The child gasped for breath as he lay in his mother's arms, and she turned her head away rather than watch him die.

When he was dead Mrs Polehampton washed and dressed the body, and in the morning they gathered flowers in the garden and laid them round him on the bed. During the day his portrait was taken by daguerreotype, just as he lay, with his head on one side and a smile as if he were happily asleep. He was buried the same evening. Mrs Bartrum broke down when she heard the first handful of earth rattle on the coffin; but afterwards she set up a gravestone to the memory of her dead, with the names and dates followed by Elisha's question and the Shunammite's reply:

> Is it well with thy husband?
> Is it well with the child?
> And she answered, It is well.

NOTES

My narrative is drawn from the sources quoted below, and I have not invented a single character, incident, speech, thought, or feeling. For instance, when I write that the onlookers laughed as Outram touched up Kavanagh's disguise, but that the laughter ceased when it was time for him to start, the dramatic detail is drawn not from imagination but from Kavanagh's own description of the scene. Again, when I mention Hope Grant's objection to Captain Ximines' parcel, it is not because I think he might have objected but because he has put his distaste on record. I am at pains to make this clear since for myself a historical or biographical work loses half its interest if I suspect that any of the detail is invented. I cannot, of course, vouch for the absolute verbal accuracy of the dialogue, some of which may have been set down from memory long after the event; but, in the light of what is known about the speakers, the circumstances, and the reporters, I believe that the conversations I have quoted are substantially correct.

In December, 1937, I had the privilege of discussing the siege with Mother Agnes (since dead, I am sorry to say) who was born on the 27th March,

1853, and who clearly remembered staring up at General Havelock on the evening of the 25th September, 1857; she is referred to in the text as Lavinia Casey. I am indebted to Mr A. F. Dashwood (who was born during the siege) and Sir Alexander Lawrence (Sir Henry's grandson) for information which they received by word of mouth from various survivors.

The value of the written sources varies considerably. Many of the authors were careless; some of them drew more or less on narratives published before their own; and some cared more for human susceptibilities than historic truth. Fortunately there are so many accounts of the siege that what is defective or misleading in one can usually be supplied or corrected by another. Among the sources used here for the first time the most notable is Private Metcalfe's spirited *Army Record*; with the trifling exception of Holloway's *Essays*, this is, so far as I know, the only narrative by one of the rank-and-file. It was written many years later, but there is no reason to doubt Metcalfe's general accuracy: the friends he mentions can be identified in the Lucknow Medal Roll, and his own account of his relations with the dog Bustle squares with and amplifies the references in Mrs Harris' diary.

So many friends and correspondents have given me valuable assistance and advice, and lent me books and documents otherwise unprocurable, that detailed acknowledgements would be unduly lengthy.

I must therefore ask them to accept the bare mention of their names in the following list as an expression of my thanks: Miss V. M. H. Adams; The Right Rev. The Lord Bishop of Allahabad; Mr H. S. Ashton; Mr E. E. Bartholomew; Mr H. Brinton; the Officer i/c Regimental Museum, The Cameronians; Mr and Mrs Stephen Chant; Fr J. Chrysostom, O.C.; Sir George and Lady Collier; Mr A. F. Dashwood; The Director General of Observatories, Poona; The Officers, Duke of Cornwall's Light Infantry; Mr N.W. Escott; Miss Constance Forbes; Miss Molly Francis; Major J. O. Fulton; Mrs P. J. Fulton; Mrs R. Fulton; Miss Freda Gaye; The Rector, Heythrop College; The Rev. E. Hull, S.J.; The Superintendent of Records, India Office; Mrs Alfred Inglis; The Secretary, Institution of Royal Engineers; Sir Carleton King; Sir Alexander Lawrence; Lt. Col. J. H. Leslie; Mr G. E. Manwaring, of the London Library; Mrs E. C. Mill; Miss H. J. Neild; Mr and Mrs Ralph Nye; Sir Francis Outram; Mr Wilfred Partington; Mr and Mrs H. Pfotenhauer; The Chief Engineer, Posts and Telegraphs (India); The Adjutant, 10th Bn. 7th Rajputs; Dr J. C. Read; The Secretary, Royal Artillery Institution; Major I. H. Mackay Scobie; Dr T. G. P. Spear; Mr Charles Stewart; Mr Mohammad Tayyab, of the Darul-Uloom, Deoband; Mr F. Wagner; Major G. Goold Walker, D.S.O., M.C.; Mrs E. F. Warburton; Mrs A. F. Warren; Miss D. Warren; Mr A. J. Waterfield; Mr R. A. Wilson; Mrs A. G. Young.

NOTES ON THE TEXT

Page viii. . . . an unfortunate report, not quite unfounded). The vexed question of the greased cartridge is dealt with at length by Rice Holmes (See his Appendix W.).

Page 1. . . . we went out eight miles to Chinhat). I have treated Lawrence's defeat merely as the prelude to the investment of the Residency by the mutineers. To give an intelligent account of the engagement would involve a preliminary sketch of the state of Oudh, an inquiry into the immediate causes of the disaster, and an examination of the effect on Lawrence's mind of Gubbins' constant cry for action—none of which are within the scope of this book.

Page 2. . . . the 13th Native Infantry). All native regiments referred to in the text are on the Bengal establishment, unless otherwise stated.

Page 3. . . . the European wounded rather than their own). See Rees, page 89. This statement is borne out by the figures I have quoted on page 31.

Page 5. . . . the kindness of the Indian women). This is one of very many instances during the Mutiny.

Page 13. . . . it will never do to retire on Allahabad). There is no doubt that Lawrence was right in thinking evacuation impossible. His critics are fully answered by Innes, *Lucknow and Oude*, pages 75 and 76.

Page 31. . . . The numbers were made up as follows). I have taken Innes' figures as correct. The official return quoted by Forrest gives a total of 1698: I cannot account for the difference.

Page 34. . . . an independent garrison). For the composition of the various garrisons and the names of the commandants see Innes, *Lucknow and Oude*, pages 110 and 120, and Gubbins, page 232.

Page 38. . . . Lawrence confirmed Major Banks and Colonel Inglis). Sir Alexander Lawrence has pointed out to me that Sir Henry had no legal right to take such a step, since there were civil and military officers senior to them, and that it was a tribute to his personal ascendancy that the arrangement met with no opposition save that of Mr Gubbins.

Page 46. . . . the Talukdars). In 1857 the Talukdar of Oudh was something between a landlord, a tax-farmer, and the chief of a clan; but as any brief description of the Talukdari system is likely to be misleading I refer the reader to Innes, Hutchinson, Gubbins, W. H. Sleeman's *A Journey through the Kingdom of Oudh*, H. C. Irwin's *The Garden of India*, and J. G. W. Sykes' *Compendium of Oudh Taluqdari Law*.

Page 49. . . . some of the engineers held him in contempt). Fulton always refers to him in contemptuous terms, and Innes, in a letter to Mrs Fulton (see page 218), calls him 'a worthless commandant'. Innes contrasted the behaviour of Inglis and Fulton in his *Rough Notes*, but his brother-in-law, who saw it through the press, feared that such personalities 'would create enemies, and therefore omitted, curtailed, or slightly altered them'. I do not know what grounds these highly intelligent and able engineers had for such a view of the Brigadier, who seems to have emerged with credit, if not distinction, from a severe ordeal, having shouldered responsibility as cheerfully as he always courted danger. Perhaps Fulton and Innes were impatient of the slower wits of the regimental officer; moreover, there was often ill-feeling between Queen's and Company's troops, and this may have embittered personal differences.

Page 62. . . . the first female nurses). See Sidney Herbert's letter to Miss Nightingale of 15th Oct., 1854: 'But the deficiency of female nurses is undoubted, none but male nurses having ever been admitted to military hospitals.' He meant in England, of course, not in Catholic countries. Miss Nightingale arrived at Scutari on the 4th November, 1854. In 1865 she drew up, at the request of the Bengal Sanitary Commission, 'Suggestions on a system of Nursing for hospitals in India,' but the matter was shelved. Up to 1887 both officers and men in military hospitals were attended by untrained orderlies, but in that year skilled female nurses were introduced, largely as the result of Lady Roberts' appeals. See Lord Roberts, *Forty One Years in India*, chapter lxvi.

Page 77. . . . carcasses). Carcasses were generally filled with some such mixture as this: Sulphur, tallow, rosin, turpentine, antimony, and saltpetre. Incendiary preparations have been used in warfare since long before the Christian era. For the connection between Greek fire, wildfire, and carcass composition, see *The Origin of Artillery*, by Lt. Col. H. W. L. Hime, Part I, chapter ii.

Page 84. . . . in the power of the Nana Sahib). The final massacre at Cawnpore was begun on the 15th July, and by noon on Johnny Inglis' birthday the last of the children had been despatched and thrown down the well.

Page 87. . . . life with neither child nor husband). But in the Autumn of 1859 Mrs Polehampton married Col. H. M. Durand, afterwards Major General Sir Henry Durand, the historian of the First Afghan War.

Page 100. . . . Dr Brydon). Brydon was, of course, the hero of Lady Butler's famous picture, 'The Remnant of an Army', now in the Tate collection.

Page 132. . . . Antiseptic surgery was unknown). Lister's first observations on the antiseptic system were not published until 1867.

Page 134. . . . known as Khaki). From the Persian,

KHAK; earth or dust. The shade varied, but was generally of a more slatey colour than it is to-day. When the troops first turned out in Khaki at Agra the children shouted 'Quakers!' after them. See Mrs Coopland, *A Lady's Escape from Gwalior*, page 241. It has been said that curry powder was the first khaki dye: see Fortescue, Vol. XIII, page 354, note.

Page 136. . . . so firmly believed that the mutineers had outraged the English women). The English community in India were not in a state of mind to question the truth of these reports, and the most repulsive details were repeated and believed both there and in England. (See the *Times* of 3rd and 25th August 1857 and 31st March 1858, for instance.) Some of the dead bodies were obscenely mutilated, but all the evidence was against the rape or torture of the victims. This is now generally admitted, but if the reader has any doubts he may consult *Records of the Intelligence Department of the Government of the North-West Provinces of India during the Mutiny of 1857* etc., Sir W. Muir and W. Coldstream, Edinburgh, 1902, Vol. I, page 49, and Vol. II, page 367. A leader in the *Times* of 6th August 1857, closes thus: 'Let it be known that England will support the officers who may be charged with the duty of suppressing this Mutiny, and of inflicting condign punishment on the blood-thirsty Mutineers, however terrible may be the measures which they may see fit to adopt.'

Page 138. . . . funnels in the ground). Or perhaps they were fired from a huge mortar which was found in the courtyard of the Kaisarbagh when Lucknow was recaptured in the following year. See I. S. A. Herford's *Stirring Times Under Canvas*, page 144.

Page 143. . . . Mr Harris' nightly duties at the churchyard). The quarrel between the Chaplain and the Brigadier seems to have been patched up later on. On the 4th August a letter was written to Father Bernard, the Catholic priest, asking why he had not of late read the funeral service over the bodies of Catholic soldiers who had been killed, or attended their remains to the burial ground. I have not printed the letter because it is not clear why he omitted these duties, and he may have had good reason. Rees (page 216) implies that the priest was a coward, but he is so ready to contrast the behaviour of the Protestant and the Catholic Chaplains that I have little faith in his judgment.

Page 158. . . . some twenty letters). Several of these reached Allahabad safely; see Forrest's *Selections*.

Page 160. . . . a respectable-looking woman). Her name was Beale. According to Rees neither she nor her baby survived the siege.

Page 165. . . . Mr Simon Martin). My authority is Sir Alexander Lawrence, who had it from Mr Martin himself.

Page 165. . . . the authorities never asked him for any figures). See Rice Holmes, page 279, note. It is hard to say who was directly to blame for Inglis' misleading statements. I think myself that, with James in hospital, either Inglis or one of his staff should have gone into the matter thoroughly, as Robert Napier did later on. Oddly enough it seems that a similar mistake was made in the early days at Kut: see *Remembering Kut*, by D. L. Neave, pages 36 and 40.

Page 185. . . . the meat rations were reduced). The scale was as follows:

	Original ration.	*Reduced ration.*
Combatant - -	1 pound.	12 ounces.
Woman - -	12 ounces.	6 ounces.
Child (over 12) -	12 ounces.	6 ounces.
Child (6 to 12) -	4 ounces.	4 ounces.
Child (under 6) -	4 ounces.	2 ounces.

Page 186. . . . a rude piece of ordnance). Bonham mounted an 8-inch mortar, bed and all, on a triangular truck with cast-iron wheels, and replaced by small wedges the large coin that had given a permanent elevation of forty-five degrees. He now had a piece of ordnance which could be fired at the lower elevation of from one to fifteen degrees, and which was effective at a greater distance than the mortars, though of course, with so short a muzzle, it had not the range of a howitzer.

Page 189. . . . Bonham). Bonham survived the siege, but his distinguished services were not rewarded by Government, though he received honourable mention in Inglis' despatch. Murray's *Guide* says: 'Colonel John Bonham, C.B., of the

Bengal Artillery, the last surviving officer of the garrison, died in Ireland on the 18th May, 1928, in his 94th year.' His *Oude in 1857: Some Memories of the Indian Mutiny*, was published in 1928, but the narrative only covers the events leading up to the siege, Colonel Bonham having been overtaken by illness in 1917 and forced to abandon the work. I tried, without success, to get into touch with his executors, in case any notes of his about the siege were in their possession.

Page 200. . . . discovered a nurse). For an account of Mr Dashwood's meeting with his old nurse in 1932 see *The Listener* of 2nd December, 1936.

Page 201. . . . Mr Gubbins, who was still chafing). This is the last we hear of the controversy. Inglis omitted Gubbins' name from his despatch, though he had played an important part in the defence, more important, certainly, than several civilians who were mentioned. This did not prevent Gubbins from writing about Inglis, in his *The Mutinies in Oude*, with moderation and even generosity.

Page 218. . . . Innes wrote afterwards). Although this eulogy was written by a partisan for the eyes of Fulton's widow, I doubt if anyone who is familiar with my sources will suggest that the note is pitched too high.

Page 222. . . . or rectum). There was good precedent for this: see Walker's *True Account of the Siege of London-Derry:* 'We sent our first answer [to Major General Kirk] made up within a piece of a

Bladder, in the shape of a Suppositor, and the same way applied to the Boy.'

Page 228. . . . Ungud was silent). This is the last we see of him. He lived to be presented to the Prince of Wales at Lucknow on the 7th January, 1876. See Fayrer, page 365.

Page 236. . . . the streets were deserted by the enemy). See Marshman, page 415, and North, page 204. There seems little doubt that the rearguard could and should have been brought in that night. The omission may have been due to the fact that Havelock was exhausted, and assumed perhaps that Outram would now take command, while Outram himself and Napier were both wounded.

Page 236. . . . the pipes of the 78th Highlanders). I am afraid that Jessie Brown, the Highland Lassie, with her 'Dinna ye hear it? Dinna ye hear it?' is a mythical figure. M. de Banneroi's letter, in which the story was told (see the *Times*, 14th Dec. 1857), does not ring true. Birch says (Lady Inglis, page 154) that, among the many rumours current immediately before the relief, it was reported that bagpipes could be heard in the still watches of the night. 'It was known that a regiment of Highlanders formed part of the relieving force, and doubtless the wish was father to the thought.' See *Notes and Queries:* Series 2, V. 147; V. 425; Series 7, III. 482; Series 11, IV. 328; IV. 416; IV. 439. Also Hilton, page 95, and *Calcutta Review*, September 1858, page 142.

Page 239. . . . Neill's order of the 25th July). Neill

himself told a friend, with evident relish, how a fat Brahman was flogged till he yelled again, and how a Mohammedan 'rather objected, was flogged, made to lick part of the blood with his tongue'. There was plenty of work for the hangman at Cawnpore: see a N.C.O.'s letter, printed in the *Times* of 29th Sept. 1857: 'As for hanging, it is nothing; it is quite a common thing to have a few to swing up every day; the least thing will do it.' The provost sergeant entered into the spirit of the thing: when Captain Maude suggested that the casual way the condemned were strung up was just a little too cruel, he replied: 'Well, I don't know, sir; I ain't heard no complaints.' There was however some supervision: a defaulter sheet of the Madras Fusileers has the following entry: 'Private ——. Hanging a native without permission—two days' C.B.' Neill's measures were approved by many of his fellow Christians. The Chief Justice of Madras was 'thankful to think that he knew he "should not bear the sword in vain as the minister of God to execute wrath on those who had done evil".' At the same meeting the Advocate General spoke as warmly in his favour. Dr Duff, the eminent missionary, wrote: 'General Neill, though naturally a mild, gentle, quiet, inoffensive man, seems to have irresistibly felt that an exhibition of stern justice was imperatively demanded. His Scottish Bible-training had taught him that justice was as absolute an attribute of Deity as mercy. . . . Dismissing, therefore, from his mind all thoughts of harmful lenity, all feelings of maudlin, sentimental pity, he sternly grasped the sword of retributive justice, and as the minister of God who ought not to bear the sword in vain, a revenger to execute wrath on them that did evil (Romans, xiii, 4), he resolved to strike terror into the souls of the evil-doers and their miscreant sympathisers. Nor did he regard it as torture or cruelty, in the ordinary sense of these terms, to cause murderers, who were still reeking with the gore of innocent women and children, to wipe up a portion of the blood which they had no scruples of conscience or of caste in so profusely shedding. Neither, may I add, need any enlightened Christian shrink from avowing that he has felt no especial indignation at a procedure so unwonted, in such strange, unwonted circumstances.' (See Kaye's *Lives*, Vol. II, page 416, note.) Duff assumed that every one of Neill's victims was a murderer of women and children, which was far from being the case. Kaye attributes Neill's measures to 'the good old Covenanter spirit' glowing within him. Sir Colin Campbell put an end to the practice, as unworthy of a Christian government; neither he nor Outram favoured the Jack Ketch school. Nor did 'Clemency' Canning, as he was called in contempt. Nor did John Lawrence, who went down from the Punjab to Delhi expressly to put an end to the reign of terror that followed our occupation of the city.

Page 240. . . . waived his military rank). I agree

with those who hold that this chivalrous gesture was ill-judged; it put both Outram and Havelock in a most awkward position, which would have become intolerable if things had gone a little worse. But I think that General MacMunn's description of it as an *illegal* act is misleading, since it was warmly approved by both the Commander-in-Chief and the Governor-General. Outram freely admitted, after the Mutiny was over, that he ought to have taken command himself.

Page 256. . . . the survivors of the Indian troops). The remnants of the 13th, 48th, and 71st Native Infantry were afterwards formed into the Regiment of Lucknow (The Bailey Guard Paltan) commanded by Colonel Palmer. This is now represented by the 10th Bn., 7th Rajputs. The regiment was awarded the battle honour 'Lucknow', with a turreted gateway.

Page 256. . . . to reward the Europeans). In addition to special field allowances, all ranks of the 32nd and 84th serving under Inglis were granted an extra year's service towards their retirement or pension. The 32nd were given the privilege of being clothed, equipped, and trained as a light infantry regiment. The battle honour 'Lucknow' was conferred upon both regiments.

Page 262. . . . but he [Outram] was mistaken). See Innes' authoritative statement: *Lucknow and Oude in the Mutiny*, page 178.

Page 284. . . . the monkeys used to swing on the

wires). The Chief Engineer of Posts and Telegraphs in India has kindly enlightened me on this point. He writes: 'It seems that in the first two or three years of the activities of this Department telegraph wires were composed of iron rods of 3/8″ diameter, it being considered at the time that in order to overcome the effects of low insulation it was necessary to use a conductor of large cross section to keep down the resistance of the line. . . . The reference to cutting line wires into slugs for muskets evidently refers to the 3/8″ iron wire lines which existed about the time of the siege of Lucknow. No reference is traceable about these large gauge wires being used so that they might support the weight of monkeys swinging on them, but you may be interested to learn that in one of the early Annual Reports of this Department, one of the advantages of this heavy gauge wire was stated to be that the conductor was not damaged in a breakdown "even if buffaloes and elephants trampled on the wire". Our telegraph and telephone practice has, of course, progressed a great deal since those days.'

Page 293. . . . Ensign Inglis). No relation, it seems, of the Brigadier. Ensign Robert Loveday Inglis was wounded on leaving Lucknow and died at Allahabad, where he was buried on the 29th December, 1857. See Polehampton, page 368.

Page 298. . . . Man Singh was still hedging). He was a successful trimmer and made his peace with the British Government in the end.

Page 299. . . . the 27th October). On this day news was received of the English prisoners in the Kaisarbagh. I have no space for their story. See Hutchinson, page 134 onwards, and *The English Captives in Oudh, 1857 and 1858,*' by M. Wylie, Calcutta and London, 1858.

Page 302. . . . our relief should be a secondary consideration). I have freely quoted those parts of Outram's despatches that deal with supplies because he has been accused of misleading the Commander-in-Chief and thus inducing him to risk his communications needlessly. The case against Outram does not bear examination. For his own defence, see Russell's *My Diary*, Vol. II, page 416.

Page 320. . . . comparing himself with the heroes of antiquity). Kavanagh's conceit was prodigious. He was mentioned in despatches, granted two thousand pounds, awarded the V.C., and made a Deputy Commissioner in the Covenanted Service—and then complained that Government had treated him shabbily. See his *How I won the V.C.*

Page 326. . . . a regimental colour appeared on the roof). That of the 2nd Punjab Infantry, placed there by the future Lord Roberts. See *Forty-One Years in India*, chapter xxiv.

Page 329. . . . 43 officers and 450 men killed and wounded). The official figures were 122 killed, 414 wounded, and 5 missing, of all ranks, from the 12th to the 18th November, inclusive: in all, 45 officers and 496 men.

Page 336. . . . Roberts felt badly snubbed). Lord Roberts wrote, in *Forty-One Years in India*, chapter xxv: 'Colonel Napier, however, was not to be appeased, and I could plainly see that I had incurred his displeasure, and that he thought me a very bumptious youngster.' Napier may have been irritable from his wound, but I gather from Roberts' *Letters Written during the Indian Mutiny* that he *was* a little bumptious at this period. The two famous soldiers worked together happily in later years.

Page 337. . . . The little white hen). Caroline Dickson wrote to 'My Dear Gabrielle', 23rd November, 1857: 'We have brought the fowl away, and, may be, it will some day be in England.' I am afraid it got lost on the way down to the coast, or drowned, perhaps, in S.S. *Ava*.

Page 346. . . . the shock had unhinged his mind). He was sent to Europe on sick certificate in the spring of 1858, under the care of an attendant, but ultimately recovered.

Page 350. . . . his grave being marked by a mound of earth). Later on Outram had the grave smoothed over so that the enemy should not find it if at any time the Alambagh were evacuated. A plan of the Alambagh, showing the exact position of the grave, was sent to Calcutta in case Government wished to move the remains to 'a holier and more honoured cemetery'. Everyone knows what grief was felt in England at the news of Havelock's death, but it may not be so well known that the ships in

New York, Boston, and Baltimore harbours flew their flags half-mast from 9 A.M. till sunset. The *New York Times* said: 'A mark of respect was shown yesterday to the memory of General Havelock, which was worth more than a peerage. The flags of the shipping in our harbour and on our public buildings were displayed at half-mast during the day, as a token of grief for his loss. It was a purely voluntary tribute paid to his memory by a people to whom he was a stranger, who were in no way interested in his career, and to whom even his name was unknown six months since. It was a tribute of respect which even the Duke of Wellington did not command, and which we believe was never before paid to a foreigner.' See Marshman, chapter x.

Page 352. . . . Mr Gubbins had a last look). This is the last we see of Mr Gubbins. He was taken ill at Cawnpore and invalided home. He returned to India at the end of 1858 and became judge of the supreme court at Agra. He resigned owing to ill-health and returned to England in January 1863. He suffered from mental depression and committed suicide at Leamington on the 6th May, 1863.

Page 354. . . . Dr Brydon, the Afghan survivor). Archibald Forbes knew him in later years, when he had retired to a Ross-shire sheep-farm—'a quiet, rather silent man, much beloved among the neighbouring shepherds and crofters, whose ailments he cared for professionally but gratuitously'. See *Havelock*, page 34, note.

Page 354. . . . the offensive against Tantia Topi). Tantia Topi was routed on the 6th December, and Lucknow was recaptured in the following March.

Page 355. . . . Inglis remained at Cawnpore). He was promoted Major General and made a K.C.B. He died on the 27th September, 1862, aged 47, his life having probably been shortened by the strain of the defence.

Page 355. . . . the dog Bustle). Metcalfe says: '. . . and did not see the dog again till November, 1860.'

Page 356. . . . Mrs Dashwood's little boy survived as well). And still survived when this book was written (1937/38).

SOURCES

Manuscript

Letter Book kept in the Deputy Assistant Adjutant General's Office, Lucknow, from 22nd May, 1857, to 22nd November, 1857, some of the entries being in Captain Wilson's own hand.

Mrs Inglis' journal, in her own hand. Sir George Collier writes: 'I clearly recollect Lady Inglis telling me, about the time when she was publishing her book, *The Siege of Lucknow*, that when she was shipwrecked after the Mutiny and was putting off in a boat from the sinking ship [S.S. *Ava*] she discovered that she had left her journal on board. Some officer [Sam Lawrence] bravely volunteered to return to the ship to get it for her, but when he brought it she found it to be the comparatively brief diary in which she had noted down the events of the siege of Lucknow, but not the fuller journal she had also kept. In consequence she wrote out at once, as best she could from that diary, a replica as nearly as was possible of the lost journal. It was from this source that the book was written.'

Letters from Ensign Robert Loveday Inglis, 63rd N.I., doing duty with 13th N.I., to his mother in Calcutta, dated from the 14th September, 1857, to 20th November, 1857.

Family papers in the possession of Sir Alexander Lawrence, Bt.

Army record of Private Henry Metcalfe, 32nd Foot; India, 1848 to 1858.

Outram's Despatch of 13th October, 1857. British Museum, Add. MSS. 43993.

Marginal Notes to *The Defence of Lucknow*, by A Staff Officer (Captain T. F. Wilson, 13th N.I.). London, 1858. Internal evidence shows that Wilson himself made the annotations, and I find that this is the copy he prepared for Sir John Kaye. See *A History of the Sepoy War in India*, Vol. III, page 540, note.

PRIVATELY PRINTED

Letters from India and China during the years 1854-1858. By R. W. Danvers, 70th B.N.I. London and Aylesbury, 1898.

Biographical Memoirs of the late Capt. G. W. W. Fulton of the Hon. E.I.C.'s Bengal Engineers' Corps. Napier, N. Zealand, 1913.

A Diary kept by Mrs R. C. Germon at Lucknow between the months of May and December, 1857. London, 1870.

A Personal Narrative of the Siege of Lucknow during the Indian Mutiny of 1857. Anonymous. No date. (By Mrs Huxham, wife of Lieutenant Huxham, 48th N.I.)

Letter Containing Extracts from a Journal kept by Mrs Inglis during the Siege of Lucknow. London, 1858.

Letters from Lucknow and Cawnpore. Anonymous. Greenwich, 1858. (By E. Delaney Lowe, 32nd Foot. I have not been able to find a copy.)

Outram's Campaign in India, 1857 to 1858. (General Orders and Despatches and Correspondence.) London, 1860.

Indian Life Sketches. 1816 to 1866. By Henry Palmer, Mussoorie, 1888.

Printed and Published

'Lord Clyde's Campaign in India.' (By Archibald Alison.) *Blackwood's Magazine*, October, 1858.

A Personal Journal of the Siege of Lucknow. By Captain R. P. Anderson. London, 1858.

A Widow's Reminiscences of the Siege of Lucknow. By K. M. Bartrum. London, 1858.

Eight Months' Campaign against the Bengal Sepoy Army. By G. Bourchier. London, 1858.

A Biographical Sketch of Sir Henry Havelock, By Rev. William Brock. London, 1858.

Day by Day at Lucknow. By Adelaide Case. London, 1858.

'Untimely Arrival at the Siege of Lucknow.' By A. F. Dashwood. *The Listener*, 2nd December, 1936.

Honoria Lawrence. By Maud Diver. London, 1936.

General Views and Special Points of Interest of the City of Lucknow. By Lt. Col. Dodgson, A.A.G. (Folio.) London, 1860.

Life of Sir Henry Lawrence. By H. B. Edwardes and H. Merivale. London, 1873.

Recollections of My Life. By Sir Joseph Fayrer. London, 1900.

Colin Campbell, Lord Clyde. By Archibald Forbes, London, 1895.

Havelock. By Archibald Forbes. London, 1891.

Selections from Letters, Despatches, and Other State Papers, etc., 1857-58. By G. W. Forrest. Calcutta, 1902.

A History of the Indian Mutiny. By G. W. Forrest. London, 1904.

James Outram. By F. J. Goldsmid. London, 1880.

Incidents in the Sepoy War, 1857-58. By Sir Hope Grant and H. Knollys. London, 1873.

The Mutinies in Oude. By Martin R. Gubbins. London, 1858.

The Story of Two Noble Lives. By A. J. C. Hare. London, 1893.

A Lady's Diary of the Siege of Lucknow. Anonymous. (By Mrs G. Harris.) London, 1858.

Mrs G. Harris. See also under Hilton.

The Tourist's Guide to Lucknow. By Edward H. Hilton. Lucknow, 1916. (Hilton reprints Mrs Harris' article on the death of Henry Lawrence from the *Anglo-Indian Magazine*, July, 1858.)

Essays on the Indian Mutiny. By John Holloway. London, 1865.

A History of the Indian Mutiny. By T. Rice Holmes. London, 1904. (Rice Holmes also contributed the chapter on the Indian Mutiny in the *Cambridge History of India*.)

Narrative of the Mutinies in Oude. By G. Hutchinson. Calcutta, 1859.

The Siege of Lucknow. By Lady Inglis. London, 1892.

Lucknow and Oude in the Mutiny. By McLeod Innes. London, 1895.

Rough Narrative of the Siege of Lucknow. By J. J. McLeod Innes. Calcutta, 1857.

The History of the Royal and Indian Artillery in the Mutiny of 1857. By J. R. J. Jocelyn. London, 1915.

How I Won the Victoria Cross. By T. H. Kavanagh. London, 1860.

Lives of Indian Officers. By J. W. Kaye. London, 1867.

A History of the Sepoy War in India, 1857 to 1858. By J. W. Kaye. London, 1876.

Kaye's and Malleson's *History of the Indian Mutiny of 1857-8*. Edited by Colonel Malleson. London, 1897.

'The Diary and Letters of A. M. Lang, 1st Lieutenant, Bengal Engineers.' *Journal of the Society of Army Historical Research*, Vol. X, 1931.

A Memoir of Lieutenant General Sir Garnet J. Wolseley. By C. R. Low. London, 1878.

The Indian Mutiny in Perspective. By Lieutenant General Sir George MacMunn, K.C.B., etc. London, 1931.

Colonel Malleson. See under Kaye.

Mrs Marriott's Narrative. *Westminster Gazette*, 27th and 28th May, 1907.

Memoirs of Major General Sir Henry Havelock, K.C.B. By J. C. Marshman. London, 1902.

Memories of the Mutiny. By F. C. Maude and J. W. Sherer. London, 1894.

Sketches and Incidents of the Siege of Lucknow. By C. H. Mecham and G. Couper. (Folio.) London, 1858.

Reminiscences of the Great Mutiny, 1857-59. By William Forbes-Mitchell. London, 1893.

Lawrence of Lucknow. By J. L. Morison. London, 1934.

Field-Marshal Lord Napier of Magdala. By H. D. Napier. London, 1927.

Narrative of the Indian Revolt. London, 1858.

A Lecture on the Relief of Lucknow. By H. W. Norman. Simla, 1867.

Journal of an English Officer in India. By Major North. London, 1858.

Parliamentary Papers. Mutinies in the East Indies, Supplement, Further Papers, and Appendix. London, 1857.

A Memoir, Letters, and Diary of the Rev. Henry S Polehampton. Edited by E. Polehampton and T. S. Polehampton. London, 1858.

Rough Recollections of Military Service and Society. By B. D. W. Ramsay. London, 1882.

A Personal Narrative of the Siege of Lucknow. By L. E. Ruutz Rees. (3rd Edition). London, 1858.

Forty-One Years in India. By Lord Roberts. London, 1908.

Recollections of a Lucknow Veteran, 1845-76. By J. Ruggles. London, 1906.

My Diary in India, 1858-9. By W. H. Russell. London, 1860.

Life of Colin Campbell, Lord Clyde. By Lieutenant General Shadwell. London, 1881.

'The Siege of Lucknow'. *Calcutta Review*, Sept. 1858.

'The Diary of an Officer's Wife.' By E. S. *Graphic*, June 15th, 1907. (Reprinted in Appendix to W. H. Fitchett's *The Tale of the Great Mutiny*, London, 1912. 'E. S.' is proved by internal evidence to be Mrs Soppitt.)

The Victoria Cross. By Lt. Col. Rupert Stewart. London, 1916.

My Journal. By A Volunteer. (Lieutenant W. O. Swanston.) Calcutta, 1858.

Historical Records of the 32nd (Cornwall) Light Infantry, 1702-1892. By G. C. Swiney. London, 1893.

The Story of Cawnpore. By Mowbray Thomson. London, 1859.

Cawnpore. By G. Trevelyan. London, 1910.

The Shannon's Brigade in India, 1857-58. By E. H. Verney. London, 1862.

The Defence of Lucknow. By A Staff Officer. (Captain T. F. Wilson, 13th N.I. Deputy Assistant Adjutant General.) London, 1858. See also under Manuscript Sources.

The Story of a Soldier's Life. By F.M. Viscount Wolseley. London, 1903.

Neill's Blue Caps. By H. C. Wylly. 1925 etc.

INDEX

T